Communications
in Computer and Information Science   42

Rory V. O'Connor   Nathan Baddoo
Juan Cuadrado Gallego
Ricardo Rejas Muslera   Kari Smolander
Richard Messnarz (Eds.)

Software Process Improvement

16th European Conference, EuroSPI 2009
Alcala (Madrid), Spain, September 2-4, 2009
Proceedings

 Springer

Volume Editors

Rory V. O'Connor
Dublin City University, Dublin, Ireland
E-mail: roconnor@computing.dcu.ie

Nathan Baddoo
University of Hertfordshire
Hatfield, Hertfordshire, UK
E-mail: n.baddoo@herts.ac.uk

Juan Cuadrado Gallego
University of Alcala, Madrid, Spain
E-mail: jjcg@uah.es

Ricardo Rejas Muslera
University of Alcala, Madrid, Spain
E-mail: rrejas@uah.es

Kari Smolander
Lappeenranta University of Technology
Lappeenranta, Finland
E-mail: kari.smolander@lut.fi

Richard Messnarz
ISCN, Graz, Austria
and ISCN, Bray, Co. Wicklow, Ireland
E-mail: rmess@iscn.com

Library of Congress Control Number: 2009933499

CR Subject Classification (1998): D.2, D.1, D.3, D.2.1, D.2.8, D.2.9

ISSN   1865-0929
ISBN   978-3-642-04132-7 Springer Berlin Heidelberg New York

Typesetting: Camera-ready by author, data conversion by Scientific Publishing Services, Chennai, India
Printed on acid-free paper   SPIN: 12748655   06/3180   5 4 3 2 1 0

Preface

This textbook is intended for SPI (software process improvement) managers and researchers, quality managers, and experienced project and research managers. The papers constitute the research proceedings of the 16th EuroSPI (European Software Process Improvement, www.eurospi.net) conference held in Alcala (Madrid region), September 2–4, 2009, Spain.

Conferences have been held since 1994 in Dublin, 1995 in Vienna (Austria), 1997 in Budapest (Hungary), 1998 in Gothenburg (Sweden), 1999 in Pori (Finland), 2000 in Copenhagen (Denmark), 2001 in Limerick (Ireland), 2002 in Nuremberg (Germany), 2003 in Graz (Austria), 2004 in Trondheim (Norway), 2005 in Budapest (Hungary), 2006 in Joensuu (Finland), 2007 in Potsdam (Germany), 2008 in Dublin (Ireland), and 2009 in Alcala (Spain).

EuroSPI established an experience library (library.eurospi.net) which will be continuously extended over the next few years and will be made available to all attendees. EuroSPI also created an umbrella initiative for establishing a European Qualification Network in which different SPINs and national initiatives join mutually beneficial collaborations (ECQA – European Certification and Qualification Association, www.ecqa.org).

With a general assembly during October 15–16, 2007 through Euro-SPI partners and networks, in collaboration with the European Union (supported by the EU Leonardo da Vinci Programme) a European certification association has been created (www.eu-certificates.org, www.ecqa.org) for the IT and services sector to offer SPI knowledge and certificates to industry, establishing close knowledge transfer links between research and industry.

An EU Certificates day of the ECQA (European Certification and Qualification Agency) took place as an associated event of EuroSPI 2009 on September 2, 2009.

The biggest value of EuroSPI lies in its function as a European knowledge and experience exchange mechanism for SPI know-how between research institutions and industry.

Since its beginning in 1994 in Dublin, the EuroSPI initiative has outlined that there is not a single silver bullet to solve SPI issues, but that an understanding of a combination of different SPI methods and approaches is needed to achieve concrete benefits. Therefore each proceedings volume covers a variety of different topics, and at the conference we discuss the potential synergy and the combined use of such methods and approaches. These proceedings contain selected research papers on six topics each comprising three papers:

Section I: SPI and the Testing Process
Section II: SPI Measurement and Assessment
Section III: Agile and Open Source Issues
Section IV: SPI and Management Issues
Section V: Process Life Cycle and Quality Issues
Section VI: Standards and Reference Models

Section I presents three studies on *SPI and the Testing Process*. Fernandex-Sanz et al. remind us that software testing is the commonest practice for software quality assurance and by implication should be fundamental to software process improvement. They argue that despite this importance and the effort expended on software testing, there is still a lack of knowledge of the real practices of testing. In this paper, they present the results of a survey conducted in two organizations in Spain, to highlight the key practices of software testing and to highlight relationships between these practices and software development successes. Almog and Heart extend this theme by concentrating on software test cases. They suggest that the process of software testing can be greatly improved if the concept of test cases is formally defined. Such formal definition will also enhance software testing assessment and make it easier for the automation of the generation and management of test cases. The theme of automation is extended by Connolly et al., who explore ways of supporting expert customers in the design and execution of tests cases in acceptance test-driven development. They identify a key challenge as the support needed by the expert in the reuse of existing documentation. They outline plans for the development of an automated testing model that improves adherence to practice through the provision of fully traceable artifacts.

Section II, *SPI Measurement and Assessment*, presents the results of three studies in this area. Bhatti et al. propose an extension to the Goal Question Metric model. They do this in response to their argument that measurements can be more successful if finely tuned to the needs of the organization collecting those measures. Their extension to the GQM is vital because this model has been derived from adopting a heuristic approach. Marín et al. address the notion of measurements in specific relation to functional size measurement and model-driven development (MDD) environments. They show how a functional size measurement procedure which has been developed for measurement of conceptual models of a specific model-driven development environment can help in the detection of defects in conceptual models. In a slight departure from measurements, Barafort and Rousseau present a sustainable service innovation framework that is used as a generic framework for supporting innovation and promoting multidisciplinary activities.

Section III emphasizes the need for incorporating innovative approaches and methods in approaches which may have become traditional or even conventional. Under *Agile and Open Source Issue* three papers bear testimony to this dictum. Hossain et al. explore how agile practices can be used to minimize the risk of coordinating global software development. Diaz et al. investigate the viability of introducing agile software development methods like SCRUM in compliance with the CMMi process model. In this paper, they set out to improve the understanding between these two development approaches by presenting empirical accounts that confirm the theoretical comparison between agile software development and plan-driven process models like CMMi. Soto and Ciolkowski touch on another innovative approach in terms of open source software (OSS) development. They present work-in-progress that details the development of process evaluation frameworks aimed specifically at OSS projects and discuss some lessons learned when the framework was applied to certain OSS projects.

In Section IV three studies on *SPI and Management Issues* are presented. Through an illustrative case study, Peisl et al. propose an approach to the management of innovation integrating business, process and maturity dimensions. Šamalíková et al. report on the application of process mining techniques to (a) discover shortcomings in the change control board process in an organization during the different lifecycle phases and (b) determine improvement activities. Välimäki et al. present current best practices for global software development (GSD) in the form of process patterns for project management—evaluated by using a scenario-based assessment method—to help companies improve their own GSD processes by incorporating the patterns presented here in their processes.

Section V addresses *Process Lifecycle and Quality Issues*. In the first paper, Kääriäinen and Välimäki present a study about the history of application lifecycle management improvement in a company. O'Connor's exploration of usability techniques in the software development process of Irish SMEs that develop Web applications found that there are no process models available that meet the specific needs of Web development, and that Web developers are confused about how to implement usability. O'Connor's study also found that definitions of usability are inconsistent and that there is still a need for a definition of usability specifically for Web applications. He concludes that there is very little awareness of usability standards. In the last paper in this section, Chiam et al. propose a framework for capturing quality attribute techniques, such as safety and security, of software development. They suggest that such a framework supports process tailoring by facilitating the selection of techniques for inclusion into process models that target specific product qualities.

Finally, Section VI presents three studies on *Standards and Reference Models*. Bru et al. present a case study of the activity of a team of six young software engineers that depicts some aspects of the building and the filling of the course-of-action observatory. They argue that observing and analyzing software engineers' activity helps to reveal their theory-in-use, i.e., what governs their behavior. Bru et al. suggest that such a study may help establish links between a project process in use and a simplified process reference model, thereby helping to reduce the fit between a project-in-action and espoused SE standards. Valdevit et al. present a guide to implementing an information security management system (ISMS) in small settings. In this study they narrate the experience of Public Research Centre Henri Tudor, Luxembourg, which was charged with finding solutions to facilitate ISMS deployment in SMEs. Finally, continuing the theme of small organizations, Pino et al. introduce an improvement framework for very small organizations (VSEs). They describe their experience of validating this framework in eight companies and provide results to support the usefulness of tailored improvement frameworks for VSEs.

Recommended Further Reading

In [1] we integrated the proceedings of three EuroSPI² conferences into one book which was edited by 30 experts in Europe. In [2] you will find the EuroSPI² research proceedings published by Springer and based on EuroSPI 2005. In [3] you will find the EuroSPI research proceedings published by Springer and based on EuroSPI² 2006. In [4] you will find the research proceedings for EuroSPI² 2007 published by Springer. In [5] you will find last year's research proceedings published by Springer.

References

1. Messnarz, R., Tully, C. (eds.): Better Software Practice for Business Benefit – Principles and Experience, 409 pages. IEEE Computer Society Press, Los Alamitos (1999)
2. Richardson, I., Abrahamsson, P., Messnarz, R. (eds.): Software Process Improvement. LNCS, vol. 3792, p. 213. Springer, Heidelberg (2005)
3. Richardson, I., Runeson, P., Messnarz, R. (eds.): Software Process Improvement. LNCS, vol. 4257, pp. 11–13. Springer, Heidelberg (2006)
4. Abrahamsson, P., Baddoo, N., Margaria, T., Messnarz, R. (eds.): Software Process Improvement. LNCS, vol. 4764, pp. 1–6. Springer, Heidelberg (2007)
5. O'Connor, R.V., Baddoo, N., Smolander, K., Messnarz, R. (eds): Software Process Improvement. CCIS, vol. 16, Springer, Heidelberg (2008).

July 2009

Rory V. O'Connor
Nathan Badoo
Juan Cuadrado Gallego
Ricardo Rejas Muslera
Kari Smolander
Richard Messnarz

Organization

Board Members

EuroSPI Board Members represent centers or networks of SPI excellence having large experience with SPI. The board members collaborate with different European SPINS (Software Process Improvement Networks).

The following six organizations have been members of the conference board in the last 9 years:

- ASQ, http://www.asq.org
- ASQF, http://www.asqf.de
- DELTA, http://www.delta.dk
- ISCN, http://www.iscn.com
- SINTEF, http://www.sintef.no
- STTF, http://www.sttf.fi

EuroSPI Scientific Program Committee

EuroSPI established an international committee of selected well-known experts in SPI who are willing to be mentioned in the program and to review a set of papers each year. The list below represents the Research Program Committee members. EuroSPI² also has a separate Industrial Program Committee responsible for the industry/experience contributions.

- Abran, Alain, Ets University of Quebec, Canada
- Ali Babar, Muhammad, Lero, the Irish Software Engineering Centre, Ireland
- Ambriola, Vincenzo, Universita Di Pisa, Italy
- Aurum, Aybüke, University of New South Wales, Australia
- Baddoo, Nathan, School of Computer Science, University of Hertfordshire, UK
- Biffl, Stefan, Technische Universität Wien, Austria
- Braungarten, Rene, Otto Von Guericke University Magdeburg, Germany
- Buglione, Luigi, Engineering Ingegneria Informatica S.P.A., Italy
- Casey, Val, University of Bournemouth, UK
- Chua, Bee Bee, University of Technology, Australia
- Ciolkowski, Marcus, Fraunhofer IESE, Germany
- Coleman, Gerry, Dundalk Institute of Technology, Ireland
- Cuadrado-Gallego, Juan J., University of Alcala De Henares, Spain
- Dalcher, Darren, Middlesex University, UK
- De Amescua, Seco Antonio, Universidad Carlos III De Madrid, Spain
- Diez, Teresa, University of Alcala, Spain
- Dingsoyr, Torgeir, Sintef ICT, Norway
- Dominguez-Alda, Mara J., University of Alcala De Henares, Spain

- Dumke, Reiner, Otto Von Guericke University of Magdeburg, Germany
- Fernandez Del Castillo, Jose Raul, University of Alcala, Spain
- Fernandez De Sevilla, Marian, University of Alcala De Henares, Spain
- Garcia, Felix, University of Castilla La Mancha, Spain
- Garcia Guzman, Javier, Universidad Carlos III De Madrid, Spain
- Gonzalez Soto, Leon A., University of Alcala, Spain
- Gorschek, Tony, Blekinge Institute of Technology, Sweden
- Gresse Von Wangenheim, Christiane, Universidade Do Vale Do Itajai – Univali, Brazil
- Haugset, Borge, SINTEF, Norway
- Hilera, Jose R., University of Alcala, Spain
- Keenan, Frank, Dundalk Institute of Technology, Ireland
- Kreiner, Christian, Graz University of Technology, Austria
- Landes, Dieter, University of Applied Sciences, Coburg, Germany
- Mäkinen, Timo, Tampere University of Technology, Finland
- Martinez, Jose J., University of Alcala, Spain
- Mas, Antonia, Universitat De Les IIIes Baleares, Spain
- McCaffery, Fergal, Dundalk Institute of Technology, Ireland
- McQuaid, Patricia, Orfalea College of Business Cal Poly, USA
- Muel, Enriqueta, University of Alcala De Henares, Spain
- Münch, Jürgen, Fraunhofer IESE, Germany
- O'Connor, Rory, Dublin City University, Ireland
- Pastor, Oscar, Technical University of Valencia, Spain
- Phalp, Keith, University of Bournemouth, UK
- Rejas, Ricardo, Universidad Francisco De Vitoria, Spain
- Richardson, Ita, Universtiy of Limerick, Ireland
- Selioukova, Yana, Helsinki University of Technology, Finland
- Siakas, Kerstin, Alexander Technological Educational Institute of Thessaloniki (A.T.E.I.), Greece
- Sillitti, Alberto, Free University of Bolzano-Bozen, Italy
- Stlhane, Tor, Norwegian University of Science and Technology, Norway
- Stapel, Kai, Leibniz Universität Hannover, Germany
- Vajde Horvat, Romana, proHUMAN, Slovenia
- Varkoi, Timo, Tampere University of Technology, Finland
- Ventura Martins, Paula, Fct-University of Algarve, Portugal
- Vondrak, Ivo, VSB - Technical University of Ostrava, Czech Republic

All six chairs, the general and the research chairs, have quite a complementary and interesting profile. Dr. Messnarz works in close collaboration with Austrian research institutions (universities of applied sciences) and large German automotive companies. Dr. Nathan Baddoo is a professor at the University of Hertfordshire, UK, and he has published scientific articles about the human factors in SPI and has performed studies at major European organizations, applying motivation techniques in SPI. Professor Juan Cuadrado Gallego is a profesor at the University of Alcala in

Spain and is a member of experience networks concerning process and product measurement. This includes experiences with and mathematical models to implement international measurement standards. Dr. Ricardo Rejas Muslera is a researcher at the University of Alcala in Spain and specialized in the field of improvement models. He recently published potential extensions for risk management in the existing assessment models. Dr. Rory O'Connor is is a senior lecturer in Dublin City University and a senior research with Lero, the Irish Software Engineering Cente. His main research interests center on software process and SPI in relation to small and very small organizations. And finally, Dr. Kari Smolander has studied software development organizations extensively and he is a professor of software engineering at Lappeenranta University of Technology.

The experience portfolio of the chairs covers different market segments, different sizes of organizations, and different SPI approaches. This strengthens the fundamental principle of EuroSPI² to cover a variety of different markets, experiences, and approaches.

Dr. Richard Messnarz
General Chair of EuroSPI
ISCN, Ireland and Austria
rmess@iscn.com

Dr. Nathan Baddoo
EuroSPI Scientific Program Committee Chair
University of Hertfordshire, UK
n.baddoo@herts.ac.uk

Professor Juan Cuadrado Gallego
EuroSPI Scientific Program Committee Chair
University of Alcala, Madrid, Spain
jjcg@uah.es

Dr. Ricardo Rejas Muslera
EuroSPI Scientific Program Committee Chair
University of Alcala, Madrid, Spain
rrejas@uah.es

Dr. Rory O'Connor
EuroSPI Scientific Program Committee Chair
Dublin City University, Ireland
roconnor@computing.dcu.ie

Dr. Kari Smolander
EuroSPI Scientific Program Committee Chair
Lappeenranta University of Technology, Finland
kari.smolander@lut.fi

Table of Contents

SPI and Management Issues

Process Lifecycle and Quality Issues

Standards and Reference Models

Factors with Negative Influence on Software Testing Practice in Spain: A Survey

Luis Fernández-Sanz[1], M. Teresa Villalba[2], José Ramón Hilera[1],
and Raquel Lacuesta[3]

[1] Depto. De C. de la Computación, Universidad de Alcalá, Ctra. Madrid-Barcelona Km 33,600,
Alcalá de Henares, 28871, Madrid, Spain
[2] Depto. de Sistemas Informáticos, Universidad Europea de Madrid,
C/Tajo s/n, Villaviciosa de Odón, 28670, Madrid, Spain
[3] Dept. of Comp. and Syst. Eng., Univ. de Zaragoza, C. Escolar s/n, 44003 Teruel, Spain
luis.fernandezs@uah.es, maite.villalba@uem.es,
jose.hilera@uah.es, lacuesta@unizar.es

Abstract. Software testing is the commonest technique for software quality assurance. It is present in every development project and concentrates a large percentage of effort, there are still not many studies which address the real practice of individuals and organizations. Anyway, practitioners usually agree with the idea that software testing efficiency and effectiveness in their organizations might be improved. Two previous studies in Spain have revealed implemented testing practices in organizations and individual performance of software professionals when designing test cases should be improved. This paper presents the results of a survey designed to know if 23 factors determined by a panel of experts in 2007 may explain this situation of testing practice. Data collected reveal that none of the factors is clearly rejected as a negative influence for testing although some of them are not generally accepted. Exploratory statistical analysis reveals relations between certain pairs of items as well as a new grouping in factors.

Keywords: Software testing, survey, influence factors.

1 Introduction

Software testing is the commonest techniques for verification and validation in development projects. Every project includes a specific phase for testing and debugging. According to different statistical studies of effort distribution throughout the life cycle [1][2][3], this phase usually requires around a large percentage, around one-third (ranging from 30 to 35%), of the total effort of the project.

Different studies have tried to analyze real practice but in many cases empirical works are focused on analyzing or demonstrating the benefits of specific methods or approaches to testing. As stated in [4], there is a need of real practice empirically-based data not vested by such purpose but aimed at providing more light on this area. This type of studies is rare although, as can be seen in the following sections, there are interesting contributions. In order to gain knowledge in this area, a series of studies centered

R.V. O'Connor et al. (Eds.): EuroSPI 2009, CCIS 42, pp. 1–12, 2009.

on software testing practices in Spain were launched in 1999 by L. Fernandez-Sanz. It began with a survey on testing practices in organizations (see Section 2) which finally collected information from 210 software professionals. After analyzing results which reveal a weak situation for organizations and as suggested by respondents, a specific study on 72 individual practitioners' performance in test case design (see Section 3) was carried out to control if professionals might get good results despite poor organizational environment. This study concluded that individual performance was also weak so as a final step a survey was launched to discover the underlying causes. This paper is focused on this final stage presented in Section 4 although a brief presentation of the two first studies is included in Sections 2 and 3. Finally, section 5 discusses results and conclusions as well as future works.

2 Analysis of Testing Practices in Organizations

In order to know something more about which the real testing practices of software organizations in Spain are, a study was carried out by the Software Quality Group of ATI (www.ati.es), the main computing professionals association in Spain, the national body of CEPIS (www.cepis.org), the Council of European Professional Informatics Societies. This study (partly published in [5]) collected, during the period 1999-2007 information, from 210 IT professionals engaged in software development projects in Spain corresponding to almost all the activity sectors as well as many different positions (see table 1). Data were collected using anonymous questionnaires during specific events (like training courses, both in-company and open access, and QA events) as well as exploiting direct relations with IT professionals in companies.

Table 1. Respondents in the study of testing practices in organizations

Sector	%	Position	%
Finance	14.3%	Tester	16.2%
Consultancy	12.8%	Analyst	12.8%
Telco/IT	10.4%	Project manager	11.1%
Energy/industry	5.2%	Manager	9.4%
Transportation/Airlines	4.3%	Software engineer	8.5%
Defense	4.3%	QA specialist	5.9%
Government	3.8%	Programmer	5.9%
Tourism	3.8%	IT director	5.1%
Health	2.3%	Others	25.1%
Others	38.8%		

Although different process models (such as CMMi[1] [6][7],TMM [8], TMMI [9][10], TPI [11] y TMap [12][13].) are applicable to testing and include specific practices, only recently [14] description for testing process improvement have been analyzed in a rigorous way. Conclusions of this study reflect that there is not a complete and well described set of practices in those models so a quick method to collect

---

[1] As stated in the areas of Product Integration, Validation and Verification.

information from a wide range of organizations is not available for a survey. Obviously, data from CMMI evaluation or similar activities would give information on real testing practice. However, it is difficult to access to details of such evaluation processes, only a small percentage of organizations have been evaluated according to this model and SEI public information does not include details of each process area.

Knowing the limitation, we decided to use as reference the list of best practices for software testing of Quality Assurance Institute (www.qaiusa.org): one of advantage is that QAI carried out several surveys using this list from 1994 to 1999 in the USA so this reference of 20 practices was refined with their results and experience. In fact, published surveys do not focus their attention in specific process models but in customized list of questions covering from detailed techniques to organizational topics. In the case of [15][16] items covered from general testing approach (independent testing, etc.), budget or standards to specific methods and possible barriers to adoption of specific practices. Other studies [17] were more focused on detailed methods (e.g. use of notations like UML, structured diagrams, etc. for documentation) and specific data on percentage of effort devoted to testing even related to project size; in the case of [18] (also based on contacts of a network of practitioners and researchers) it was focused on extremely detailed aspects of software unit testing although some conclusions might be common to general testing practices.

Table 2. Summary of results from survey on testing practices implemented in organizations

QAI practice	Implem
1. Identified responsibility for testing processes in the organization?	28.57%
2. Is there and is used a standard for test plans?	23.33%
3. Is there and is used a standard for unit testing?	18.10%
4. Is there and is used a standard for test reports?	27.14%
5. Testing planning and execution process parallel to the whole development process?	28.57%
6. Check if software specifications are correct?	39.05%
7. Besides being correctly implemented. check if customer expectations are fulfilled?	48.57%
8. Testing staff check if development documents are complete and correct?	21.43%
9. Testing staff report defects to developers (and not to managers)?	41.43%
10. Testing staff identifies business risks before developing test plan?	11.43%
11. Are there measurable objectives for each tested system?	14.76%
12. Testing objectives are clearly linked to business risks?	14.29%
13. Are detected defects recorded, reported and used to improve development and testing processes?	28.10%
14. Has testing staff defined defect expectations according to paste experience?	17.62%
15. Is there a testing processes improvement process?	18.10%
16. Defects are identified with a unique code?	20.95%
17. Does the organization record, report and used defect data to asses test effectiveness?	17.62%
18. Are metrics used for planning and evaluating testing processes?	9.05%
19. Are there specific training processes for the testing staff?	17.62%
20. Do testing tools represent a significant element of testing process?	12.50%

Organizations			Implem
No. Practices from 0 to 4	10.95%	No. Practices from13 to 16	19.05%
No. Practices from 5 to 8	31.90%	No. Practices from17 to 20	13.33%
No. Practices from 9 to 12	24.29%		

Results updated to 2007 from the survey [5] are summarized in Table 2: each practice is described with a short description. Although QAI suggests that organizations would be classified in a scale of five levels according to the number of practices implemented, we think this is scheme is not rigorous enough although results are shown below as an indicator of aggregated number of practices per respondent. The survey also included information on two additional items:

- Specialized training in software testing: only 30.61% of respondents had attended such training. Similar formal [16] and informal surveys referred to testing training revealed slightly higher percentage of those with training).
- Relationship between training and answers to questions on testing foundations: number of people with specific training who passed the questions is twice the number of those with no training at all.

Looking at the result in table 2 with general low percentages in all items, it is clear there is still a wide margin of improvement for software testing practices: poor testing practices are not exclusive of Spain as can be seen in [14][15][16]. Trying to go further, we wanted to investigate if individual performance of testers would be good despite the weak organizational practices so we devised a specific study (Section 3).

3 Analysis of Individual Performance in Test Case Design

To check if software professionals were good at designing functional test cases, a small size case study (4 use cases) was created to control such activity with selected IT professionals contacted in seminars and events. The problem to be solved was the design of test cases for a basic DVD list management application where several defects were injected. A website with the following features was created:

- Access to the natural-language specification for the application
- Collection of anonymous data of the participants: position, sector, experience, etc.
- Interactive recording of test cases with options to create cases, to "execute" (by simulation) showing the list of stored DVDs after it, to determine if a defect is detected and to review the list of "executed" cases.
- Recording of time devoted by each participant.
- Presentation of a list of suggested correct test cases (to assure full coverage of the application) and recording of priority of each test case suggested by each participant according to his/her vision of the program objectives.

Table 3. Participants in the study of individual test case design

Sector	%	Position	%
Consultancy and IT	36.1%	Researcher	28%
Education	12.4%	Tester	27%
Internet	16.2%	Project manager	17%
Energy/industry	9.8%	Software engineer	13%
Finance	5.5%	Programmer	9%
Government	5.5%	Systems analyst	6%
Transportation/Airlines	1.5%		
Others	29.2%		

This experience had also a secondary objective as a check of the acceptance of test generation based on UML activity diagrams: "correct" solution presented at the end of the experience was generated using this method. The sample of 71 IT professionals (discarding unreliable tryouts and incomplete data) who participated in the first wave is shown in Table 3. Average development experience of respondents is 5.6 years and average time devoted to the experience was 27 minutes.

Results were presented at [18] and [19] and they can be summarized as follows:

- Only 1 participant covered more than 75% of the options of the program. 70.4% of participants did not reach the 50% of coverage of functional options, 13% did not detect any of the 4 injected defects and 40.8% detected at least 3. As an average, 50% of defects were detected and participants claim detection of 8 not real defects.
- As an average, around 50% of the cases designed by a tester were oriented to test program options previously controlled in similar cases executed by him/her. This was especially intense in test cases oriented to enter data in the program (e.g. insert new DVD data) rather than when deleting or modifying records.
- On one hand, among the 10 most executed test cases, there was only one of the ten most important ones according to participants' own rank of priority. On the other hand, among the 10 least executed cases, there were 3 of the most important ones.
- As additional information, it was also shown that practitioners considered a trade-off to invest in detailed UML models like Activity Diagrams for software specifications in order to gain productivity and effectiveness in test case generation using the AQUABUS method and its associated Eclipse plug-in [19].

These results reveal a weak situation and an opportunity for improving both effectiveness and efficiency through a more systematic design of cases. Nor organizational practices neither individual abilities of developers offer good results for productivity and quality in software so our next logical step was the investigation of possible causes of this situation: a detailed study was launched in 2007.

4   Survey on Factors Which Influence Testing Practice

Although some information on which is the state of practice in software testing is available, it is really difficult to find analysis on which can be the causes of the situation. In general, it is possible to locate articles (e.g. [20] [21]) based on subjective personal analysis of experts analyzing or explaining the contributing factors that impede efficient and effective application of software testing best practices. However, it is difficult to find works based on evidences, quantitative data or, at least, analysis of experiences (e.g. [22] or [23]) although specific surveys (e.g. [15]) have included questions on which are some of the barriers for better performance in software testing. Another interesting approach is the use of ethnographic methods to capture and analyze the work of software developers in projects [4] as they allow realizing a distance between theory and practice exists in real testing practices.

In our case, analyzing the results in organizations (Section 2) and the ones of individual performance in test case design (Section 3), we decided to investigate the possible causes of such situation. As part of the research network REPRIS (focused on software testing in software engineering and funded by the Spanish Ministry of

Science), we exploited the opportunity of promoting a debate with a panel of experts from industry (9 specialists) and academia (16 researchers) during a workshop hold in Zaragoza (Spain) in 2007. After an intensive session and refining and consolidating conclusions (reviewed by participants), 23 factors arose as possible causes of problems in software testing real practice. Although it was an interesting result, we decided to check if software professionals in Spain really confirm such factors were applicable to their professional environment. A questionnaire was created (see Table 5) where respondents had to indicate if they consider each item an effective factor of influence; they also ranked influence in a three-level scale: total/partial/ none.

Table 4. Factors of influence as items of questionnaire with ID for factorial analysis

Id	Factor
Q1.1.	When delays or finance problems appear, it is usual to shorten quality and testing effort.
Q1.2.	It is not strange a QA position disappears transferring people to software development roles
Q2.1	Testing is not creative: it is something annoying and not attractive which you have to do. Even it is negative (looks for defects) and destructive (goes against developers' work)
Q2.2	It is an area without good opportunities of career development or promotion.
Q2.3	Career development in testing does not guarantee the same salary or conditions as in other professional careers in software development (even you may expect worse conditions).
Q2.4	It is not usually recognized this work on testing, it is not usually accounted to be paid by customers, it is usually an internal service with no direct relationships with customers, etc.
Q2.5	Low level testers do not require a university degree, maybe only a basic professional education so this tend to project an image of not attractive professional career
Q3.1	Many IT university graduates have not attended specific training on testing
Q3.2	Many IT professionals have not also received specific training on testing
Q3.3	Courses on software testing are not usual in company training programs for software professionals (more focus on technology, new versions of products or in software development methods)
Q3.4	Testing is not a hot topic in universities: many teachers mention it and encourage students to do but few of them understand the correct philosophy and techniques of testing.
Q3.5	Specific testing training tend to focus on unit/detailed testing while functional/system testing is addressed as a marginal topic
Q3.6	Low importance or absence of specific training/qualification in testing (materials, certifications, etc.)
Q4.1	Junior tend to focus on programming and code: reject to work in other activities like testing
Q4.2	Many managers did not attend good training on software testing so they do not appreciate its interest or potential for efficiency and quality
Q5.1	People tend to execute testing in an uncontrolled manner until the total expenditure of resources in the belief that if we test a lot, in the end, we will cover or control all the system
Q5.2	It is not usual to plan and design efficient cases with minimum cost or to link tests to priorities or risks; there is not control on incurred risks depending on tests, no control of evidences, etc.
Q5.3	Test design usually means a rework of what analysts did not completed or documented because testing is totally dependent on a good requirements specification
Q5.4	Software test phase is located at the end of the project suffering shortened schedule due to delays of the previous development phases and the impossibility of postpone delivery to customer
Q5.5	Relationship between software models and testing is not exploited, specially for test design: "testing is something we do at the end once we have code"
Q5.6	It is not usual to design tests once we have a specification (although it is possible to do it in parallel with analysis): in fact, they document knowledge on functionality and requirements
Q6.1	Market is not mature enough so certain software quality problems are not sufficiently penalized
Q6.2	Best business is possible when customer pays maintenance of defects delivered with the developed software (getting money for repairing defects one has created)

Table 5. Respondents in the survey of factors of influence on software testing

Sector	%	Position	%
Government	22.9%	Project manager	21.8%
Telco/IT	21.8%	Tester	14.6%
Consultancy	14.5%	Manager	14.6%
Finance/insurance	9.8%	Programmer	12.5%
Defense	5.2%	QA specialist	9.4%
Tourism	5.2%	Systems analyst	7.3%
Health	3.1%	Others	20.6%
Transportation/Airlines	3.1%		
Others	14.4%		

Again, through direct contact with software professionals in events and training courses, we got a varied sample of 127 practitioners to collect opinion on the proposed list of factors of influence (see Table 4). The following sections will present both the general descriptive results and the detailed statistical data analysis.

4.1 Descriptive Data

As a first step, a simple descriptive analysis of data is done. Percentages of respondents who chose each option (i.e., confirmation of factor as a fact in professional settings and each level of possible influence) are presented in Table 6.

Table 6. Results of survey on factor of influence on testing

Factor	Confirm.	Rank of influence			Factor	Confirm.	Rank of influence		
		Total	Partial	None			Total	Partial	None
Q3.1	96,1%	40,94%	39,37%	19,69%	Q5.2	74,0%	40,94%	33,07%	25,98%
Q3.2	93,7%	39,37%	40,16%	20,47%	Q2.4	71,7%	23,62%	37,80%	38,58%
Q5.4	92,1%	61,42%	22,05%	16,54%	Q6.1	70,1%	31,50%	40,94%	27,56%
Q1.1	90,6%	61,42%	25,98%	12,60%	Q2.5	66,9%	25,98%	37,01%	37,01%
Q3.3	90,6%	37,01%	44,09%	18,90%	Q3.5	63,8%	30,71%	33,86%	35,43%
Q3.4	85,8%	30,71%	44,09%	25,20%	Q5.1	58,3%	29,13%	33,86%	37,01%
Q4.2	85,8%	48,03%	30,71%	21,26%	Q6.2	57,5%	31,50%	28,35%	40,16%
Q5.5	85,0%	48,82%	26,77%	24,41%	Q2.3	54,3%	14,96%	35,43%	49,61%
Q5.3	80,3%	40,16%	33,07%	26,77%	Q1.2	48,0%	30,71%	25,98%	43,31%
Q3.6	78,0%	33,86%	44,09%	22,05%	Q2.1	48,0%	25,20%	35,43%	39,37%
Q5.6	78,0%	30,71%	45,67%	23,62%	Q2.2	41,7%	18,90%	35,43%	45,67%
Q4.1	77,2%	29,92%	41,73%	28,35%					

As can be seen in Table 6, only three factors are not confirmed by at least 50% of respondents: Q1.2 (unstability of QA positions), Q2.1 (testing is not attractive) and Q2.2 (poor career development). However, in our opinion, they should not be rejected because there are a significant percentage of respondents supporting the idea. Another group of factors (Q 53.6, Q 5.6, Q 4.1, Q 5.2, Q 2.4, Q 6.1, Q 2.5, Q 3.5, Q 5.1, Q 6.2, Q 2.3) have a greater proportion of support although an important percentage of people are not convinced of their presence in professional environments. And finally, a group of factors (Q 3.1, Q 3.2, Q 5.4, Q 1.1, Q 3.3, Q 3.4, Q 4.2, Q 5.5, Q 5.3) have a confirmation percentage above 80% so they can be considered as real facts in the software development world. As an additional action, for some of the respondents (33), we collected information about testing training. Combining with the first survey (Section 2), a global 36% of professionals have attended specific testing training.

4.2 Detailed Analysis of Results

A first objective is the validation of the questionnaire used to collect data analyzing correlations between pairs of questions. First of all, reliability of the scale should be tested through the Cronbach´s alpha coefficient. This measure helps to verify if the questions are related between them, i.e., all the questions measure the same concept. Then factorial analysis will be applied to verify which concept measures each group of questions. This allows determining the structure of the scale [24].

4.2.1 Previous Analysis
Exploratory analysis enables the detection of possible errors during data collection as well as the checking of feasibility of factorial analysis. Subsequently we examine descriptive statistics (means, standard deviation, median, minimum and maximum and absolute and relative frequencies) of all the variables in the study. Moreover, box plots can help to determine data entry errors and the coefficient of variation can be used to check the homogeneity of data. The correlation matrix gives information about factorial analysis applicability: correlations higher than 0.30, significance levels and determinants close to 0 shows there are correlated variables [25].

SPSS 16.0.1 and LISREL 8.80 statistical programs have been used to analyze the collected data. A first visual inspection of correlation matrix showed us that there was an essential number of correlations higher than 0.30; consequently, we concluded that there were interrelated variables [25]. Moreover, as almost all significance levels are close to zero, we had to reject the null hypothesis and concluded there was linear relationship between the variables. The determinant is near zero too (9,06E-005): it confirms these variables are highly correlated so factorial analysis is applicable.

4.2.2 Reliability Analysis
The first validation is the reliability analysis of the used factors. The reliability is the degree in which the observed variable measures the real value and is free of error. The reliability analysis includes the examination of corrected item-to-total correlations to find out if each factor measures the same issue than the rest of the factors. We eliminate specific items to improve reliability alpha coefficient. In this case, questions 1.1 (Q1.1) and 3.5 (Q3.5) have been eliminated. The final Cronbach´s alpha coefficient value after these eliminations is 0.908 demonstrating high consistency and reliability of the model[2].

---

[2] The conventional minimum for Cronbach's alpha coefficient is established in 0.7 [26].

Q1.1 had provoked some comments during data collection because some people were reluctant to recognize this practice. Comparing with descriptive analysis (section 4.1) Q1.1 was confirmed as a real fact (90.6%) and its influence on testing is high enough (only the 12,60% rank influence as none). Although it is an important factor, it is not related to the scale here presented: maybe this question should be better formulated. Anyway more research is needed to verify the importance of this factor.

Q3.5 experienced problems due to people without specific testing training. 63.8% of the respondents considered it as a real fact but the influence on testing is not clear because the data are very similar for the three categories.

4.2.3 Exploratory Factorial Analysis (EFA)

EFA enables to identify the underlying structure of the relations obtaining a predictive validation of the model. To investigate acceptability of factorial analysis results the

Table 7. EFA Results for the model

Factor	EFA Loadings (after varimax rotation)[a]				
	C1	C2	C3	C4	C5
Q1.1.					,673
Q1.2.			,382	,590	
Q2.1				,812	
Q2.2				,602	,328
Q2.3		,367		,302	,572
Q2.4				,715	
Q2.5		,850			
Q3.1		,824			
Q3.2		,728			
Q3.3	,446	,368	,347		
Q3.4	,487		,471		
Q3.5	,513		,372		
Q3.6	,562		,325		
Q4.1	,448				,565
Q4.2			,430		,576
Q5.1			,646		
Q5.2			,701		
Q5.3			,685		
Q5.4	,376		,408		
Q5.5	,658			,353	
Q5.6	,820				
Q6.1					,673
Q6.2			,382	,590	

Cronbach´ alpha	0.908
Kaiser-Meyer-Olkin (KMO) Measure of Sampling Adequacy	0.853
Bartlett's Test of Sphericity (Approx. Chi-Square)	1099,9(df = 210)[b]
Correlation Matrix Determinant	9,06E-005

Note: EFA=Exploratory Factor Analysis, loadings < 0.32 not shown;
a.Total variance extracted by the five factors = 60,995%, b. p<0.001

Kaiser-Meyer-Oklin (KMO) index[3] and the Bartlett's Test of Sphericity are checked. Then, principal components as extraction method with Varimax (with Kaiser normalization) as rotation method and the breaks-in-eigenvalues criterion [25] is used to decide the initial number of factors to keep. Factor loadings equal to or greater than 0.5 are considered strong [25]. Items with low loadings on all components (the cut-off value for loadings was 0.32 [26]) are eliminated too. Table 7 shows the KMO and Bartlett´s Test and the extracted components with their loadings. KMO was clear with value greater than 0.80 and Bartlett´s Test indicates a meaningful relationship among the variables. The extracted components have been labeled as follows:

Q3.4 Q3.6 Q4.1 Q4.2 Q6.1 Q6.2 = C1 (Market and attitude toward testing)
Q3.1 Q3.2 Q3.3 = C2 (Education and training)
Q5.3 Q5.4 Q5.5 Q5.6= C3 (Integration with development)
Q2.1 Q2.2 Q2.3 Q2.5 = C4 (Career)
Q1.2 Q2.4 Q5.1 Q5.2 = C5 (Attractiveness)

Note that EFA has extracted one factor less than the initial set of the questionnaire: initial grouping was done by the expert in charge of coordination based on his own experience and was not object of debate but it was confirmed by experts.

4.2.4 Confirmatory Factorial Analysis

The predictive validation obtained after applying EFA in previous section should be confirmed to obtain the final model. Confirmatory Factor Analysis (CFA) through Structural Equation Model (SEM) and Maximum Likelihood (ML) estimation method is used in order to assess the validity of the model. Several indicators were used to assess model fit in order to compare the alternative models such as the Root Square Error of Approximation (RMSEA), Comparative Fit Index (CFI), the Normed Fit Index (NFI), the Non-Normed Fit Index (NNFI) and the Relative Fit Index (RFI).

Table 8. Goodness of Fit indicators for the model

	Suggested cut-off Values	Factor´s questionarie
χ^2 (df)		189,036 (179)
S- χ^2	>1, <2	1.05
RMSEA	< 0.08	0.0021
CFI	> 0.9	0.997
NFI	> 0.9	0.954
NNFI	> 0.9	0.997
RFI	> 0.9	0.946

Table 8 shows minimum recommended values for good fit [28] as well as the calculated values for the model. All the indicators exceed the minimum recommended values for good fit providing evidence of discriminate validity.

5 Conclusions

One of the usual shortcomings of the area of software engineering is the lack of trustable data about which is the state of practice in general and more specifically in

---

[3] KMO: above 0.5, it should be accepted, 0.7-0.8, good value; above 0.8, meritorious [27].

software testing. Data from industry tend to be collected and processed in an informal and even slanted way so they are not trustable as an accurate view of reality; academia usually experience many problems to access software professionals and organizations to get information. The above presented studies are a contribution to overcome the mentioned absence of information.

In general, besides the need of improvement of organizational and individual practices, many of the 23 explicative factors have been confirmed by a varied and significant sample of 127 software professionals so there is now a guideline for improving software testing conditions. One of the most evident barriers is the lack of training and expertise, something consistent with other surveys [14] although market maturity and career issues are also considered very important factors. It is remarkable the traditional divorce between the development deliverables and test case design methods, something also detected in the data from individual practices (section 2).

We are now working to launch this survey across Europe with the help of CEPIS to check if the factors are common or if local differences arise. To support this effort, we intend to use results of the factorial analysis of the questionnaires for the grouping of items as well as for establishing the final model of factors to be applied. Anyway the model would be useful also for other researchers who may collect data in this area.

Acknowledgments

This study was supported by the projects TIN2007-67843-C06-01 and TIN2007-30391-E partially funded by the Spanish Ministry of Science and Innovation.

References

1. Jones, C.: Estimating software costs. McGraw-Hill, New York (1998)
2. Grindal, M., Offutt, J., Mellin, J.: On the Testing Maturity of Software Producing Organiza-tions: Detailed Data. Technical Report ISE-TR-06-03, Department of Information and Software Engineering, George Mason University (2006)
3. McGarry, F., Pajerski, R., Page G., Waligora, S., Basili V., Zelkowitz, M.: Software Process Improvement in the NASA Software Engineering Laboratory, Technical Report, CMU/SEI-94-TR-22, SEI Carnegie-Mellon University (1994)
4. Martin, D., Rooksby, J., Rouncefield, M., Sommerville, I.: 'Good' Organisational Reasons for 'Bad' Software Testing: An Ethnographic Study of Testing in a Small Software Company. In: Proc. of 29th Int. Conf. on Soft. Engin., pp. 602–611 (2007)
5. Fernandez-Sanz, L.: Un sondeo sobre la práctica actual de pruebas de software en España. REICIS 2, 43–54 (2005)
6. SEI: CMMi® for Development. SEI-Carnegie Mellon University (2006)
7. Paulk, M., Weber, C., Curtis, B., Chrisis, M.: The Capability Maturity Model. Addison-Wesley, Reading (1995)
8. van Veenendaal, E.: Test Maturity Model Integration (TMMi) Versión 1.0. TMMI Foundation (2008), http://www.tmmifoundation.org
9. Burnstein, I.: Practical Software Testing. Springer, Heidelberg (2002)
10. VanVeenendaal, E.: Guidelines for Testing Maturity. STEN IV, 1–10 (2006)

11. Koomen, T.: Test process improvement: a practical step-by-step guide to structured test-ing. Addison Wesley, Reading (1999)
12. Pol, M., Teunissen, R., van Veenendaal, E.: Software Testing. A guide to the TMap Ap-proach. Addison-Wesley, Reading (2002)
13. Koomen, T., van der Aalst, L., Broekman, B., Vroon, M.: TMap Next for result-driven testing. UTN Publishers (2006)
14. Sanz, A., Saldaña, J., García, J., Gaitero, D.: TestPAI: A proposal for a testing process area integrated with CMMI. In: European Systems and Software Process Improvement and Inno-vation (EUROSPI 2008), pp. 3–5 (2008)
15. Ng, S.P., Murnane, T., Reed, K., Grant, D., Chen, Y.: A Preliminary Survey on Software Testing Practices in Australia. In: ASWEC, Proceedings of the 2004 Australian Software Engineering Conference, pp. 116–125 (2004)
16. Geras, A.M., Smith, M.R., Miller, J.: A survey of software testing practices in Alberta. Canadian J. of Electrical and Computer Engineering 29, 183–191 (2004)
17. Groves, L., Nickson, R., Reeves, G., Reeves, S., Utting, M.: A Survey of Software Prac-tices in the New Zealand Software Industry. In: Proceedings of the 2000 Australian Soft-ware Engi-neering Conference, pp. 189–101 (2000)
18. Runeson, P.: A Survey of Unit Testing Practices. IEEE Softw. 23, 22–29 (2006)
19. Lara, P., Fernández-Sanz, L.: Un experimento sobre hábitos de pruebas artesanales de soft-ware: Resultados y Conclusiones. In: Taller sobre Pruebas en Ingeniería del Software PRIS 2007, pp. 23–30 (2007)
20. Lara, P., Fernández-Sanz, L.: Test Case Generation, UML and Eclipse. Dr.Dobbs Jour-nal 33, 49–52 (2008)
21. Whittaker, J.A.: What Is Software Testing? And Why Is It So Hard? IEEE Software 17, 70–79 (2000)
22. Glass, R.L., Collard, R., Bertolino, A., Bach, J., Kaner, C.: Software Testing and Industry Needs 23, 55–57 (2006)
23. García, A., de Amescua, M.V., Sanz, A.: Ten Factors that Impede Improvement of Verifi-cation and Validation Processes in Software Intensive Organizations. Software Process Improvement and Practice 13, 335–343 (2008)
24. Taipale, O., Karhu, K., Smolander, K.: Observing Software Testing Practice from the Viewpoint of Organizations and Knowledge Management. In: First Intern. Symp. on Em-pirical Software Engineering and Measurement, pp. 21–30 (2007)
25. Hair, J.F., Tatham, R.L., Anderson, R., Black, W.: Multivariate Data Analysis. Prentice Hall, Englewood Cliffs (1998)
26. Tabachnick, B.G., Fidell, L.S.: Using Multivariate Statistics. Pearson, London (2006)
27. Nunnally, J., Bernstein, I.: Psychometric Theory. McGraw-Hill, New York (1994)
28. Hu, L., Bentler, P.M.: Cutoff: Criteria for Fit Indexes in Covariance Structure Analysis: Conventional Criteria vs new alternatives. Structural Equation Modeling 6, 1–55 (1999)

What Is a Test Case? Revisiting the Software Test Case Concept

Dani Almog and Tsipi Heart

The Department of Industrial Engineering and Management
Ben Gurion University of the Negev
almog.dani@gmail.com, heart@bgu.ac.il

Abstract. Since the 1980s the term "Test Case" (TC) has been recognized as a building block for describing testing items, widely used as a work unit, metric and documentation entity. In light of the centrality of the TC concept in testing processes, the questions this paper attempts to answer are: What are the uses of TC in software testing? Is there a general, commonly agreed-upon definition of a TC? If not, what are the implications of this situation?

This article reviews and explores the history, use and definitions of TCs, showing that while extensively used in research and practice, there is no one formal agreed upon definition of a TC. In this paper we point at undesirable implications of this situation, suggest four criteria for a 'good' TC definition, and discuss the benefits accrued from such a definition. We conclude by urging the academic and professional community to formalize a TC definition for the benefits of the industry and its customers, and strongly believe that this review paves the way to articulating a formal TC definition. Such a definition, when widely accepted, will clarify some of the ambiguity currently associated with TC interpretation, hence with software testing assessment which relies on TCs as metrics. Furthermore, a formal definition can advance automation of TC generation and management.

1 Introduction

A research initiated by the US Department of Commerce [1] estimated an annual economic damage equivalent to $20 – $52 billion as a result of inadequate software testing infrastructure and processes. The authors classified two primary categories of damages: damages users incurred because of software malfunction, and damages associated with software modification, fixing and re-testing. Although published some six years ago, there is a sound indication that the situation has not significantly improved. Hence, the alarming magnitude of damages caused by inappropriate software testing merits closer investigation into plausible reasons and explanations to this undesirable situation in a quest for solutions and improvement.

Because software testing is a broad topic which cannot be grasped in a single work, this study focuses on one specific aspect of the software testing domain – the test case (TC), since TC is a cornerstone in software testing processes, and because, as shown later on, it is posited that inconsistencies in TC definitions and use throughout the testing process is perhaps a cause for fundamental flaws.

The questions this paper attempts to answer are: What is the role of TC in software testing? Is there a general agreement about the definition of TC? If not, what are the consequences of this situation?

R.V. O'Connor et al. (Eds.): EuroSPI 2009, CCIS 42, pp. 13–31, 2009.
© Springer-Verlag Berlin Heidelberg 2009

We believe that answering these questions will clarify some of the ambiguity currently associated with TC interpretation, and pave the way to articulating a formal TC definition. If and when widely accepted, it can relieve some of the ambiguity associated with software testing metrics that commonly relies on counting TCs. Furthermore, an appropriate formal definition can drive automation of TC generation and management. Therefore, this work is clearly a contribution to software process improvement by dealing with an important aspect of testing – the test case.

The rest of the paper is organized as follows: common software testing processes and practices are briefly described in the next chapter, showing the importance of testing processes in software engineering, and the TC as the testing building block. We then describe the literature survey methodology employed. Next, several definitions for TCs are presented as a result of the literature survey, showing the conceptual variability of these definitions. We then proceed to a review of the literature discussing the centrality of TCs in testing processes, concluding with a suggestion of dimensions by which a TC definition can be evaluated, as well as an evaluation of existing definitions based on these dimensions. The paper concludes with a discussion of the implications of the lack of a unified approach to TCs and whether there is a need to re-define this term.

2 Common Practices in Software Testing

In the following section the importance of testing in terms of its substantive role in software development on the one hand, and of its complexity, on the other hand, is briefly presented. This background clarifies the merit in further looking into TC use and definitions, since TCs are building blocks of testing.

The testing effort undoubtedly comprises a significant portion of the programming effort. For example, an early research conducted at NASA [2] found that testing efforts comprise 30% of the time invested by programmers, and 37% of their actual work days (Figure 1).

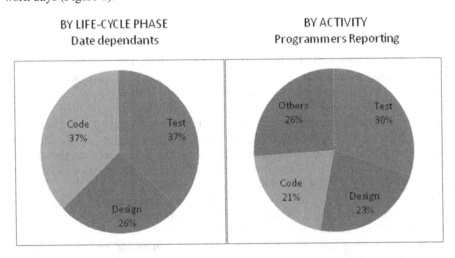

BASED ON 11 PFROJECTS IN FLIGHT DYNAMICS
ENVIRONMENT (of Similar Size and Complexity)

Fig. 1. Distribution of the effort among programmers' tasks (NASA) [2]

A more recent study conducted in Alberta, Canada [3] identified large variance among projects regarding testing resources in terms of the ratio of developers to testers, showing that about 50% of the studied projects allocated around two developers to one tester (~50%), whereas 35% invested much less personnel resources in testing (five developers to one tester, ~20%). Other studies generally support these findings, substantiating the positive correlation between software development process maturity and the degree of investment in software testing – around 35% of the overall investment [4, 5].

Testing tasks have been traditionally classified into three phases [6]: 1) Preparation: plan, design, construct, 2) Execution, and 3) Verification: verify results against expected outcomes and report. These three stages were often performed sequentially as in structured software development process models, demanding rather equal resource investment. Recently, however, there is a tendency to change this structured model due to several reasons [7]. One reason is the growing popularity of new software development models and techniques, such as agile methods, service oriented architecture (SOA), and test driven development (TDD), all three indicating testing processes that somewhat deviate from the structured process models. Along changes in development models, testing automation has matured and is now more prevalent, potentially easing the execution phase. Finally, verification and validation processes become more complex due to the growing complexity of the developed applications and the data units involved. For example, growing complexity can be attributed to data representation simultaneously using various techniques as databases, XML files, encryption, compression, coding, dynamic data location, etc. Consequently, a deeper understanding of the data structure and characteristics is required during testing, as well as more sophisticated tools and processes.

In light of the growing complexity of the testing process, Bach [8] advocated exploratory testing, defined as "any testing to the extent that the tester actively controls the design of the tests as those tests are performed and uses information gained while testing to design new and better tests" (p. 2). This methodology addresses the assertion that complete testing preparation is unlikely at an initial phase of the testing process. Thus, Kaner [9] explained the advantages of exploratory testing in allowing testers to learn while they test, to get more sophisticated as they learn, interpret and design their tests differently as they learn more about the product, the market, the variety of uses of the product, the risks, and the mistakes that are likely to be made by the humans who wrote the code. Under exploratory testing the test plan evolves during the test development and execution, rather than pre-planned before the actual complexity of the product is realized. This realm, however, might be practically problematic when having to pre-estimate testing efforts as part of the overall project estimation. Evidently, there is a broad agreement that testing is a complex task, hence difficult to estimate and quantify. In-depth examination of various testing processes and techniques is beyond the scope of this work, instead, we focus on the common building block of all software testing techniques – the TC. Thus, in order to better understand the problem at hand, we next bring a review of the literature, elaborating on the single concept common to all testing processes and techniques – the TC.

3 Methodology

The following methodology has been employed in order to identify the literature relevant for this review. First, Google and Google Scholar were used as search engines to find sources with the keywords: "software testing", "software reliability", "testing methodology", "black box testing", and "test case". This first search effort yielded about 150 papers and about 25 books dated 1982 onwards, which were scanned for relevance by reading their abstracts. Looking at citations appearing in the elicited papers implied that there is merit in further expanding the search by using the following keywords: "TDD", "SOA", "agile", "software cost estimation", "software project management", "testing projects", "test case generation", and "testing automation". This search yielded about 100 additional papers and about 10 books spanning the years 1980 till 2008.

A similar search has been conducted on leading journals and conferences, for example relevant IEEE and EMSE journals and ICST conferences that directly or indirectly included topics represented by the above keywords. These three rounds of literature search resulted in a database of about 300 papers, books, and conference proceedings. Endnote 9.0 has been used as the reference management tool, where research notes have been added for classification purposes.

This reference database has been then reviewed, and each reference has been classified to sub-topics as in Table 4 (a paper could be related to more than one sub-topic), as well as whether or not it included a formal definition of a TC. Those papers which contained such a definition were further categorized based on the nature of the definition, as appears in Table 3.

While classifying the papers, additional references and topics were searched by scanning their reference list, which resulted in about 40 additional papers, bringing the total number of papers and books reviewed to about 340, of which 267 directly referred to TCs.

4 Literature Review

4.1 Historical Overview of the TC Concept

The TC concept appeared as a central concept underlying testing processes since the beginning of formal software testing, for example as part of the Systematic Test & Evaluation Processes (STEP) model [10], which defined feedback loops between software development and testing. Three sources for TC generation were identified: directly from the requirements, stemming from performance requirements, and based on system's design [10]. A formal definition of a TC, however, was not included. In a study published in the same year, Ostrand & Balcer [11] suggested to build TCs as a collection of test frames and test scripts, yet these two terms were not precisely defined although TCs were perceived to be measureable by their size. Weyuker [12] brought a quite different approach when she maintained that TCs are formed by decision statements, and recognized that the more the number of decision statements in the tested code, the more complex is the TC, recommending to limit the average number of decision statements tested by one TC to 3.6. Interestingly, in spite of frequent use of the term TC in her paper (76 times) it was not formally defined.

The centrality of the TC is evident in the work of Harrold, Gupta & Soffa [13], who used TCs as the basis of a methodology to minimize testing efforts, realizing that the testing process could in fact become indefinite because of the lack of indicators for absence of errors. They developed a structured methodology to identify redundant TCs and merge them into TC suites or execute these TCs in pairs. In this work TCs were identified as *TC requirements* assuming that TCs stem from requirements. Adopting an analogous line of thinking, Rosenberg, Hammer & Huffman [14] maintained that TC content should reflect the requirements, and therefore should be controlled by a TC coverage matrix, which maps requirements to TCs, aimed at optimizing the testing effort. Clearly, TCs and the resulting coverage matrix tend to become more complex relative to the number and complexity of the requirements. In an effort to handle this growing complexity, Iberle [15] developed a TC hierarchy methodology at HP labs, where the test plan was formed by test groups based on the system's functionality as defined by the requirements, the system's design and other sources, and each test group is then further detailed into tests composed of TCs in the leaves (Figure 2). Here again, the TC was the fundamental building block of the testing process, yet no formal definition was provided.

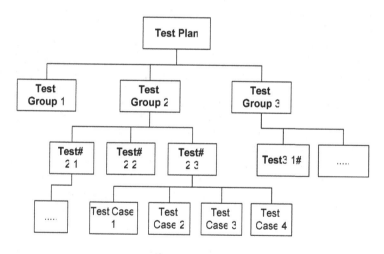

Fig. 2. Test plan hierarchy [15]

Aichernig [16] was among the few researchers who attempted a formal TC definition by developing a mathematical description of a TC, although he suggested that TCs were in fact abstractions of the requirements, or "highly abstract contracts" (p. 6). Aichernig's mathematical approach to TC definition (brought later on in section 4.4) was aimed at advancing a formal language essential for automation of TC generation.

In the first chapter of his book "Software Testing: A Craftsman Approach" Jorgensen [17] reviewed the TC concept, noting that the TC was the key to the success of the testing process. He distinguished between TCs identified by the functional requirements (functional testing) and TCs identified by the software structure (structural testing).

In an attempt at identifying "what is a good test case?" Kaner [18] maintained that a good TC was one that gave the required *information* which was the objective of the particular test. He counted several testing objectives each requiring a different type of TCs, and acknowledged that TCs greatly vary and hence using them as metrics is problematic: "Also, under this definition, the metrics that report the number of test cases are meaningless. What do you do with a set of 20 single-variable tests that were interesting a few weeks ago but now should be retired or merged into a combination? Suppose you create a combination test that includes the 20 tests. Should the metric report this one test, twenty tests, or twenty one?" (p. 2).

Later works by Grindal and Colleagues [19, 20] included a review of mechanisms to render software testing more efficient and effective, heavily relying on TC selection and execution, since they maintained that testing is "loosely considered to be the dynamic execution of test cases" [19, p. 2]. An interesting approach has been adopted by the aerospace industry where the Conformance and Fault Injection (CoFI) methodology has been used [21, 22]. Under this methodology, TCs were differentiated between those that aim at confirming the appropriate behavior of the tested product and those that are aimed at creating faulty situations. The authors suggested a structured approach to the definition of the two types of testing, and as a result, a systematic creation of the relevant TCs.

Because of the centrality of the TC in the testing process, and due to the significant effort invested in designing and generating TCs especially in large or complex projects, several studies have elaborated on TC management processes and tools. For example, Desai [23] from Bell Laboratories described a tool which managed the configuration and inventory of TCs separately from the testing tasks, compatible with the IEEE 829 standard. A later work described a TC management and tracking tool, where the term 'test item' is used in a context similar to TC [24], making the TC concept even more ambiguous in the absence of a formal definition. The need to automate the generation and management of TCs was demonstrated in Jorgensen's [25] work, where he noted that it took 141,306 TCs to test version 5.0.1 of Acrobat Reader. It is noteworthy that Jorgensen did not define a TC unit in this work as the basis for the counting method although the term was extensively used in this commentary.

The likely variability among TCs has been acknowledged by Nagappan [26] who developed the Software Testing and Reliability Early Warning (STREW) metric suite for software testing effort estimation, using TCs as one of the model metrics. He warned, however, that using TCs as a metric might not be well defined since "....one developer might write fewer test cases each with multiple asserts checking various conditions. Another developer might test the same conditions by writing many more test cases, each with only one assert" (p. 39). This variability among TCs should be taken into account when defining effort estimation model parameters. Table 1 shows that TCs can greatly vary, for example by complexity, size (whether containing many asserts or one assert), or by origin (requirements or other), hence cannot be unified as indicating a singular metric.

Table 1. Software rating – defect density, [27]

Rating	Very Low Defect Density	Very High Defect Density
Test Cases	Few test cases	Many test cases
Test case asserts	Asserts that only exercise "success" behavior of the product or do not adequately cover the functionality of the product	Asserts that exercise various behaviors of each requirements
Requirements	Test cases do not relate to requirements	At least one test case per requirement
Code coverage	Minimal coverage of important functions	100% coverage

A further warning in this regard has been advocated by Hoffman [28], who pointed at the possibility that definitions of TCs, as well as their number and content, might change during the course of the project, jeopardizing the validity of metrics based on these TCs.

4.2 TC Use and Generation in Modern Software Development

Not only have TCs been important in traditional software development processes, they also continue to play an important role in more modern software development methodologies and techniques.

Similar to the more traditional software development environments, the TC is a fundamental entity in testing software in the *object oriented* environment. For example, Binder [29] first developed a methodology for TC generation in an object oriented environment, by introducing the 'testing points' concept, a mechanism used to define test requirements and the relevant TCs. Later in his book Binder suggested to define the TC as a method thereby including the test itself as part of the design of the objects.

Agile software development methods have quite revamped traditional testing concepts, particularly the division between testers and developers [30], since on-going testing is one of the principles guiding development of very small and frequent software iterations common to the agile methodology. Nonetheless, the centrality of the TC concept has not changed as a result of utilizing these methodologies, although the test planning method has.

TDD or TDM are software development methods that advocate writing TCs prior to the actual software development to assure developing software that is testable [31, 32]. Here, the role of the TC is even magnified, yet evidence about the effectiveness of this method is still mixed [31, 33].

Service oriented architecture (SOA) has introduced new testing challenges [34] demonstrated for example by the inclusion of a testing mechanism in the SOA infrastructure delivered by IBM [35]. Especially challenging is testing composed and complex services that require new testing methods [36], making estimation of testing scope and effort more difficult. The recent move to SOA has raised the interest in software componentization [37, 38] and component-based testing, adding additional ambiguity to the TC concept.

Some research has focused on *automatic TC generation*, a process requiring TC formalization [39-42]. As use cases largely reflect functional requirements in the UML environment, Nebut, Fleurey, Le Traon & J'z'quel [43] suggested TC generation from use cases, after incorporating the contract element they claim is a component essential for translating a use case into a TC. Likewise, test objectives and sequence diagrams also serve as sources for TC generation. Generally, several works have developed techniques to generate TCs from UML diagrams, termed Model Based Testing (MBT), mostly based on transforming use cases and states into TCs [44, 45]. Although the attempts to automate TC generation resulted in some level of formalization, the difficulties pertaining to the TC concept were not solved by this mechanism, since use cases and scripts all suffer from the same fuzziness of definition regarding size, complexity, number of states, etc.

4.3   TCs as Metrics

During the testing phase, there is a need to manage and control the process, by measuring its size, complexity, and quality, as a minimum. This, however, is easier said than done, due to reasons brought in the previous sections. Thus, for example when using the Goal – Questions – Metrics (GQM) method [1]developed by V. Basili and D. Weis for measurement development, Management strives to find metrics to answer questions such as 'how long would it take to complete testing?', or 'how much resources should be allocated to testing?', aimed at achieving managerial goals such as appropriate resource allocation and adhering to schedules. Measures developed to answer these questions often rely on number of TCs, for example "total number of planned white/black box test cases run to completion, number of planned integration tests run to completion, or number of unplanned test cases required during the test phase" [26, p. 15]. The Software Testing Reliability Early Warning Model for Java (STREW-J) developed by Nagappan [26] to estimate expected problems as a means to estimate testing efforts used at least two estimation parameters that are based on number of TCs: 1) *number of test cases divided by source lines of code (R1)* as an indication of whether there are too few test cases written to test the body of source code; and 2) *number of test case divided by number of requirements (R2)* as an indication of the thoroughness of testing relative to the requirements. Other TC-based metrics recommended as reflecting the status of the testing project were number or percent of TCs run since testing started, number or percent of TCs run since the last status report, number of percent of TCs that passed since the beginning of the testing project, number or percent of TCs passed since the last status report, number or percent of failed TCs, total number of open issues or TCs not run [46].

Elsewhere, eight of thirteen reports recommended as tools for testing monitoring and control were based on TCs count, completion status, results etc. [47]. Further, these same authors suggested eighteen indicators to monitor the project status, eleven of which are based on tests or TCs. Two real-world examples of using TCs as the unit for testing progress monitoring are presented in Figures 4 and 5. Figure 4 illustrates

---

[1] We thank the reviewer for suggesting using GQM as a metric-generation methodology.

NASA's recommendation for test execution monitoring, and Figure 5 was drawn from a real-world project at a large telecom enterprise, where three different projects were tracked based on the number of TCs not yet executed (test backlog). Evidently, not only all TCs were equally counted, but also TCs from different projects were compared under the same unit of analysis, regardless of potential variance among TCs stemming from the dissimilarity of the projects.

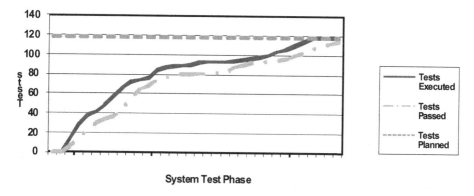

Fig. 3. Testing execution progress monitoring, [48]

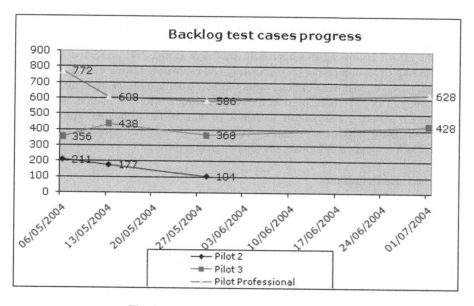

Fig. 4. Testing execution progress monitoring

In the next example (Table 2), number of tests was recommended as a metric to track and control testing execution. Since tests are composed of TCs it is reasonable to assume that this metric implies actually counting TCs from different software features ignoring their likely differences.

Table 2. Number of tests is used as a metric for testing monitoring and control [46]

Project online trade				Date: 5/23/2007	
Feature tested	Total Tested	# Complete	% Complete	# Success	% Success
Open Acct	46	46	100	41	89
Sell Order	36	25	69	25	69
Buy Order	19	17	89	12	63
......					
Totals	395	320	81	311	79

Similarly, IBM published reporting metrics for testing the software developed by various vendors under IBM's supervision for the Sydney Olympic Games, all based on counting number of TCs [49]: 1) Number of test cases defined, 2) Number of test cases executed, 3) Number of test cases with failures but no associated defect records 4) The percentage of test cases attempted, used as an indicator of progress relative to the completeness of the planned test effort.

TCs has also been used for testing effort estimation in few works where overall project effort has been estimated based on distinctive estimation of the various development phases [50-52]. In an attempt to overcome the problem of counting TCs of various size and complexity Nageswaran [53] suggested using function points where the number of TCs can be determined by the function points estimate for the corresponding effort. Following this approach Aranha & Borba [54] presented a scheme for collecting execution points for calculating and estimating testing efforts. It should be noted, however, that none of these works formally defined the TC term although.

Evidently, TCs have been used as metrics for testing effort estimation, as well as for testing monitoring and control. Common to most of the techniques suggested in these works is the reliance on counting TCs, with only minimal reference to the fact that TCs lack a standard definition and tend to greatly differ.

4.4 Test Case Definitions

As stated earlier, a thorough literature survey has been conducted in order to study where and how TCs are defined. Interestingly, in spite of a plethora of research about software quality assurance, few works formally define a TC, although most use this term quite intensively. Perhaps most notable is the fact that an explicit definition of a TC could not be located in the 2004 version of SWEBOK. Rather, the TC appears as an integral part of the general software testing definition:"ïSoftware testing consists of the dynamic verification of the behavior of a program on a finite set of test cases, suitably selected from the usually infinite executions domain, against the expected behavior" [55, p. 5-1]. Nonetheless, several definitions have been retrieved, classified into four dominant approaches: 1) input-process-output-objectives, 2) states and transitions, 3) contractual approach, and 4) other definitions.

The *input-process-output-objectives* perspective conceptualizes a TC as a set of inputs into a pre-defined process, aimed at yielding a desired output, based on the test

Table 3. Test Case Definitons and Sources

Category	Definition	Source
Input-Process-Output-Objectives	"A set of conditions or variables under which a tester will determine if an application or a software system meets specifications.... It may take many test cases to determine that a software program or system is functioning correctly"	www.wikipedia.org
	"A test case is the combination of test data and oracle information to determine the validity of the test"	[56, p. 9]
	"A set of test inputs, execution conditions, and expected results developed for a particular objective, such as to exercise a particular program path or to verify compliance with a specific requirement"	[24, p. 187]
	"Test case is a test vector consisting of a set of test inputs and the corresponding test outputs (pre and post conditional assertions)"	[45, p. 2]
	"Test Case is an identified set of information including inputs and expected outputs associated with a particular program behavior"	[17, p. 7]
	"A test case is a finite structure of input and expected output: a pair of input and output in the case of deterministic transformative systems, a sequence of input and output in the case of deterministic reactive systems, and a tree or a graph in the case of non-deterministic reactive systems	[32, p. 2]
States and Transitions	"A sequence of one or more subtests executed as a sequence because the outcome and/or final state of one subtest is the input and/or initial state of the next. The word 'test' is used to include subtests, tests properties, and test suites".	[57, p. 13]
	"A test case specifies the pretest state of the implementation under test (IUT) and its environment, the test inputs or conditions, and the expected result. The expected result specifies what the IUT should produce from the test inputs. This specification includes messages generated by the IUT, exceptions, returned values, and resultant state of the IUT and its environment. Test cases may also specify initial and resulting conditions for other objects that constitute the IUT and its environment."	[29, p. 47]
	"Test case is composed of several components: test case values, prefix values, verify values, exit commands and expected outputs"	[58, p. 28]
	"Test Case is a verification of some aspect of the System Under Test (SUT). Test Case for any feature of any SUT can be defined as follows: Perform verification, Vv Which may be preceded by a sequence of actions, Aa Which may require a set of data, Dd	[59, p. 51]

Table 3. (*continued*)

Contract	Which may require preconditions, Pp All of which runs in environment, Ee Hence, a Test Case, Tt = Ee Pp Dd Aa Vv"	
	"Test-cases common in software engineering are in fact contracts (highly abstract contracts)... However, our result that test-cases are abstractions holds for general contract statements involving user inter-action".	[16, p. 8]
	"a form of contract between a service provider and a service user"	[60, p. 2]
Other	"An empirical frame of reference, rather than a theoretical one"	[61, p.359]
	"...test case is a question that you ask of the program. The point of running the test is to gain information, for example, whether the program will pass or fail the test"	[18, p. 2]
	"A test idea is a brief statement of something that should be tested. For example, if you're testing a square root function, one idea for a test would be 'test a number less than zero'. The idea is to check if the code handles an error case"	[18, p. 2]
	"a specific set of attribute values that tests a given logical situation"	[62, p. 3]
	"a test case can be considered as a predator while a mutant program is analogous to a prey"	[63]

objective. The *states and transitions* approach considers a TC as a set of transition patterns among states. The *contractual* approach defines TC as a contract since the outcomes of pre-defined conditions are fully defined. Finally, there are several *other definitions* stemming from various contexts. Table 3 lists examples of definitions in each category. The implications of this variability are discussed next.

5 Discussion

The TC serves as the backbone of testing processes, and is a fundamental unit for test planning, execution, monitoring and control. It is also used as a common metric in quantifying testing effort, scope and status. Furthermore, there is a growing quest to automate TC generation, execution and management. Nonetheless and quite interestingly, there is no consensus regarding the formal definition of a TC.

From the papers reviewed for this work it is evident that the TC concept is frequently used in various contexts, yet infrequently formally defined (Table 4). Please note that numbers in Tables 4 and 5 do not add up because papers could be classified to more than one sub-topic.

Table 4. TC-related papers, definitions and contexts used

Topic	Cost/ROI Estimations	Manage-ment	UML/MBT OO/SOA	Metrics	Automation/ Generation	Total
TCs Papers Reviewed	86	69	46	25	44	267
Formal TC Definition	11 (13%)	19 (28%)	26 (57%)	4 (16%)	14 (32%)	38 (14%)

Table 4 shows that 267 reviewed papers referring to TCs covered five different topics, yet only in 38 papers (14%) a formal definition of TC was attempted, particularly in studies focusing on OO related issues and TC automation and Management. It is thus valid to wonder why only 14% of authors bothered to formally define the central concept of their work in spite of heavily using this term (some mention TC more than a hundred). Thus, in the 38 papers where TC was defined, various definitions were employed representing all four definition categories: input-process-output-objective, states & transitions, contract, and other. It is thus interesting to examine whether there is an association between the definition category used and the specific context (Table 5). For example, it could be expected that works in the UML/MBT/OO context would use states & transitions definitions that stem from the OO world. This, however, could not be substantiated by the present literature review, as those few authors who have used the TC definition in their OO-related work chose definitions from all categories (Table 5). Moreover, no author has articulated the reasons for choosing one definition or another. As seen in Table 5, authors using TCs in the context of OO/MBT/UML more frequently used the input-process-output-objective (termed hereinafter process-based for brevity sake) definitions rather than the more naturally related states & transitions definitions, which turn out as the most popular definition category. Evidently, no correlation could be deduced between the definition category and the context, possibly attesting to the arbitrary choice of the former.

Table 5. TC definition distribution by research context

Context	Definition category				
	Process	States	Contract	Other	Defined
Cost/ROI	6	1	1	3	11
Management / Project	11	4	1	3	19
OO/ MBT/UML/SOA	12	6	2	6	26
Measurements/Metrics	1	1	1	1	4
Automation/Regression	10	1	1	2	14
Total	18	11	2	8	38

The lack of formal TC definition and the fact that most studies do not include any definition raise several questions: Is such a definition required? Are there deficiencies in the existing definitions? What are the implications of the lack of a formal definition?

We maintain that a formal definition is indeed required, encouraged by the fact that in real-world testing of life-threatening projects a formal definition is an important part of the testing guidelines. For example, based on the IEEE standard, chapter 6 of a manual for testing safety applications in a nuclear reactor environment greatly elaborates on TC types, definitions, content, and documentation [64]. Four types of TCs are specified: 1) verification TC, 2) validation TC, 3) demonstration TC, 4) general suitability TC. Each TC is defined by a general description including reference number, geometry, flow features, experimental data, existing simulations, related experiments, and rating of the challenge the test case poses. These details should be accompanied by further documentation describing the test environment for each TC.

It is suggested that a formal TC definition could render several benefits if satisfying at least four requirements: 1) Unambiguousness: such TCs would be uniformly understood by the various stakeholders participating in a testing endeavor, 2) Generalizability: TCs would hold upon transforming from one platform to another, from one testing domain to another, and so on, 3) Quantifiability: only quantifiable TCs would be sensibly measured, and 4) Automatability: some might argue that this trait is an outcome of the above three characteristics, yet we chose to explicitly indicate it as a desirable feature because of its importance.

Unambiguousness ensures a unified view shared by all professionals involved in software testing regardless of their prior experience, background, testing environments, methods and techniques. This trait is important because it will ease the current 'Tower of Babylon' dominating the testing world, and rive sharing expertise among various testing schools and perceptions. *Generalizability* ensures maintaining testing assets and investments along various testing efforts, namely, TC generation tools and techniques would be valid in different testing environments. *Quantifiability* is clearly beneficial because of the importance of the TC as a fundamental metric. Currently, measurements involving counting TCs are clearly inconsistent. Finally, there is no need to explain the benefits rendered by the ability to *automate* TC generation, execution and management. Several attributes are mandatory for TC automation, among them is a formal definition of the TC structure.

Examining the existing definitions by the four categories illustrates the deficiencies in each type. The *input-process-output-objective* definitions are generally unambiguous, but not necessarily generalizable. For example, non-functional requirements, such as testing a user experience, are difficult to define using this type of definition. Likewise, the 'process' part of the TC can vary in size and complexity hence difficult to quantify and measure. For instance, a process can be as simple as 'check for existence of a certain value' or quite complex as 'create a customer order'. Consequently, this type of definition is problematic to automate. The *state & transitions* definitions may satisfy the unambiguousness and quantifiability traits but are hardly generalizable since they stem from the state-machine world, therefore not transferrable to other testing domains. For example states and transitions that are a result of dynamic environmental conditions and data would be rather impossible to define as a finite number of states and transitions. TCs defined as States & Transitions, however, are quite convenient to quantify and automate due to their origination in the state-machine domain. The *contract* group of definitions is becoming popular, mainly in SOA platforms, yet these definitions clearly violate the unambiguousness criterion. For example, Aichernig [16] defined a test as a contract between the user and the software provider, Mikhailova et al. [65] defined testing as a contract between the system under test and its environment, and Bruno et al. [66] thought it was a contract ensuring service compliance between releases. Clearly, only a formal definition of the contract, such as the one attempted by Aichernig [16] is unambiguous. For similar reasons it cannot be generalized, quantifiable or automatable unless formalized. Finally, it is quite obvious that the *other* definitions do not meet most of the above requirements.

We maintain that the absence of a formal definition for TCs causes test planning, execution, and monitoring malfunctioning. For example, reporting testing effort estimation or testing progress by number of executed TCs is clearly misleading, often resulting in projects not meeting time and budget constraints, or in inadequate software quality. Testing automation efforts are likewise contingent upon formal definition of TCs, hence its absence is possibly one of the barriers to a broader diffusion of automation tools. These shortcomings are quite likely among the causes for the huge annual economic damage as a result of inadequate software testing infrastructure and processes reported by the US Department of Commerce [1]. Hence, further work towards a formal TC definition that meets the above requirements is advocated.

6 Conclusions

TC is a cornerstone for planning, designing, and monitoring testing projects, as well as a means for work, effort and cost estimation. This work demonstrated not only the centrality of the TC but also the variance among TC definitions. Further, the official professional taxonomies, for example those presented in the joint ISO-IEEE Guide to the Software Engineering Body of Knowledge – SWEBOK does not explicitly define TC.

This situation is possibly a barrier to improving the testing infrastructure leading to higher software quality, therefore decreasing the enormous resulting damage. It is suggested that establishing a formal, unambiguous, generic, quantifiable and structural definition for a TC would be a significant contribution to the world of software testing, and software quality in general. Such a definition would pave the way to standard TC generation techniques, as well as to measurement and evaluation tools.

Referring to Kaner's [18] question "what is a good Test case?" and his assertion that "good TC is one that gives the required information", we see benefits in formalizing a unified, well defined and structured TC entity that satisfies all the above dimensions. We suggest pursuing, determining and proposing an improved and comprehensive definition of a test Case.

References

[1] Tassey, G.: The Economic Impacts of Inadequate Infrastructure for Software Testing. National Institute of Standards and Technology (2002)

[2] Basili, V., Caldiera, G., McGarry, F., Pajerski, R., Page, G., Waligora, S.: The software engineering laboratory: an operational software experience factory. In: Proceedings of the 14th international conference on Software engineering. ACM, New York (1992)

[3] Geras, A.M., Smith, M.R., Miller, J.: A survey of software testing practices in alberta. Canadian Journal of Electrical and Computer Engineering 29(3), 183–191 (2004)

[4] Grindal, M., Offutt, J., Mellin, J.: On the Testing Maturity of Software Producing Organizations. In: Proceedings of the Testing: Academic and Industrial Conference-Practice and Research Techniques TAIC PART (2006)

[5] Ng, S.P., Murnane, T., Reed, K., Grant, D., Chen, T.Y.: A Preliminary Survey on Software Testing Practices in Australia. In: Software Engineering Conference (2004)

[6] Illes, T., Herrmann, A., Paech, B., Rockert, J.: Criteria for Software Testing Tool Evaluation. A Task Oriented View. In: Proceedings of the 3rd World Congress for Software Quality (2005)

[7] Almog, D.: Verification Points for Better Testing Efficiency. In: StarEastSQE (2007)

[8] Bach, J.: Exploratory Testing Explained,
http://www.satisfice.com/articles/et-article.pdf

[9] Kaner, C.: The Ongoing Revolution in Software Testing. In: Software Test & Performance Conference (2004)

[10] Gelperin, D., Hetzel, B.: The Growth of Software Testing. Communications of the ACM 31(6), 687–695 (1988)

[11] Ostrand, T.J., Balcer, M.J.: The Category-Partition Method for Specifying and Generating Functional Tests. Commun. ACM 31(6), 676–686 (1988)

[12] Weyuker, E.J.: The Cost of Data Flow Testing: An Empirical Study. IEEE Transactions on Software Engineering 16(2), 121–128 (1990)

[13] Harrold, M.J., Rajiv, G., Mary Lou, S.: A Methodology for Controlling the Size of a Test Suite. ACM Trans. Softw. Eng. Methodol. 2(3), 270–285 (1993)

[14] Rosenberg, L., Hammer, T.F., Huffman, L.L.: Requirements, Testing and Metrics. In: 15th Annual Pacific Northwest Software Quality Conference (1998)

[15] Iberle, K.: Divide and Conquer: Making Sense of Test Planning. In: The International Conference on Software Testing, Analysis and Review, STARWEST (1999)

[16] Aichernig, B.K.: Test-Case Calculation through Abstraction. In: International Symposium of Formal Methods. Springer, Heidelberg (2001)

[17] Jorgensen, P.: Software Testing: A Craftsman's Approach. CRC Press, Boca Raton (2002)

[18] Kaner, C.: What Is a Good Test Case? In: Star East (2003)

[19] Grindal, M., Offutt, J., Andler, S.F.: Combination Testing Strategies: a Survey. Software Testing Verification and Reliability 15(3), 167 (2005)

[20] Grindal, M., Lindstrom, B., Offutt, J., Andler, S.F.: An Evaluation of Combination Strategies for Test Case Selection. Empirical Software Engineering 11(4), 583–611 (2006)

[21] Ambrosio, A., Mattiello-Francisco, F., Santiago, V., Silva, W., Martins, E.: Designing Fault Injection Experiments Using State-Based Model to Test a Space Software. In: Bondavalli, A., Brasileiro, F., Rajsbaum, S. (eds.) LADC 2007. LNCS, vol. 4746, pp. 170–178. Springer, Heidelberg (2007)

[22] Ambrosio, A.M., Martins, E., Vijaykumar, N.L., de Carvalho, S.V.: Systematic Generation of Test and Fault Cases for Space Application Validation. In: DASIA: Data Systems in Aerospace, European Space Agency (2005)

[23] Desai, H.D.: Test Case Management System (TCMS). In: IEEE Conference Global Telecommunications GLOBECOM: 'Communications: The Global Bridge' (1994)

[24] Craig, R.D., Jaskiel, S.P.: Systematic Software Testing. Artech House (2002)

[25] Jorgensen: Testing with Hostile Data Streams. ACM Sigsoft Software Engineering Notes 28(2), 1 (2003)

[26] Nagappan, N.: A Software Testing and Reliability Early Warning (STREW) Metric Suite, Thesis: Computer Science, North Carolina University (2005)

[27] Sherriff, M., Boehm, B.W., Williams, L., Nagappan, N.: An Empirical Process for Building and Validating Software Engineering Parametric Models. North Carolina State Univeristy CSC-TR-2005-45, October, 19 (2005)

[28] Hoffman, D.: The Darker Side of Metrics. In: Conference of the Association of Software Testing, CAST (2006)

[29] Binder, R.: Testing Object-Oriented Systems: Models, Patterns, and Tools. Addison-Wesley Professional, Reading (2000)

[30] Talby, D., Hazzan, O., Dubinsky, Y., Keren, A.: Agile Software Testing in a Large-Scale Project. IEEE Software, 30–37 (2006)

[31] Beck, K.: Test-driven Development: By Example. Addison-Wesley Professional, Reading (2003)

[32] Utting, M., Legeard, B., Pretschner, A.: A Taxonomy of Model-based Testing. Dept. of Computer Science, University of Waikato Hamilton, New Zealand (2006)

[33] Bohnet, R., Meszaros, G.: Test-Driven Porting. In: Proceedings of the Agile Development Conference (2005)

[34] Lewis, G.A., Morris, E., Simanta, S., Wrage, L.: Common Misconceptions about Service-Oriented Architecture. In: Proceedings of the Sixth International IEEE Conference on Commercial-off-the-Shelf (COTS)-Based Software Systems (2007)

[35] Hiebert, D., Klaedtke, R.A., Lowery, E., Nartovich, A., Raut, N., Sandberg, M.J.: Building SOA-based Solutions for IBM System i Platform. IBM (2007)

[36] Karam, M., Safa, H., Artail, H.: An Abstract Workflow-Based Framework for Testing Composed Web Services. In: IEEE/ACS International Conference on Computer Systems and Applications, AICCSA (2007)

[37] Rehman, M.J., Jabeen, F., Bertolino, A., Polini, A.: Testing Software Components for Integration: A Survey of Issues and Techniques. Software Testing, Verification & Reliability 17(2), 95–133 (2007)

[38] Weyuker, E.J.: Testing Component-Based Software: A Cautionary Tale. IEEE Software 15(5), 54–59 (1998)

[39] Cai, K.Y., Zhao, L., Hu, H., Jiang, C.H.: On the Test Case Definition for GUI Testing. In: Fifth International Conference on Quality Software, QSIC (2005)

[40] Boujarwah, A.S., Saleh, K.: Compiler Test Case Generation Methods: A Survey and Assessment. Information and Software Technology 39(9), 617–625 (1997)

[41] Calam, J.R., Ioustinova, N., Pol, J.: Towards Automatic Generation of Parameterized Test Cases from Abstractions. Technical Report SEN-E0602, Centrum voor Wiskunde en Informatica (2006)

[42] Byers, D., Engstrom, M., Kamkar, M.: The Design of a Test Case Definition Language. Automated and Algorithmic Debugging, 69–78 (1997)

[43] Nebut, C., Fleurey, F., Le Traon, Y., Jezequel, J.M.: Automatic Test Generation: A Use Case Driven Approach. IEEE Transactions on Software Engineering, 140–155 (2006)

[44] Prasanna, M., Sivanandam, S.N., Venkatesan, R., Sundarrajan, R.: A Survey on Automatic Test Case Generation. Academic Open Internet Journal 15 (2005)

[45] Coulter, A.C.: Graybox Software Testing Methodology: Embedded Software Testing Technique. In: Proceedings of the18th Digital Avionics Systems Conference (1999)

[46] Craig, R.: Measurement and Metrics for Test Managers. In: STAR East. SQE (2007)

[47] Kaner, C.: Measurement Issues and Software Testing (2001)

[48] Landis, L., Waligora, S., McGarry, F.: Recommended Approach to Software Development. Software Engineering Laboratory Series, pp. 81–305. NASA (1992)

[49] Bassin, K., Biyani, S., Santhanam, P.: Metrics to Evaluate Vendor-Developed Software Based on Test Case Execution Results. IBM Systems Journal 41(1), 13–30 (2002)

[50] Jorgensen, M., Shepperd, M.: A Systematic Review of Software Development Cost Estimation Studies. IEEE Transactions on Software Engineering 33(1), 33–53 (2007)

[51] Binkley, D.: Semantics Guided Regression Test Cost Reduction. IEEE Transactions on Software Engineering 23(8), 498–516 (1997)

[52] Leung, H.K.N., White, L.: Insights into Regression Testing [software testing]. In: Conference on Software Maintenance (1989)

[53] Nageswaran, S.: Test Effort Estimation Using Use Case Points. In: 14th International Internet & Software Quality Week (2001)

[54] Aranha, E., Borba, P.: An Estimation Model for Test Execution Effort. In: International Symposium on Empirical Software Engineering and Measurement, ESEM 2007 (2007)

[55] Abran, A., Bourque, P., Dupuis, R., Moore, J.W.: Guide to the Software Engineering Body of Knowledge - SWEBOK. In: Alain, A., et al. (eds.). IEEE Press, Los Alamitos (2004)

[56] Stocks, P.A., Carrington, D.A.: Test Templates: A Specification-Based Testing Framework. In: Proceedings of the 15th International Conference on Software Engineering. IEEE Computer Society Press, Los Alamitos (1993)

[57] Beizer, B.: Black-Box Testing: Techniques for Functional Testing of Software and Systems. John Wiley & Sons, Inc., Chichester (1995)

[58] Offutt, J., Abdurazik, A.: Generating tests from UML specifications. In: Proc. Second International Conference on the Unified Modeling Language (1999)

[59] Taylor, C.M.: EPDAV – A Model for Test Case Definition. In: Conference of the Association of Software Testing (2006)

[60] Bruno, M., Canfora, G., Di Penta, M., Esposito, G., Mazza, V.: Using Test Cases as Contract to Ensure Service Compliance Across Releases. In: Benatallah, B., Casati, F., Traverso, P. (eds.) ICSOC 2005. LNCS, vol. 3826, pp. 87–100. Springer, Heidelberg (2005)

[61] Kaner, C., Falk, J.L., Nguyen, H.Q.: Testing Computer Software. John Wiley & Sons, Inc., New York (1999)

[62] Maletic, J.I., Soliman, K.S., Moreno, M.A., Mercer, W.M.: Identification of Test Cases from Business Requirements of Software Systems. In: American Conference on Information Systems AMCIS (1999)

[63] Baudry, B., Fleurey, F., Jezequel, J.M., Le Traon, Y.: Genes and Bacteria for Automatic Test Cases Optimization in the .NET Environment. In: Proceedings of the13th International Symposium on Software Reliability Engineering, ISSRE (2002)

[64] Menter, F.: CFD Best Practice Guidelines for CFD Code Validation for Reactor- Safety Applications. CFX, Germany (2002)

[65] Mikhailova, A., Doche, M., Butler, M.: Contracts for Scenario-Based Testing of Object-Oriented Programs (2002)

[66] Bruno, M., Canfora, G., Di Penta, M., Esposito, G., Mazza, V.: Using Test Cases as Contract to Ensure Service Compliance Across Releases. In: Benatallah, B., Casati, F., Traverso, P. (eds.) ICSOC 2005. LNCS, vol. 3826, pp. 87–100. Springer, Heidelberg (2005)

Automating Expert-Defined Tests: A Suitable Approach for the Medical Device Industry?

David Connolly[1], Fergal Mc Caffery[2], and Frank Keenan[1]

[1] Software Technology Research Centre
[2] Regulated Software Research Group,
Dundalk Institute of Technology, Dublin Road, Dundalk, Ireland
{david.connolly,fergal.mccaffery,frank.keenan}@dkit.ie

Abstract. Testing is frequently reported as a crucial stage in the software development process. With traditional approaches acceptance testing is the last stage of the process before release to customer. Acceptance Test Driven Development (ATDD) promotes the role of an expert customer in defining tests and uses tool support to automate and execute these tests. Here the challenge is to support such an expert in the reuse of existing documentation. This paper details an experiment in a generic domain while outlining plans for development of an automated testing model that could assist medical device companies to adhere to regulatory guidelines by providing them with a fully traceable testing artifacts.

1   Introduction

A large part of software development expenditure is attributed to *testing*. Traditionally, with plan-driven development, acceptance testing, the process of testing functional requirements with "data supplied by the customer" [1] occurs as the final stage of the development process long after the initial investigation has completed [2]. Many reports, however, highlight that costs can be reduced by detecting errors earlier in development [3]. Also supporting this, in many domains, such as the medical device industry, software is developed subject to a regulatory environment with a tendency for extensive documentation. This regulatory environment features guidelines and standards such as [4] - [9]. Despite many constraints already being specified, this is often ignored with tests written from scratch after implementation is complete. In contrast, agile approaches require constant customer collaboration throughout development, with customer provision of acceptance tests being an important part of this role. Often, it is recommended that tests be identified before implementation commences. In eXtreme Programming (XP) [10], for example, acceptance tests are defined as a part of the User Stories practice and, as such, are written before coding of the story begins. In this context, functional tests are synonymous with acceptance tests [11]. Further, for accurate user stories, Cohn recommends customers themselves specify acceptance tests with developers and testers providing support as required [12]. The XP practice of Continuous Integration, that is, building and testing a system frequently, maximizes the use of the executable and automated

R.V. O'Connor et al. (Eds.): EuroSPI 2009, CCIS 42, pp. 32–43, 2009.

products of Test Driven Development (TDD) [13]. TDD visibly links executable unit tests to the overall development process. TDD is widely practised and has many reported benefits [14] but successful use does rely on tools such as JUnit [15]. ATDD adds to this established test-first philosophy with acceptance testing of an automated and executable nature. In keeping with agile principles, ideally customers write acceptance tests guided by developers. Its practice "allows software development to be driven by the requirements" [16]. A key advantage of ATDD in its wider context is that it leverages existing agile infrastructure supporting continuous integration. As with TDD, support from tools makes ATDD feasible. However, Andrea [17] claims that existing tools exhibit several deficiencies and produce tests that are "hard to write and maintain". To overcome this Andrea also suggests that the next generation of functional testing tools need to support writing (and reading) functional tests in multiple formats. Given the widespread adoption of information and communication technology, in many organisations business rules are documented in numerous formats, for example, including Medical Devices . However, ATDD is currently not well supported with tools that enable reusing such existing documents, without rewrites, to create executable tests. A challenge, therefore, is to support a suitably informed expert to perform the agile *customer role* and in easily creating tests from existing material. However, successful identification of accurate acceptance tests in this manner is not necessarily straightforward.

2   Importance of "Well Tested" Medical Device Software

The risk of patient injury from software defects is a concern due to the manufacture and deployment of increasing numbers of software-embedded medical devices [18] - [20]. There have been a number of major medical device product recalls over this past 25 years that were the result of software defects [21]. Highly traceable testing and change control procedures within medical device software development is important as such modifications can occur frequently and may occur at different levels (e.g. design, interface or code), therefore increasing the risk of software failure [21]. It is therefore important that a medical device company has an efficient software development process in place that include change control practices. According to the Institute of Medicine report "To Err is Human" [22], between 44000 to 98000 people die in hospital from preventative medical errors. The report also says that more people die every year as a result of medical errors than from motor vehicle accidents, breast cancer or AIDS. Like most industries, the medical device industry depends on computer technology to perform many of the functions ranging from financial management to patient treatment [23]. The use of software in medical devices has become widespread in the last two decades. Medical devices with software include those that are supplied and used entirely in hospitals and other health facilities, as well as consumer items such as blood pressure monitors. Many medical devices, and their software, operate in real time - monitoring, diagnosing, or controlling a physiological process as it changes. The complexity and risk profile of medical devices varies widely and range from a consumer digital thermometer for minor diagnosis, and an implanted artificial heart that is critical to preserving a patient's life, to a therapeutic X-ray machine with a computer user interface, programmable software controlled therapy and anatomical and biophysical modelling in the software, which is operated under a high level of professional staff supervision [24]. Analysis of medical device recalls highlights the diverse nature of medical device software failures. The FDA found that during 1983 - 1987 approximately 44% of the quality problems that led to voluntary recalls of medical devices were attributed to errors or deficiencies designed into particular medical devices rather than having been inserted during the manufacturing phase. The study also recognised software quality management practices as a means to prevent failure [25]. In the medical device industry, the software used to control a device takes on an additional role - it must help ensure the safety of the user. There are many challenges to implementing safe software. Software design needs to include deliberate engineering practices and rigorous approaches for software testing such as an expert customer defining suitable tests before development begins.

3   Related Work

Many approaches to conducting acceptance testing exist. Some concentrate on acting as a "recording device" allowing user actions to be replayed against a system, checking for deviations. However, this approach is mainly limited to Graphical User Interface (GUI) testing of a specific version of a system, using a tool such as the Selenium IDE [26]. Tools for writing acceptance tests in a customer friendly format and appropriate for continuous integration exist. RSpec, for example, is a "Behaviour Driven Development framework for Ruby" [27]. It promotes a workflow that involves writing stories in a somewhat prescriptive natural language style and then manually translating these steps into Ruby. While the authors consider this approach interesting for new stories, it has limitations in dealing with pre-existing documents. Other open source tools aimed at supporting ATDD exist including EasyAccept which supports both tabular and sequential styles [28].

Generally, the Framework for Integrated Tests (FIT) is the most widely accepted tool for managing acceptance tests in agile development and therefore practising ATDD [29]. In FIT's simplest workflow a user, places inputs and some expected output into a tabular format, a *ColumnFixture* [30]. The developer then writes code (*fixtures*) that executes this data against the system's production code. Other built-in fixture included in FIT include *ActionFixtures* for testing a "sequence of commands" and *RowFixtures* for "comparing test data to objects in the system" [30]. FitNesse is a Wiki framework developed to support FIT [31]. It facilitates the editing of FIT tables in a browser allowing non-programming experts to add content. While FIT tables can be written in any tool that can export HTML, such as Microsoft Excel, these generic tools do not have any authoring features directly supporting the task domain. Existing tools that support either FIT or FitNesse include AutAT and FitClipse. AutAT seeks to assist "business-side people" taking a visual approach to building Acceptance Tests [32]. As FitClipse [33] builds on FitNesse tests are entered using its wiki syntax. Mugridge introduces a process based around a library of *fixtures* named FitLibrary, which improves FIT's "business-level expressiveness" to emphasise a "domain-driven design approach" [34]. It supports a type of fixture, *DoFixtures*, which approach natural language in readability. Commercial software also supports such a workflow, with GreenPepper [35] supporting "executable specifications" while providing an expressive library of table types. For clarity, it is important to note that GreenPepper uses code annotations (Java and C#) that are unrelated to the annotations in this paper. However, none of these tools is focused on reusing existing documentation, so unlike the proposed approach these approaches require re-writes of content.

In the requirements authoring process, Melnik and Maurer found that the use of FIT helped students to "learn how express requirements in a precise, unequivocal manner" [36]. In a number of experiments aimed at evaluating the impact of FIT tables on the implementation of change requests Ricca et al. [37], found improvement in the correctness of code produced. The addition of FIT Tables to plain text descriptions had the most impact on more experienced students, and they found no significant increase in time taken to implement the changes. The use of annotations was proposed because it provides users with a simple conceptual framework allowing them to add detail to text descriptions of tests. Annotations are used here to allow for links to be made between descriptions and corresponding FIT Tables. These annotations are based on elements of an acceptance test description recommended by Jain [29]. There are four basic types, covering most elements of an individual acceptance test:

- *Precondition*: event that must occur before a test is run.
- *Actor + Action*: part of system and functionality.
- *Observerable Result*: a verifiable response generated by the system.
- *Examples*: represent the input data given to a test.

The passing or failure of a test rests with variance from specified *Observable Results*. A visual representation of the annotations is contained in Figure 1.

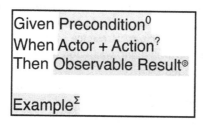

Fig. 1. Annotations

4   Annotations Experiment

This experiment was designed to evaluate the impact of annotations on the process of authoring acceptance tests. The scenario used to write the question descriptions given to respondents concerned the management of software packages on a computer system, such as GNU/Linux [38]. There were six participants, each experienced in computing as either a postgraduate or professional. However, none had prior experience of writing FIT tables. All were given a short, two-hour training session on FIT Tables and ATDD. Participants were tasked to create tests using either annotated descriptions or from non-annotated plain text descriptions. The plain text descriptions serve as a reference for comparison against annotations. The only difference between descriptions was the presence or absence of annotations. Each participant was randomly assigned to Group A and Group B, with each group assigned in total three participants and receiving four questions. Group B started with annotated descriptions while Group A were given a non-annotated version. For subsequent exercises the groups alternated between annotated and non-annotated. Apart from a common assignment of question, to their group, participants worked alone. In providing these descriptions, the first author acted in the role of a customer on an agile project. The experiment considered annotations in paper-based experiment in isolation aside from usability considerations of prototypes.

4.1   Design

For comparison purposes, the first author wrote reference tests, providing an "ideal" test description against which the participants' tests were compared. Each was in the form of high-level descriptions of how a system should function, including handling of error conditions and intended to be of approximately equal difficulty: Question 1 covered *initial bootstrap* of the package management system; Question 2 covered *installation* of new packages; Question 3 covered *removal* of packages; Question 4 covered *upgrading* of packages. The metrics used to assess the experiment were gathered under the following headings:

- *Errors*: elements that should not appear in the test. From participants' answers, all error occurrences counted towards the average.
- *Correct Elements*: From participants' answers an elements first occurrence. Participants were free to reuse structural elements (for example the first row in a FIT Table) as this only affects readability. However, repeated data elements are counted as *Errors*. Presence of a data element irrespective of corresponding structural element was enough for it to count as correct, so two penalising respondents twice.
- *Missing Elements*: defined as elements that were omitted by the participants compared to the reference test.
- *Time*: amount of time taken to complete FIT table.

4.2   Question and Responses

A reproduction of Question 2 with annotated text is presented in Figure 2. This version was provided to Group A while Group B received it non-annotated.

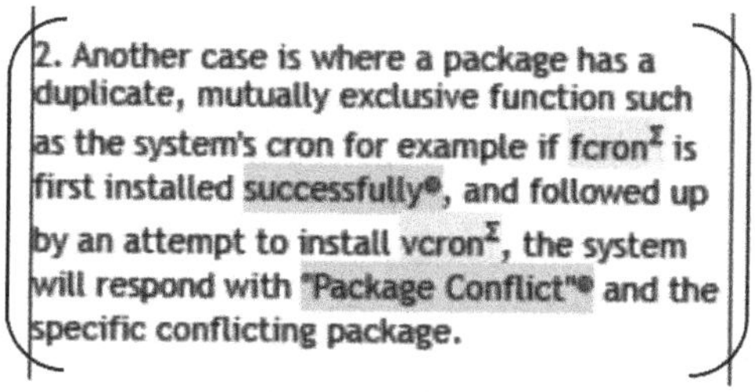

2. Another case is where a package has a duplicate, mutually exclusive function such as the system's cron for example if fcron[Σ] is first installed successfully[●], and followed up by an attempt to install vcron[Σ], the system will respond with "Package Conflict"[●] and the specific conflicting package.

Fig. 2. Sample Question

A simple FIT Table (ColumnFixture) has been transcribed in Figure 3, it represents the text of Figure 2. This acknowledges the flow of events encoded in the text and unambiguously represents the specific package name of the "conflicting package".

package	install()	failReason?	failPackages?
fcron	TRUE		
vcron	FALSE	Package conflict	fcron

Fig. 3. Sample 'Ideal' Answer

For illustration and comparison with the "ideal" response, two respondent answers are transcribed in Figure 4 and Figure 5. Figure 4 the answer attempt from respondent A2, who had been provided an annotated version of Question 1.

package	success?	
fcron	TRUE	
vcron	FALSE	"Package Conflict"

Fig. 4. Respondent answer (annotations)

Here, the respondent A2 correctly identifies the sequence of events, but fails to include the name of the package, "fcron", causing the failure. However, the chosen label heading "success?" does not reflect the action name but this is

Install	Result
Duplicate (vcron)	Package Conflict

Fig. 5. Respondent answer (non-annotated)

not considered an error because the respondent correctly labelled the table. Respondent A2 achieved the fewest Errors and both the most Correct Elements and fewest Missing Elements in Question 2.

The corresponding snippet from respondent B1, who had used a non-annotated version, is transcribed in Figure 5. Here, the respondent B1 failed to identify from the text that the "install()" action should fail due to the prior installation of a conflicting package. Indeed respondent B1 didn't correctly identify "install()" as an action at all, instead specifying the package name "vcron" combined with the error detail as data to be verified. In comparing these answers with the reference answer in Figure 4 one element was missed by respondent A2 while four elements were missed by respondent B1 in Figure 5. Finally, it should also be noted that respondent B1 performed better when using annotated texts and respondent A2 performed worse when using non-annotated texts. The next section summarises the overall results for the experiment.

4.3   Results

The results gathered from the respondents answers, are summarised in Table 1. For clarity, the *row number* is included in column 1. Columns 2, 3 and 4 introduce the *question number*, which *group* is responding (A or B) and the *type* of description provided in the group's question. Columns 5, 6 and 7 contain the arithmetic mean of the counts for each group's *Errors, Correct Elements* and *Missing Elements*, respectively. The presence of *Errors* indicates *Over-Specification* while that of *Missing Elements* indicates *Under-Specification*. In all cases, *Correct Elements* plus *Missing Elements* equals *Total Elements* of the "ideal" answer.

We analysed both the data element and the structural element of the responses. An *Error* occurs whenever a response is matched against the "ideal" answer and a mistake is identified. A mistake may be identified in either the data element or the structural element. All mistakes that occur in the data element are counted as errors, whereas only the first occurrence is counted as an error in the structural element. For example, if we matched an individual's response against the "ideal" response and discovered that a data element "fcron" had been included by a respondent three times; the first two match the "ideal" response counting as *Correct* but the third element would be incorrect and count as one error.

Each row in Table 1 presents the results of one group for a particular question. For example, Row 1 represents the arithmetic mean of responses from Group B for Question 1 (annotated). The use of median would not reverse the overall results.

Table 1. Results from annotations experiment

Row	Q	Group	Type	Errors	Correct	Missing
1	Q1	B	Annotated	7.33	12	14
2	Q1	A	Plain	13	14	12
3	Q1	-	Difference	55.74%	(15.38%)	(15.38%)
4	Q2	A	Annotated	4.67	14	7
5	Q2	B	Plain	9.67	10.67	10.33
6	Q2	-	Difference	69.77%	27.03%	38.46%
7	Q3	B	Annotated	9.67	9.67	3.33
8	Q3	A	Plain	11.67	9	4
9	Q3	-	Difference	18.75%	7.14%	18.18%
10	Q4	A	Annotated	11.5	14	6
11	Q4	B	Plain	14	8.67	11.33
12	Q4	-	Difference	19.61%	47.06%	61.54%
13	-	-	Average Difference	40.97%	16.46%	25.70%

Further, the percentage difference (55.74%) between Group A and Group B is represented in row 3. This is obtained from as follows:

$$Row3 = ((|Row1 - Row2|)/(Row1 + Row2)/2) * 100. \qquad (1)$$

For example, in the case of the obtaining the percentage difference of Errors:

$$55.74\% = (|7.33 - 13|)/((7.33 + 13)/2) * 100 \qquad (2)$$

In the case of a worse performance when given annotations, such a result has been enclosed with parenthesis in Table 1. This pattern continues for each question given to respondents. The final row, Row 13, contains the overall percentage difference; these results included the cases of decreased performance in Row 3 as negative numbers. In each case, the occurrence of *Errors* is reduced for the annotated versions. This holds across both groups even with a pattern of Group A taking less time on average compared to Group B. For example, the figure of 55.74% in row 3 indicates that there were 55.74% less errors identified in the annotated version. This means responses with a lower incidence of *Over-Specification* occurred when respondents were provided with annotations. In Question 2 to Question 4, the average number of *Correct Elements* for the annotated version is greater than that for the non-annotated version. A similar reduction in the number of *Missing Elements* occurred. For example, 27.03%, *Correct* in Row 6 means that there were 27.03% more elements identified by the group given annotations. Similarly, 38.46%, *Missing* in Row 7 means that there were 38.46% less missing elements identified by the group given annotations. As with *Error Rates*, the number of *Correct Elements* achieved by respondents appears unrelated to the amount of time spent. However, the effect of annotations on *Correct Elements* and *Missing Elements* was smaller than on the *Error Rates*, therefore annotations had less of an impact on *Under-Specification*.

4.4   Selection of a Domain

The initial results are promising however the chosen domain used in the experiment is one of largely unregulated innovation; therefore the large tracts of documentation required for the approach do not exist. However, medical device companies must produce a design history file detailing the software components and processes undertaken in the development of their medical devices. Due to the safety-critical nature of medical device software it is important that highly efficient software development practices are in place within medical device companies. Medical device companies who market within the USA must ensure that they comply with medical device regulations as governed by the FDA (FDA - Food and Drug Administration) [39] - [6]. The medical device companies must be able to produce sufficient evidence to support compliance in this area. To this end, the (CDRH - Center for Devices and Radiological Health) has published guidance papers for industry and medical device staff which include risk -based activities to be performed during software validation [4], pre-market submission [5] and when using off-the-shelf software in a medical device [6]. Although the CDRH guidance documents provide information on which software activities should be performed, including risk based activities; they do not enforce any specific method for performing these activities. The FDA have defined the following eleven software development areas:

- *Level of Concern*
- *Software Description*
- *Device Hazard and Risk Analysis*
- *Software Requirements Specification*
- *Architecture Design*
- *Design Specifications*
- *Requirements Traceability Analysis*
- *Development*
- *Validation, Verification and Testing*
- *Revision Level History*
- *Unresolved Anomalies*

The research outlined in this paper with tool support could greatly assist medical device software development companies to have traceability of all requirements throughout the testing phase and to ensure that all requirements are thoroughly tested. In particular, this would assist medical device companies to adhere to the FDA demands in relation to "Requirements Traceability Analysis" and "Validation, Verification and Testing".

4.5   Conclusions and Future Work

The annotations experiment in this paper was designed to evaluate the impact of annotations on the process of authoring acceptance tests. Future work in the form of case studies will be aimed at measuring the stages of error detection encountered on projects applying digital annotations; this will asses if the approach helps to highlight deficient documents in-place, encouraging correction at source rather than through creation of second generation artefacts (for example, by writing new acceptance tests). While the size of groups in this study has limited the statistical conclusions, the results presented in this paper indicate that using annotated documents helped to identify more elements that are *Correct* with fewer *Missing* elements and *Errors* when creating acceptance tests.

Due to the applicability of this research to medical device software we would now like to re-design this experiment so that it concerned medical device software requirements. This work will specifically help medical device companies to address two of the eleven areas defined by the FDA i.e. "Requirements Traceability Analysis" and "Validation, Verification and Testing".

Acknowledgments

This research is partially supported by Institutes of Technology, Technological Sector Research Programme, Strand 1 Fund and Science Foundation Ireland through the Stokes Lectureship Programme, grant number 07/SK/I1299.

References

1. Sommerville, I.: Software Engineering, 8th edn., pp. 80–81. Addison-Wesley, Reading (2007)
2. Pressman, R.S.: Software Engineering: A Practitioner's Approach, European Adaption, 5th edn. McGraw-Hill, New York (2000)
3. Tassey, G.: The economic impacts of inadequate infrastructure for software testing, National Institute of Standards and Technology (NIST) (May 2002)
4. CDRH, General Principles of Software Validation; Final Guidance for Industry and medical device Staff (January 11, 2002)
5. CDRH, Guidance for the Content of Premarket Submissions for Software Contained in Medical Devices; Guidance for Industry and medical device Staff (May 11, 2005)
6. CDRH, Off-The-Shelf Software Use in Medical Devices; Guidance for Industry, medical device Reviewers and Compliance (September 9, 1999)
7. ANSI/AAMI/ISO 14971, Medical devices - Application of risk management to medical devices, 2nd edn. (2007)
8. ANSI/AAMI/IEC 62304, Medical device software - Software life cycle processes (July 19, 2006)
9. ISPE, GAMP Guide for Validation of Automated Systems (December 2001)
10. Beck, K., Andres, C.: Extreme Programming Explained: Embrace Change, 2nd edn. Addison Wesley, Boston (2005)
11. Sauvé, J.P., Neto, O.L.A.: Teaching software development with ATDD and Easy-Accept. In: SIGCSE 2008: Proceedings of the 39th SIGCSE technical symposium on Computer Science Education, pp. 542–546 (2008)
12. Cohn, M.: User Stories Applied. Addison-Wesley, Boston (2005)
13. Beck, K.: Test Driven Development: By Example. Addison-Wesley Professional, Reading (2002)

14. Jeffries, R., Melnik, G.: Guest editors introduction: TDD- the art of fearless programming. IEEE Software 24(3), 24–30 (2007)
15. Beck, K., Gamma, E., Saff, D.: JUnit 4, http://junit.sourceforge.net/ (last accessed January 16, 2009)
16. Park, S.S., Maurer, F.: The benefits and challenges of executable acceptance testing. In: APOS 2008: Proceedings of the 2008 international workshop on Scrutinizing agile practices or shoot-out at the agile corral, pp. 19–22 (2008)
17. Andrea, J.: Envisioning the next generation of functional testing tools. IEEE Software 24(03), 58–66 (2007)
18. Crumpler, E.S., Rudolph, H.: FDA software policy and regulation of medical device software. Food Drug Law Journal 52, 511–516 (1997)
19. Munsey, R.R.: Trends and events in FDA regulation of medical devices over the last fifty years. Food Drug Law Journal 50, 163–177 (1995)
20. Medical device reporting: Improvements needed in FDAs system for monitoring problems with approved devices, US General Accounting Office, GAO/HEHS-97-21 (1997)
21. Bovee, M.W., Paul, D.L., Nelson, K.M.: A Framework for Assessing the Use of Third-Party Software Quality Assurance Standards to Meet FDA Medical Device Software Process Control Guidelines. IEEE Transactions on Engineering Management 48(4), 465–478 (2001)
22. Kohn, L., Corrigan, J., Donaldson, M.: To Err is Human: Building a Safer Health System. National Academy Press (2000)
23. Wallace, D.R., Kuhn, D.R.: Failure Modes in Medical Device Software: An analysis of 15 Years of Recall data. NIST,
http://csrc.nist.gov/staff/kuhn/final-rqse.pdf (last accessed, January 2007)
24. Jamieson, J.: Regulation of medical devices involving software in Australia - an overview. In: 6th Australian Workshop on Safety Critical Systems and Software, Brisbane (2001)
25. Leffingwell, D.A., Widrig, D.R., Morrissey, W.T.: Applying requirements management to medical devices utilizing software, Rational Software Corporation (1997)
26. Kasatani, S.: Selenium IDE, http://seleniumhq.org/ (last accessed December 1, 2008)
27. RSpec Development Team, http://rspec.info (last accessed December 1, 2008)
28. Sauvé, J.P., Cirne, W., Osorinho, Coelho, R.: EasyAccept Sourceforge Project, http://easyaccept.sourceforge.net (last accessed December 3, 2008)
29. Jain, N.: Acceptance Test Driven Development. Presentation,
http://www.slideshare.net/nashjain/
acceptance-test-driven-development-350264/
(last accessed November 30, 2008)
30. Cunningham, W.: Framework for Integrated Test, September 2002,
http://fit.c2.com (last accessed January 16, 2009)
31. FitNesse.org., http://fitnesse.org (last accessed February 7, 2008)
32. Schwarz, C., Skytteren, S.K., Øvstetun, T.M.: AutAT: an eclipse plugin for automatic acceptance testing of web applications. In: OOPSLA 2005: Companion to the 20th annual ACM SIGPLAN conference on OOPSLA, pp. 182–183 (2005)
33. Deng, C., Wilson, P., Maurer, F.: FitClipse: A FIT-based Eclipse plug-in for Executable Acceptance Test Driven Development. In: Concas, G., Damiani, E., Scotto, M., Succi, G. (eds.) XP 2007. LNCS, vol. 4536, pp. 93–100. Springer, Heidelberg (2007)

34. Mugridge, R.: Managing agile project requirements with storytest-driven development. IEEE Software 25, 68–75 (2008)

35. Pyxis Technologies inc., GreenPepper Sofware,
http://www.greenpeppersoftware.com/confluence (last accessed January 19, 2009)

36. Melnik, G., Maurer, F.: The practice of specifying requirements using executable acceptance tests in computer science courses. In: OOPSLA 2005: Companion to the 20th annual ACM SIGPLAN conference on OOPSLA, pp. 365–370 (2005)

37. Ricca, F., Penta, M.D., Torchiano, M., Tonella, P., Ceccato, M., Visaggio, C.A.: Are fit tables really talking?: a series of experiments to understand whether fit tables are useful during evolution tasks. In: ICSE 2008: Proceedings of the 30th international conference on Software engineering, pp. 361–370 (2008)

38. Free Software Foundation, About the GNU Project,
http://www.gnu.org/gnu/the-gnu-project.html (last access January 16, 2009)

39. FDA's Mission Statement,
http://www.fda.gov/opacom/morechoices/mission.html (last access March 18, 2009)

A Model for Selecting an Optimum Set of Measures in Software Organizations

Ansar Malook Bhatti, Hafiz Muhammad Abdullah, and Cigdem Gencel

Blekinge Institute of Technology, School of Engineering,
372 25 Ronneby, Sweden
{ambh07,hmabh07}@student.bth.se, cigdem.gencel@bth.se

Abstract. Most of the software organizations face difficulties in choosing the measures to collect since there is no universal set of measures for all types of organizations and projects. Experience shows that measurement can be more successful if the measures are collected based on the goals of the organization or the project which it will serve. However, one of the major constraints for the organizations is the associated cost for the resources needed when collecting the measures. Therefore, based on their goals, the software organizations require collecting not only as few measures from a large number of possible measures as possible but an optimum set of measures as well. In this paper, we propose a model, called 'Optimum Measures Set Decision (OMSD) Model', which is an extension of the well-known Goal Question Metric (GQM) paradigm using a heuristics approach. We performed a survey by distributing a structured questionnaire to a number of people from the industry in order evaluate and get feedback on these factors. We evaluated the rules of the model by means of some sample cases we created. In this paper, we discuss OMSD as well as the empirical studies we conducted in order to develop it.

Keywords: Software Measurement Program, Software Measures, Software Process Improvement, Goal Question Metric.

1 Introduction

Software measurement process has become an integral part for software process due to its significance in project estimations, decision making and software process improvement [1]. However, in spite of the fact that many organizations started measurement programs to benefit from it; the failure rates for software measurement programs in software organizations are still very high.

About 80% of the measurement programs were reported to fail to either helping in decision making or delivering performance improvements for numerous reasons [2], [3]. Some of the most significant reasons stated are as follows [2], [4], [5]:

- Focusing on collecting process rather than having clear action plans for improving the organizational processes and/or making decisions,
- Inappropriate measures selection; a misunderstanding of what is to be measured, why and how it is to be measured,

R.V. O'Connor et al. (Eds.): EuroSPI 2009, CCIS 42, pp. 44–56, 2009.
© Springer-Verlag Berlin Heidelberg 2009

- Inadequate data collection and wrong interpretations of data that leads to ineffective decision making,
- Lack of trained and expert resources required to dedicate to measurement,
- Lack of management support for the measurement program,
- The cost for measurement not planned according to the organization's budget.

Various frameworks and models have been developed to overcome some of the above mentioned difficulties software organizations are facing, such as Goal Question Metric (GQM) paradigm [6], [7], Goal Question Indicator Model (GQIM) [8] and Measurement Information Model [9]. GQM; developed by Basili and Weiss [6] and then improved by Basili and Rombach [7], is one of the well-known frameworks used in deriving measures from organization or business goals. Two reasons for the success of GQM are stated in [10] as that it is adaptable to many different organizations and environments and it aligns with the organizational directions and goals.

However, although these frameworks help the organizations to collect data on the measures which are required to fulfill the goals of the organization, none of those explicitly support the need to limit the number of measures to be collected [10]. In fact, one of the major constraints for the organizations which are also one of the significant reasons for measurement programs failure is the associated cost for the measurement programs.

A well-known figure, Tom De Marco said [11]; *"Metrics are good, more would be better and most is best but the importance of cost and time factor cannot be denied. Faced with a high number of measures to be collected for software process improvement reasons, most organizations want to know whether all those measures are equally important or some are more important than the others"*. Two out of ten problems leading to failure in the implementation of software measurement programs are reported by Howard Rubin to be: the intensive use of a single measure or, conversely, the use of too many [12].

According to [13], software measurement programs usually fail as they require expert judgment for selecting appropriate number of measures in relation to the organizational goals. The mapping of goals with appropriate measures requires experienced resources in the field of software measurement. These goals are required to be prioritized. One important point to be considered is that this prioritization might also be influenced by the cost associated to measures collection. Therefore, software organizations require deciding on an optimum set of measures which are good enough and at the same time less costly.

This paper suggests a model named 'Optimum Measure Set Decision (OMSD) Model' which extends the GQM approach and aims to fill in the gap discussed above by facilitating the managers in selecting an optimum set of measures from a large number of possible measures. To develop the model, we identified the factors which are significant when deciding on the measures to be collected as well as optimizing the cost associated based on the findings of an extensive literature review and getting feedback from the industry by conducting a survey. Then, we tested the model by means of some sample cases we created.

The paper is divided into five main sections. Section 1 provides an introduction. Section 2 explains the proposed OMSD model. Section 3 presents the empirical studies we made in order to test the model and discusses the results we obtained. Finally, we present the conclusions in Section 5.

2   Optimum Measures Set Decision (OMSD) Model

The Optimum Measures Set Decision (OMSD) Model [14], which is extending the GQM approach, is based on a heuristics approach. Heuristics is defined as a technique which seeks near optimal solution at a reasonable cost [15]. It is a rather flexible, easy to understand and implement technique. Constraints [16] regarding the costs and resources are defined early in the measurement process and it plays an important role during the final decision making on an optimum measures set selection. These constraints act as thresholds which are utilized as process terminators in OMSD Model.

The constraints for the heuristics rules are collected after the first level of GQM is implemented; i.e. when the goals are identified. After implementing levels in GQM, all the measures decided are ensured to be collected for a purpose and hence also reflect interesting and useful measurements for an organization. OMSD consists of five main steps shown as follows (Fig. 1 below):

- Category Selection
- Attributes Identification
- Measures Selection
- Collecting Data on the Measures Based on Factors
- Decision Making

2.1   Category Selection

In order to perform any measurement activity we need to identify the entity to be measured and the associated attributes [17]. This step involves mapping of the questions identified in the questions level of GQM paradigm on their respective entity categories. In [17], three main categories of entities are defined as: Process, Product and Resource.

Process category includes different activities and these activities are associated with a timescale. There is a particular order defined for these activities which means activity B requires the completion of activity A. This timing could be implicit or explicit. Resources and Product categories are associated with the process category. Every process has certain resources and products that it utilizes. This step results in the identification of measurement entities (questions) on their respective classes which serves as input to the next phase of 'Attribute Identification'.

2.2   Attribute Identification

Attributes associated with the entities are identified that can be divided into two main categories as external and internal attributes [17]. Internal attributes are those which could be measured only by observing the product. External attributes include processes, products, resources and its behavior which tells how these attributes relate to the environment. Category selection and attributes identification provide deep understanding regarding behavior of the respective questions.

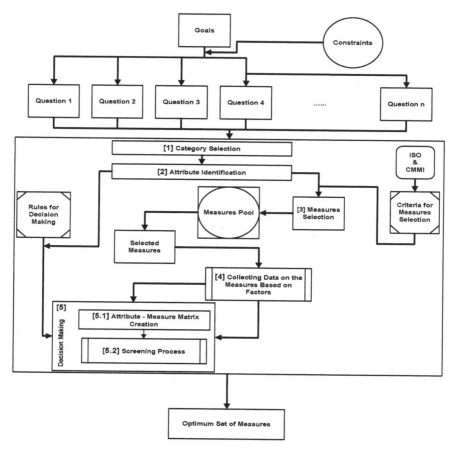

Fig. 1. Optimum Measures Set Decision (OMSD) Model

This step results in the following two outputs regarding the questions:

- Respective categories of questions
- Associated attributes depicting their behavior and relation with environment.

These identified attributes facilitate in Decision Making (Step 5) later on. At least one attribute is identified for each question because these attributes represent its respective questions in decision making. It is possible that one question can be related to more than one attribute and one attribute can be associated with more than one question. These dependencies are also identified and used later in the decision making process.

2.3 Measures Selection

The main aim of this step is the selection of all possible measures from a 'Measures Pool' using identified categories attributes and measures selection criteria (explained below). This step is conducted at the third level of GQM when the measures are identified.

We define the 'Measures Pool' as the repository which contains a finite set of measures defined for the attributes of software entities. Since this set might contain hundreds of measures, as our first attempt in this study, we included the ones provided in ISO 9126 [18], [19], [20], [21], ISO 25000 [22], the ones suggested as the minimum set of measures defined in CMMI [23] and the measures which are best known by the organization itself in their experience factory. Every organization can tailor the attributes and measures set in the Measures Pool based on their needs.

We defined these criteria for the measures selection from the Measures Pool based on the guidelines defined by the standards such as ISO 15939 [9] and CMMI [23]. We incorporated the following criteria in our model:

- Feasibility of collecting data in an organization
- Availability of human resources to collect and manage data
- Extent of intrusion and disruption of staff activities
- Availability of appropriate tools and equipment
- Personal preference
- Ease of interpretation by measurement users and measurement analysts
- Ease of presentation and relevancy to the audience

The criteria serve as a base for measures selection, but these do not tell which of the available measures should be collected for a specific attribute. For example, if a measure for software size is required to be collected, all size measures available in the Measures Pool such as Function Points, SLOC, Bytes, are selected.

2.4   Collecting Data on the Measures with Respect to the Identified Factors

Once the measures are selected based on the basic criteria defined in the previous section, the factors (Fig. 2) which we identified to be significant in deciding on the optimum set are considered for further decision.

A number of factors have been suggested to be considered when selecting the measures such as cost, time, resource requirements, tools, special trainings etc. [24], [25], [11]. We have selected the most basic ones having significant impact on the measurement process. These factors are general and can be applied to any process that involves measurement irrespective of its domain i.e. software process, management process, manufacturing process etc.

Factors proposed in the OMSD Model are the core of the model and play a key role in getting important data for selected measures which is vital for deciding on the optimum measures set. By means of the survey[1], we received industrial feedback on the identified factors. Survey was conducted in 10 different software organizations from different countries and which have different maturity levels. Respondents are selected on the basis of their experience regarding software measurement activities in order to create better understanding of our defined factors and having reliable feedback from them.

In this step, for each measure, the relevant data for each factor are to be entered by the measurement responsible and used in final decision making.

---

[1] For the questionnaire design, see http://sites.google.com/site/omsd09/survey

Factor 1: Collection Time. The collection time for a measure is composed of two sub-factors which are Duration and Frequency.

Duration describes the time required to collect a measure 'A'. Frequency describes how many times that specific measure 'A' is needed to be collected. Based on these data, the cumulative collection time weight (CCTW) is calculated by the following formula;

$$CCTW = Duration \times Frequency \tag{1}$$

Factor 2: Cost. The cost of a measure is determined based on the resources required (both human and non-human). It is comprised of one sub-factor: Utilization. Utilization factor is related to two sub-factors which are 'Resources' and 'Expense'. Resources contain the details regarding the number of resources required as well as their cost as; No of Resources and Resource Cost. Expense involves any other additional expenses such as the requirements for training, tools, hardware, etc.

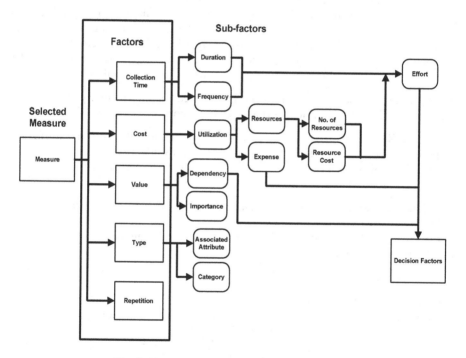

Fig. 2. Significant Factors for Measures Selection

We defined three classes of resources with respect to their roles in an organization as Upper Management Resource (UMR), Middle Management Resource (MMR) and Resource [Developer, Tester, Analyst] (R). Individual resource cost (IRC) is calculated by the following formula;

$$IRC = \frac{Salary}{Working\ Hours\ per\ Month} \tag{2}$$

Resource cost is used with the cumulative time weight in calculating effort of a particular measure. It is calculated by adding the cost of different resources involved in it.

$$Resource\ Cost\ (RC) = \sum_{i=1}^{n} IRCi \qquad (3)$$

In these calculations, we assumed that the working hours in a month depend on the organizational work policy. Currently we assumed that resources work 8 hours daily and 22 days per month means they work total 176 hours per month.

Factor 3: Value. Value is defined as a measure's dependency to other measures (direct and derived measures [26]) and its importance in a client organization's view as its Dependency and its Importance. This dependency identification is critical for effectiveness of final decision making. In OMSD, we used only direct measures in order to make decision process easier. If a derived measure came up we adjust it by calculating the cost of each base measure and then add them together. For example, cost of 'Development effort' measure is calculated by adding cost of measuring 'number of persons' and 'number of hours'. By means of that, we avoided complexity of dependency between measures. On the other hand, Importance of a measure (it is related to the priority of the goals identified) depicts the significance of a particular measure in the view of customer. We have defined four levels of importance which includes Level 1: Minor, Level 2: Essential, Level 3: Major, Level 4: Critical.

Factor 4: Type. The type of a measure is collected for information purposes only. The type is defined as associated attributes and Category.

Factor 5: Repetition. Data on this factor is also collected only for information purposes. It facilitates in decision making later on by identifying the multiple usage/repetition of the same measure. In this way, it reduces the probability of redundancy.

Decision Factors: Decision factors include the effort required to collect a particular measure.

Effort is calculated in terms of person-hours through cumulative collection time weight and resource cost as;

$$Effort = CCTW \times RC \qquad (4)$$

Then, the effort is used to calculate the cumulative cost (CC) for collecting a particular measure. And it is calculated by the following formula; (see also Factor 2: Cost).

$$CC = Effort + Expense \qquad (5)$$

2.5 Decision Making

Decision making is the final step in the OMSD model. Decision making is a process that shows expertise of an individual in selecting one solution out of the possible alternatives [27]. There are different categories given in the literature [27] that differentiate different decision making problems.

Decision making in OMSD model includes controlled inputs in the form of constraints (time and cost limits) and variables as factors such as usage and importance. This cost limit is used as Constraint cost (Ccost) while executing 7 steps of the screening process (explained below). So, the problem addressed by OMSD model is deterministic and decisions are made by constructing rules (7 steps explained below) in order to solve the defined problem. The Decision Making step consists of Attribute – Measure Matrix Creation and Screening Process. Main purpose of this step is to decide on an optimum set of measures from the selected measures. It utilizes the identified attributes (Step 2 of OMSD) and selected measures (Step 3 of OMSD) for decision making. Some ground rules are defined which facilitate in the final decision making.

Attribute – Measure Matrix Creation: This is first step for decision making and identified attributes and the selected measures are its inputs. It is a two dimensional matrix that depicts the relation of the measures with their respective attributes (see Fig. 3 below).

Measure / Attributes	Measure 1	Measure 2	Measure 3		....				Measure n
Attribute 1	0	0	1	0	0	0	0	0	1
Attribute 2	1	0	0	0	0	0	0	0	0
Attribute 3	0	1	0	0	0	0	1	0	0
:	1	0	0	0	0	0	0	0	0
	0	0	0	0	1	0	0	0	0
	1	0	0	0	0	0	0	1	0
Attribute n	0	0	0	1	0	1	0	0	0
Usage	3	1	1	1	1	1	1	1	1
Importance	4	4	3	3	2	2	1	1	1
Cumulative Cost	50 €	70 €	10 €	15 €	40 €	35 €	180 €	100 €	5 €

Fig. 3. Attribute – Measure Matrix

First, the dependencies of the measures are identified. The reason for this is that OMSD in this current form cannot handle dependencies between the base and the derived measures. Therefore, the model might exclude a particular measure in the screening process, on which many measures could be dependent. Therefore, first consider only direct measures in this step and when any derived measure comes up, instead of using its base measures, we use the derived measure itself.

Attribute – Measure Matrix creation consist of the following steps:

1. Sort measures on the basis of their importance. Highest importance (4-Critical) measure comes first.
2. If Measure 'X' is used to measure Attribute 'Y', then fill in the respective cell with '1' otherwise with '0' (see Fig. 3 above).
3. Calculate the number of usages of each measure by adding the values in that column.
4. Add Importance weight and cumulative cost of each measure in the respective cells.

Screening Process: Screening process is the last step in OMSD Model. It utilizes attribute – measure matrix and a set of pre-defined decision factors in order to decide on the optimum set of measures. The defined screening rules are implemented during the final screening process. These rules are based on a number of factors such as the Number of usage, Importance and Cost. A heuristics approach is used to make a tradeoff. After every selection, a comparison is made with the constraints (cost and time) [16] in order to control the progress. Certain tradeoffs are also needed with respect to the importance of the measure and the cost for the measure, but these trade-offs are primarily dependent on the organizational business needs and priorities.

The model selects at least one measure for each attribute because each attribute represents a particular question. Order of these rules could be changed based on the organizational requirements. Steps include in screening process are given below:

Step 1: Select Attribute 'Ai' Where i = {1,2,3,4.....n}

Step 2: Select each measure 'mi' which satisfy attribute 'Ai'
Ai= {m1, m2, m3.....mn}

Step 3: Calculate the usage Umi of each measure mi
Usage of mi (Umi)=How many time it is used in Attribute-Measure Matrix.

Step 4: Perform Comparisons on the base of Decision factors.

- Compare the Use of each measure mi with all selected measures
- Compare the Importance of each measure with all selected measures
  Importance = weight assigned to Measure mi (Step 4: Factor-Value)
- Compare the Cost of each measure with all selected measures
  Cost = Calculated through Step 4 of the Model

Step 5: Measures are selected after step 4. Note that measure selection is completely dependent on the organizational decision (means which decision factor is of high importance for organization).

Step 6: Check the selected measure against the pre-defined constraints. Primary aim of this step is to control the measurement process in order to make sure that cost of the selected measures remains under the cost limits. This step is repeated at the end of each iteration during the screening process.

Step 7: Check the following conditions:

- If Cost of selected measure (Cms) is less than Constraint Cost (Ccost) then continue from step 1

$$Cms < Ccost \tag{6}$$

- If Cms > Ccost terminate the process.

Step 6 and 7 are mutually exclusive. Once the selected measure is analyzed against the defined constraints, decision about continuation or termination of measurement process is made on the basis of condition in step 7. An optimum measure set is selected after completion of these steps (either termination condition is met or all measures are gone through).

A Sample Case. In order to evaluate this model, we created a sample case[2] and executed it to obtain the optimum set of measures for a specified set of goals. Specifically, 5 goals were defined and 11 questions were identified which would provide the information required. Each question can be answered by means of a number of measures associated with it. For this case, we identified 23 suitable measures from the Measures Pool.

Then, we collected the data for each measure according to the factors defined in OMSD. Among those measures, we observed that 3 of the measures are to be used for answering more than one question. Therefore, we had 20 measures for the further decision making process. After this step, we calculated the effort required to collect each measure, checked the dependencies of the measures, and at the end calculated the cumulative cost for each measure by adding any additional expenses if exist. We performed the same calculations for the all 22 measures.

Next, we created the 'Attribute-measure matrix' and then made the decisions using the screening rules in the OMSD model. In this matrix, cumulative costs for all of the measures are obtained in the previous step along with the Importance value decided by the managers according to the importance of each goal. For example, 'Productivity' measure had a cumulative cost 350$ and its importance value is 3. These measures are then mapped to the relevant attributes. For example, Development effort measure as well as any product size measure is required to derive the measure for answering the question related to the productivity attribute. Using the screening rules, we saw that two size measures can be chosen to derive the measure for the productivity. Therefore, we first considered all three measures (Development Effort, SLOC, FP). Then, we checked the 'No. of usage' attribute for each measure globally. FP is to be used more than SLOC, which means that it can be used to satisfy other goals as well. Here, SLOC and FP are equally important and the cost for measuring FP is higher. Based on this information, the OMSD model decided to choose FP since it can be used to answer a couple of questions which reduces the total cost.

After each execution for each measure, there checked the Constraint cost. After selection of each measure, the remaining available budget is re-calculated by deducting the cost for the selected measure from it. It is important to note that if two measures have the same 'No. of usage' but different importance and cost, then a tradeoff between importance and cost is made by the measurement responsible(s) and/or managers.

At the end of the whole process, OMSD model decided on 8 measures from suitable 23 measures. This is the optimal set of measures as it helps achieving the goals under the defined constraints and identified factors.

Although we obtained a smaller measures set in this experiment, our main purpose in this case study was not to show the model's efficiency but rather to test the applicability and the rules of the model. The model is dependent on the initial measures set as well as the constraints set by the measurement responsible.

3 Conclusions

Measurement process is one of the critical processes, which leads organizations towards process improvement. Since numbers of measures are available, it is needed to

---

[2] The sample case can be found at: http://sites.google.com/site/omsd09/sample-case

have an approach guiding organizations for selecting an optimum set of measures. This paper presented a model called "OMSD Model", a systematic approach for dealing with the challenge of 'finding an optimum measures set' out of the possibly large set of measures.

In a nutshell, this model is developed to address one of the challenges organizations are facing; the risk for the failure of measurement programs due to improper time and cost estimates, by minimizing the cost by supporting efficient and effective measures selection process in organizations. There is little explicit discussion in the literature about what constitutes a reasonable overhead for a measurement program. In [6], it is stated that 90% of the practitioners reported to spend less than 3% of their time on metrics-related work. OMSD model can also help the organizations to collect such information so that they can also calculate the Return on Investment (ROI) for initiating such programs.

Even though we evaluated the OMSD model by means of an industrial survey we made to determine the factors considered in the model and by means of a thorough experimentation of the rules of the model, in order to show evidences that the model is valuable for the organizations, industrial case studies should be conducted.

One of the current constraints of the OMSD Model is that high levels of human interaction are needed to enter the input required by the model such as measures dependency, time and cost limits. Improvement and automation of this process can reduce human effort resulting in less time and cost expense.

Other future works related to this study includes measures prioritization based on the priority of the goals at Step 1 of GQM, developing a Measures pool that will make initial measures selection easier (Step 3 of OMSD Model), incursion of new factors based on more industrial surveys, industrial experimentation of the OMSD Model and its integration with measurement frameworks other than GQM.

Acknowledgements. We would like to thank Johan Holmgren for his support in the development of the heuristics approach. We also thank the survey respondents for their feedback on the model.

References

1. Wang, Q., Li, M.: Measuring and improving software process in China. In: International Symposium on Empirical Software Engineering, p. 10 (2005)
2. Bundschuh, M., Dekkers, C.: The Measurement Compendium: Estimating and Benchmarking Success with Functional Size Measurement. Springer, Heidelberg (2008)
3. Goethert, W., Hayes, W.: Experiences in Implementing Measurement Programs. Technical Note, Software Engineering Institute, Carnegie Mellon University, CMU/SEI-2001-TN-026 (2001)
4. Gopal, A., Krishnan, M.S., Mukhopadhyay, T., Goldenson, D.R.: Measurement Programs in Software Development: Determinants of Success. IEEE Transactions on Software Engineering 28(9), 863–875 (2002)
5. Hall, T., Fenton, N.: Implementing Effective Software Metrics Programs. IEEE Software 14(2), 55–65 (1997)

6. Basili, V.R., Weiss, D.M.: A Methodology for Collecting Valid Software Engineering Data. IEEE Transactions on Software Engineering SE-10(6), 728–738 (1984)

7. Basili, V.R., Rombach, H.D.: The TAME Project: Towards Improvement-Oriented Software Environments. IEEE Transactions on Software Engineering SE-14(6), 758–773 (1988)

8. Park, R.E., Goethert, W.B., Florac, W.A.: Goal-Driven Software Measurement - A Guidebook. Handbook. Software Engineering Institute, Carnegie Mellon University, CMU/SEI-96-HB-002 (1996)

9. ISO/IEC 15939 International Standard 1st Edition 2002: Software engineering — Software measurement process. Reference Number ISO/IEC 15939:2002(E) (2002)

10. Berander, P., Jönsson, P.: A goal question metric based approach for efficient measurement framework definition. In: Proceedings of the 2006 ACM/IEEE international Symposium on Empirical Software Engineering. ISESE 2006, Rio de Janeiro, Brazil, September 21 - 22, pp. 316–325. ACM, New York (2006)

11. DeMarco, T.: Why does software cost so much? Essay 2: Mad about Measurement, pp. 11–25. Dorset House Publishing, Co., Inc., New York (1995)

12. Rubin, H.A.: The Top 10 Mistakes in IT Measurement. IT Metrics Strategies II(11) (1996), http://www.cutter.com/benchmark/1996toc.html

13. Lavazza, L., Barresi, G.: Automated support for process-aware definition and execution of measurement plans. In: 27th international Conference on Software Engineering. ICSE 2005, St. Louis, MO, USA, May 15 - 21, pp. 234–243. ACM, New York (2005)

14. Abdullah, H.M., Bhatti, A.M.: Deciding on Optimum set of Measures in Software Organizations. Master's Thesis MSE-200901, Blekinge Institute of Technology, Ronneby, Sweden. pp. 1–66 (2009)

15. Principles of heuristics optimization, http://www.mm.helsinki.fi/kurssi/Marv/MSUU14/Heuristic.pdf

16. Rina, D.: Constraint Processing. Morgan Kaufmann, San Francisco (2003)

17. Fenton, N.E., Pfleeger, S.L.: Software Metrics: A Rigorous and Practical Approach, 2nd edn. Course Technology (1998)

18. ISO/IEC 9126-1 International Standard 1st Edition 2001: Software engineering — Product quality — Part 1: Quality model. Reference Number ISO/IEC 9126-1:2001(E) (2001)

19. ISO/IEC 9126-2 International Standard 1st Edition 2003: Software engineering — Product quality — Part 1: Quality model. Referenc Number ISO/IEC 9126-2:2003(E) (2003)

20. ISO/IEC 9126-3 International Standard 1st Edition 2003: Software engineering — Product quality — Part 1: Quality model. Reference Number ISO/IEC 9126-3:2003(E) (2003)

21. ISO/IEC 9126-4 International Standard 1st Edition 2004: Software engineering — Product quality — Part 1: Quality model. Reference Number ISO/IEC 9126-4:2004 (E) (2004)

22. ISO/IEC 25000 International Standard 1st Edition 2005: Software engineering — Software product Quality Requirements and Evaluation (SQuaRE) — Guide to SQuaRE. Reference Number ISO/IEC 25000:2005(E) (2005)

23. CMMI Product Team: CMMI for Development Version 1.2 (CMMI-Dev, V1.2): Improving processes for better products. CMU/SEI-2006-TR-008, ESC-TR-2006-008, Software Engineering Institute, SEI (2000)

24. Lamouchi, O., Cherif, A.R., Lévy, N.: A framework based measurements for evaluating an IS quality. In: Hinze, A., Kirchberg, M. (eds.) Proceedings of the Fifth on Asia-Pacific Conference on Conceptual Modelling - Volume 79. Wollongong, NSW, Australia, January 01. Conferences in Research and Practice in Information Technology Series, vol. 325, pp. 39–47. Australian Computer Society, Darlinghurst (2008)

25. Thakkar, D., Hassan, A.E., Hamann, G., Flora, P.: A framework for measurement based performance modeling. In: Proceedings of the 7th international Workshop on Software and Performance. WOSP 2008, Princeton, NJ, USA, June 23 - 26, pp. 55–66. ACM, New York (2008)

26. Kaner, C., Bond, W.P.: Software Engineering Metrics: What Do They Measure and How Do We Know? In: 10th International Software Metrics Symposium, Metrics (2004), http://www.kaner.com/pdfs/metrics2004.pdf

27. Murty, K.G.: Optimization Models For Decision Making, Dept. of Industrial & Operations Engineering, vol. 1. University of Michigan, Ann Arbor (2003), http://www.ioe.engin.umich.edu/people/fac/books/murty/opti_model/junior-0.pdf

Applying a Functional Size Measurement Procedure for Defect Detection in MDD Environments

Beatriz Marín, Giovanni Giachetti, and Oscar Pastor

Centro de Investigación en Métodos de Producción de Software,
Universidad Politécnica de Valencia,
Camino de Vera s/n, 46022 Valencia, Spain
{bmarin,ggiachetti,opastor}@pros.upv.es

Abstract. Nowadays, is widely accepted that functional size measurement is essential to manage and control software projects. In order to obtain early indicators for software projects, many functional size measurement procedures have been developed to measure the functional size of conceptual models. To do this, the measurement procedures assume that models do not present defects. However, this is an unreal assumption because, in practice, the conceptual models can have defects that may affect the implementation of final applications. This is especially important for software production processes based on MDD technology, where the conceptual models are key artifacts used as inputs in the process of code generation. Therefore, this paper presents how a functional size measurement procedure (which has been developed for the measurement of conceptual models of a specific MDD environment) can help in the detection of defects in conceptual models.

Keywords: Conceptual Model, Functional Size, Measurement Procedure, COSMIC, Model-Driven Development, Defect Detection.

1 Introduction

During the last few years, software production processes have evolved from the solution space (software product) to the problem space (conceptual models). Models are abstractions of the reality that help to understand complex problems and their potential solutions [34]. Thus, Model-Driven Development (MDD) methods have been emerged to take advantage of the benefits of the use of models, such as a simplified view of the problem (using concepts that are much less bound to the underlying implementation technology and are much closer to the problem domain); and an easy way to specify, understand, and maintain the systems.

In a software production process based on MDD technology, the conceptual models are key artifacts that are used as input in the process of code generation. These conceptual models must provide a holistic view of all the components of the final application (including the structure of the system, the behavior, the interaction between the users and the system, etc.) in order to be able to automatically generate the final application. To do this, the models (conceptual models) must have enough semantic formalization to specify all the functionality of the final application and also to

R.V. O'Connor et al. (Eds.): EuroSPI 2009, CCIS 42, pp. 57–68, 2009.

avoid different interpretations for the same model. Therefore, it is very important to be able to evaluate and improve the quality of the conceptual models in order to improve the quality of the software products generated by using MDD technologies.

One important quality issue to be evaluated is the amount of defects that the conceptual models used in MDD environments can have. In many cases, the defect detection is performed by the MDD compilers, which presents disadvantages such as the extra complexity included in the compiler, and also the identification of defects with regard to specific technical platforms (i.e. Java, C#, etc.). To overcome the limitations of the defect detection procedures embedded in MDD compilers, it is necessary a defect detection procedure that can be applied directly in the conceptual models. Taking into account that in terms of the management of software projects: (1) it is widely accepted that is essential to know the functional size of applications in order to successfully apply estimation models, effort models, and budget models [26], and (2) the measurement of the functional size in conceptual models allows the project leader to generate indicators in early stages of the development cycle of a software product; we advocate the use of a measurement procedure to detect defects in early stages of the software product. Thus, the aim of this work is to present how a functional size measurement procedure that allows the measurement of conceptual models can helps in the detection of defects that can have the conceptual models used in MDD environments.

The rest of the paper is organized as follows: Section 2 presents a brief background and a set of relevant related works. Section 3 presents the functional size measurement procedure for the conceptual model of a specific MDD approach that is used to apply the introduced ideas into practical settings. Section 4 presents how a measurement procedure can be used to identify types of defects of the conceptual models. Finally, Section 5 presents some conclusions and points out future work.

2 Background and Related Work

The ISO/IEC 14143-1 [11] standard defines *functional size* as the size of the software derived by quantifying the functional user requirements. This standard also defines a Functional Size Measurement (FSM) as the process of measuring the functional size. In addition, this standard defines a FSM method as the implementation of a FSM that is defined by a set of rules, which is defined in accordance with the mandatory features defined in the ISO/IEC 14143-2 [12].

In order to measure the functional size of software applications, four measurement methods have been recognized as standards: IFPUG FPA [18], MK II FPA [19], NESMA FPA [20], and COSMIC FFP [17]. The first three methods are based on the Function Point Analysis proposal [3]. These FPA-based methods have several limitations for the correct measurement of systems: for instance, they only consider the functionality of the system that the human user observes, they have units that are hard to understand; they do not consider the functionality that allows communication between layers in systems with a layer-based architecture, etc. To overcome the limitations of FPA-based measurement methods, the COSMIC measurement method was defined as the second generation of functional size measurement methods. COSMIC uses a mathematical function to aggregate the functional size of the functional processes specified in the conceptual models and is not limited by maximum values to measure the size of conceptual models: this helps to better distinguish the size of large conceptual models.

Currently, there are some approaches that apply COSMIC in order to estimate the functional size of future software applications from the requirement models, such as [4]. However, these models do not have enough semantic expressiveness to specify all the functionality of involved systems. There are other proposals designed to measure the functional size of conceptual models, which have more functional expressiveness than requirement models and are used to the automatic generation of final applications. This is the case of Diab's proposal [7] and Poels' proposal [33]. Diab's proposal presents a measurement procedure to measure real time applications modeled with the ROOM language [35]. Poels' proposal presents a measurement procedure to object-oriented applications of the domain of Management Information Systems (MIS) that are modeled with an event-based method called MERODE [6]. Other FSM procedures (based on COSMIC) to measure the functional size of conceptual models can be found in the survey presented in [25].

Summarizing, none of the proposals of measurement procedures based on COS-MIC allows an accurately measurement of the functional size of MIS applications from the related conceptual models. Moreover, none of them take into account the improvements made to the COSMIC measurement method, for instance, the capability to measure the functional size of a piece of software of the application depending on the functionality that needs other piece of software. The main limitation of the approaches presented above comes from the lack of expressiveness of the conceptual models that are involved in the generation of the final application, for instance, the conceptual models do not allow the specification of presentation aspects. For this reason, we have selected the OO-Method approach as the reference MDD environment. The OO-Method approach is an object-oriented method that puts the MDA technology in practice [31], separating the business logic from the platform technology, allowing the automatic generation of final applications by means of well-defined model transformations [32]. It provides the semantic formalization needed to define complete and unambiguous conceptual models, allowing the specification of all the functionality of the final application at conceptual level. This method has been implemented in an industrial tool [4] that allows the automatic generation of fully working applications. The applications generated can be desktop or web MIS applications and can be generated in several technologies (for instance, java, C#, visual basic, etc.). In the next section we present a measurement procedure that is based on this MDD approach.

3   A FSM Procedure for Conceptual Models of an MDD Approach

OOmCFP (OO-Method COSMIC Function Points) [23] is a measurement procedure that was developed for measuring the functional size of the applications generated by the OO-Method MDD environment. The OOmCFP procedure measures the functional size focusing on the conceptual model of the OO-Method MDD approach, which is comprised of an object model, a functional model, a dynamic model, and a presentation model.

The OOmCFP measurement procedure was defined in accordance with the COS-MIC measurement manual version 3.0 [2]. Given that the OOmCFP procedure was designed in accordance with COSMIC, a mapping between the concepts used in COSMIC and the concepts used in the OO-Method conceptual model has been defined [22]. The OOmCFP FSM procedure is structured in the three phases of the COSMIC method: the strategy phase, the mapping phase, and the measuring phase.

With respect to the *strategy phase*, the scope of the measurement can be determined by the functional processes, the layers, or the whole application. Since the OO-Method applications are generated with a three tier architecture (presentation, logic, and database), each tier of the architecture is associated with the other tiers in a superior/subordinate hierarchical dependency. Therefore, the presentation tier can use the services of the logic tier because the logic tier is beneath the presentation tier in the hierarchy. In the same way, the logic tier can use the services of the database tier because the database tier is beneath the logic tier in the hierarchy. Thus, the layers correspond to the hierarchical tiers of the OO-Method applications: the presentation tier, the logic tier, and the database tier.

In addition, the OO-Method applications have at least one software component in each tier of the architecture: the client component, the server component, and the database component. For this reason, the pieces of software correspond to the software components: the client component, the server component, and the database component. Finally, the users are the human users, the client component, and the server component of the applications. The users are separated from the pieces of software by a boundary.

With respect to the *mapping phase*, the functional processes are groups of functionality that can be directly accessed by the users. These groups of functionality correspond to the interaction units specified in the menu of the presentation model. The data groups correspond to the classes of the object model that participate in the functional processes. The data attributes correspond to the attributes of the classes identified as data groups.

With regard to the *measuring phase*, the data movements correspond to the movements of data groups between the users and the functional processes. Each functional process has two or more data movements. Each data movement moves a single data group. A data movement can be an Entry (E), an Exit (X), a Read (R), or a Write (W) data movement. This proposal has 29 rules to identify the data movements that can occur in the OO-Method applications. Each rule is structured with a concept of the COSMIC measurement method, a concept of the OO-Method approach, and the cardinalities that associate these concepts. The rules for the data movements can be visualized in [22]. These mapping rules detect the data movements (E, X, R, and W) of all the functionality needed for the correct operation of the generated application, which must be built by the developer of the application. Finally, this proposal has a set of rules to obtain the functional size of each functional process of the application, of each piece of software of the application, and of the whole application.

Therefore, the OOmCFP procedure has been designed to obtain accurate measures of the applications that are generated from the OO-Method conceptual model. This is feasible because we have selected a conceptual model that has enough semantic expressiveness to specify all the functionality of the final application (the conceptual model of the OO-Method MDD approach). Thus, the measures obtained are accurate because all the data movements that occur in the final application could be traceable to the conceptual model. This measurement procedure has been automated, providing the measurement results in a few minutes and using minimal resources [24]. However, the OOmCFP measurement procedure assumes that the conceptual model has high quality, that is, the OOmCFP procedure assumes that the conceptual model is correct, complete, and without defects. Obviously, this is an unreal assumption because several times the conceptual models present defects. In the following section we discuss this issue in order to use the measurement procedure to improve the quality of the conceptual models.

4 Improving the Quality of Conceptual Models Using a FSM Procedure

In the literature, there is no consensus for the definition of quality of conceptual models. There are several proposals that use different terminology to refer to the same concepts. There are also many proposals that do not even define what they mean by quality of conceptual models. In order to achieve consensus about the definition of quality of conceptual models and then improve the quality of these kind of models, we have adopted the definition proposed by Moody [29]. This definition is based on the definition of quality of a product or service in the ISO 9000 standard [10]. Therefore, we understand the quality of a conceptual model to be *"The total of features and characteristics of a conceptual model that bear on its ability to satisfy stated or implied needs"*.

To evaluate the quality of software products, the ISO 9126 standard [13] has been defined. This standard defines a set of characteristics and sub-characteristics that are oriented to evaluate the quality of software products from three perspectives: the internal quality of software products [15], the external quality of software products [14], and the quality in use of software products [16]. However, since the ISO 9126 standard has been illustrated in the evaluation of the quality of final applications, it is necessary to select the characteristics, sub-characteristics and metrics that can be applied to the conceptual models in order to evaluate their quality.

In the last few years, several proposals have emerged to evaluate the quality of conceptual models based on the ISO 9126 standard: for instance, Genero et al., Li and Henry, Lorenz and Kidd, Bansiya and Davis, Chidamber and Kemerer, etc. A detailed description of these proposals can be found in [21]. These proposals focus on the evaluation of the maintainability of conceptual models [21]. In addition, there are also proposals that attempt to evaluate the usability of software products in the conceptual models, for instance, Panach et al. [30], and Abrahao et al. [1]. Despite the great number of proposals that present metrics to evaluate the internal quality of conceptual models, none of the proposals has performed an analysis of the defect types that can be identified in conceptual models, and the conceptual constructs that must be measured in order to achieve quality characteristics in the conceptual model.

Defect detection refers to found anomalies in software products in order to correct them and, therefore, obtain software products of better quality. The IEEE 1044 standard classification for software anomalies [9] define an anomaly as *any condition that deviates from expectations based on requirements specifications, design documents, user documents, standards, etc. or from someone's perceptions or experiences.* This definition is very broad, so that different persons can found different anomalies in the same software artifact, and even the anomalies that found one person could be don't perceived as anomalies for other person. This situation has caused that many researchers redefine the concepts of error, defect, failure, fault, etc.; and that many times these concepts have been used indistinctly [8]. In order to avoid the proliferation of concepts related to the software anomalies, in this paper we analyzes the proposals of defect detection in conceptual models adapting the terminology defined by Meyer in [27]:

- Error: It is a wrong decision made during the development of a conceptual model.
- Defect: It is a property of a conceptual model that may cause the model to depart from its intended behavior.
- Fault: It is the event of a software system departing from its intended behavior during one of its executions.

Taking into account that the costs of faults correction increase exponentially over the development life cycle [29], it is of paramount importance to discover faults as early as possible, which means detect errors or defects. The next section shows how a measurement procedure can be used to identify defects in the conceptual models.

4.1 Using the OOmCFP Measurement Procedure to Detect Defects

Since the measurement of the functional size using the OOmCFP approach has defined rules to perform the mapping between the concepts of COSMIC and OO-Method, and rules to identify the data movements of the final application in the conceptual model; it is possible to identify some defects that impede the compilation of the conceptual model or that cause faults in the generated application.

The main concepts of the models that comprise the OO-Method conceptual model are well-known because they are the same as those used in the UML diagrams [10]. However, for a better understanding of the defects that can be identified, the OO-Method models and their conceptual constructs (which are used by OOmCFP) are briefly described in the following paragraphs.

The object model of the OO-Method approach describes the static part of the system. This model allows the specification of classes, attributes, derived attributes, events, transactions, operations, preconditions, integrity constraints, agents, and relationships between classes. In this model, the *agents* are active classes that can access specific attributes of the classes of the model and that can execute specific services of the classes of the model.

The functional model of the OO-Method approach allows the specification of the effects that the execution of an event has over the value of the attributes of the class that owns the event by means of a *valuation formula*.

The presentation model allows the specification of the graphical user interface of an application in an abstract way [28]. To do this, the presentation model has a set of abstract presentation patterns that are organized hierarchically in three levels: access structure, interaction units, and auxiliary patterns. The first level allows the specification of the system access structure. Based on the menu-like view provided by the first level, the second level allows the specification of the interaction units of the system. The interaction units are groups of functionality that allow the users of the application to interact with the system. Thus, the interaction units of the interaction model represent entry-points for the application, and they can be:

- A *Service Interaction Unit* (SIU). This interaction unit represents the interaction between a user of the application and the execution of a system service.
- A *Population Interaction Unit* (PIU). This interaction unit represents the interaction with the system that deals with the presentation of a set of instances of a class.
- An *Instance Interaction Unit* (IIU). This interaction unit represents the interaction with an object of the system.
- The three previous elementary interaction units can be composed to build a *Master Detail Interaction Unit* (MDIU).

The third level of the presentation model allows the specification of the auxiliary patterns that characterize lower level details about the behavior of the interaction units. These auxiliary patterns are: entry, selection list, arguments grouping, masks, filters, actions, navigations, order criteria, and display set. The *display set* pattern is used to specify which attributes of a class or its related classes will be shown to the user in a PIU or an IIU.

Table 1 lists a set of rules of the OOmCFP measurement procedure that are related to the mapping between COSMIC and OO-Method, and how these rules help to find defect in the conceptual models.

Table 1. Mapping Rules of OOmCFP

COSMIC	OO-Method	Defects
Functional User	Rule 1: Identify 1 functional user for each **agent** in the OO-Method object model.	Defect 1: An object model without a specification of an agent class.
Functional Process	Rule 5: Identify 1 functional process for each **interaction unit** that can be **directly** accessed in the menu of the OO-Method presentation model.	Defect 2: An OO-Method Conceptual Model without a definition of the presentation model. Defect 3: A presentation model without the specification of one or more interaction units.
Data Group	Rule 6: Identify 1 data group for each **class** defined in the OO-Method object model, which does not participate in an inheritance hierarchy.	Defect 4: An object model without the specifications of one or more classes. Defect 5: A class without a name. Defect 6: Classes with a repeated name.
Attributes	Rule 9: Identify the set attributes of the **classes** defined in the OO-Method object model.	Defect 7: A class without the definition of one or more attributes. Defect 8: A class with attributes with repeated names.

Based on the Conradi el al. proposal [5], we classify the defect types into: Omission (missing item), Extraneous information (information that should not be in the model), Incorrect fact (misrepresentation of a fact), Ambiguity (unclear concept), or Inconsistency (disagreement between representations of a concept). Thus, Defects 1, 2, 3, 4, and 7 correspond to *omissions*; Defect 5 corresponds to an *incorrect fact*; and Defects 6 and 8 correspond to *ambiguities*.

Table 2 lists a set of rules of the OOmCFP measurement procedure that are related to the identification of data movements. This table also indicates how the presented rules help to find defect in the conceptual models.

Table 2. Rules to identify the data movements of OOmCFP

OO-Method Conceptual Element	OOmCFP Rules	Defects
Display Pattern	Rule 10: Identify **1X** data movement for the client piece of software for each **display pattern** in the interaction units that participate in a functional process.	Defect 9: An instance interaction unit without display pattern. Defect 10: A population interaction unit without display pattern.
	Rule 11: Identify **1E** data movement for the client piece of software, and **1X** and **1R** data movements for the server piece of software for each different **class** that contributes with attributes to the display pattern.	Defect 11: A display pattern without attributes.
	Rule 13: Identify **1R** data movement for the server piece of software for each different **class** that is used in the **effect** of the **derivation formula** of derivate attributes that appear in the display pattern.	Defect 12: Derived attributes without a derivation formula.
Filter Pattern	Rule 16: Identify **1R** data movement for the server piece of software for each different **class** that is used in the **filter formula** of the filter patterns of the interaction units that participate in a functional process.	Defect 13: A filer without a filter formula.
Service	Rule 20: Identify **1R** data movement for the server piece of software for each different **class** that is used in the **effect** of the **valuation formula** of events that participate in the interaction units contained in a functional process.	Defect 14: An event of a class of the object diagram without valuations.
	Rule 21: Identify **1W** data movement for the server piece of software for each **create event, destroy event**, or **event that has valuations** (represented by the class that contains the service) that participate in the interaction units contained in a functional process.	Defect 15: A class without a creation event.
	Rule 22: Identify **1R** data movement for the server piece of software for each different **class** that is used in the **service formula** of transactions, operations, or global services that participate in the interaction units contained in a functional process.	Defect 16: Transactions without a specification of a sequence of services (service formula). Defect 17: Operations without a specification of a sequence of services (service formula). Defect 18: Global services without a specification of a sequence of services (service formula).

Table 2. (*continued*)

Rule	Defect
Rule 23: Identify **1E** data movement and **1X** data movement for the client piece of software, and **1E** data movement for the server piece of software for the **set of data-valued arguments** of the services (represented by the class that contains the service) that participate in the interaction units contained in a functional process. Rule 24: Identify **1E** data movement and **1X** data movement for the client piece of software, and **1E** data movement for the server piece of software for each different **object-valued argument** of the services that participate in the interaction units contained in a functional process.	Defect 19: A service without arguments. Defect 20: A service with arguments with repeated names.
Rule 31: Identify **1R** data movement for the server piece of software for each different **class** that is used in the **precondition formulas** of the services that participate in the interaction units contained in a functional process.	Defect 21: A precondition without the specification of the precondition formula.
Rule 32: Identify **1X** data movement for the client piece of software for all **error messages** of the **precondition formulas** of the services that participate in the interaction units contained in a functional process.	Defect 22: A precondition without an error message.
Rule 34: Identify **1R** data movement for the server piece of software for each different **class** that is used in the **integrity constraint formulas** of the class that contains each service that participates in the interaction units contained in a functional process.	Defect 23: An integrity constraint without the specification of the integrity formula.
Rule 35: Identify **1X** data movement for the client piece of software for all **error messages** of the **integrity constraint formula** of the class that contains each service that participates in the interaction units contained in a functional process.	Defect 24: An integrity constraint without an error message.

The list of defect types presented in Table 2 also have been classified using the Conradi et al. [5] classification. Thus, Defects 9, 10, 15, 19, 22, and 24 correspond to *omissions*; Defects 11, 12, 13, 14, 16, 17, 18, and 21, and 23 correspond to an *incorrect fact*; and Defect 20 corresponds to an *ambiguity*. Therefore, we can state that the OOmCFP measurement procedure helps in the identification of defects types of conceptual models, which are related to omissions, incorrect facts, and ambiguities.

It is important to note that Defects 1, 2, 4, 5, 6, 7, 8, 9, 10, 12, 13, 14, 16, 17, 18, 19, 21, and 23 allow the definition of measures that contribute to the evaluation of the sub-characteristic of *compliance* of the conceptual models (in accordance with the ISO 9126 standard), because it is possible to determine if the conceptual model is adhered to the rules and conventions of the model compiler. In the same way, Defects 3, 11, 15, 20, 22, and 24 allow the definition of measures that contribute to the evaluation of the sub-characteristic of *analyzability* of software products (in accordance with the ISO 9126 standard), because it is possible to diagnostic the possible faults of the final application in the conceptual models.

4.2 General Comments

For many years, software industry has applied different techniques for the requirement modeling and definition of conceptual models in order to identify and correct software defects. Otherwise, these defects could propagate to later development phases, which imply an extra cost to fix them. This situation is also present in the new software production processes, such as MDD methods. Therefore, it is very important to use different techniques in order to found defects in the conceptual models, avoiding their propagation to the final application. The use of a unique technique to found defects does not guarantee that all the defects be found. Thus, it is recommended that organizations use several verification techniques [36].

Since in MDD approaches the quality of conceptual models has a direct impact in the quality of generated applications, the use of the OOmCFP measurement procedure for defects detection provides a new technique to improve the quality of conceptual models, and hence, the quality of final applications.

The defect types presented in sub-section 4.1 where identified by applying the OOmCFP FSM procedure to five different case studies of the OO-Method approach, which correspond to a publishing system, a rent-a-car system, an invoice system, a camping system, and a photography agency system. These five case studies have been selected because they (all together) cover all the modeling possibilities of the OO-Method approach. However, it is important to perform controlled experiments to compare our results with the results obtained from other subjects in order to complete the list of defects that can be identified using the OOmCFP measurement procedure.

In addition, the OOmCFP measurement procedure has a tool that automates its application. Therefore, this tool can be adapted to automatically report the defects that may have the conceptual models, and, once the model is free of defects, to obtain the functional size of the final application. This helps to demonstrate that the OOmCFP measurement procedure is not based on an unreal assumption, and that it could really help in the quality improvement of conceptual models used in software projects.

With regard to the generalization of this approach, in spite of the OOmCFP measurement procedure has been developed for a specific MDD environment (called OO-Method), many of the conceptual constructs used in the conceptual model of this environment can be found in other object-oriented MDD approaches, specially in those oriented to the development of management information systems. Thus, the OOmCFP procedure can be easily generalized to other MDD approaches.

5 Conclusion

In this paper, we have presented the applicability of the COSMIC standard method to perform the detection of defects of object-oriented conceptual models used in MDD environments. This identification is obtained through the application of a FSM procedure (called OOmCFP), which allows the measurement of functional size from conceptual models related to an MDD approach called OO-Method. This approach has been selected because it allows the whole specification of the final application in a conceptual level, and because it has been successfully applied to industrial software development.

The application of the OOmCFP measurement procedure to shows how the COS-MIC specification can be applied in the defects detection is precisely the main contribution of this paper, since this approach can be used for other MDD proposals as reference to improve the quality of their generated applications.

As future work, we plan to complete the definition of a list of defect types that may be introduced in object-oriented conceptual models, and the evaluation in use (by means of empirical studies) of the application of the OOmCFP measurement procedure for the detection of these defects. This also implies the reengineering of the tool that automates the OOmCFP procedure in order to automate the detection of defects.

Acknowledgments. This work has been developed with the support of MEC under the project SESAMO TIN2007-62894.

References

1. Abrahao, S., Insfrán, E.: Early Usability Evaluation in Model Driven Architecture Environments. In: 6th Conference on Quality Software (QSIC), pp. 287–294 (2006)
2. Abran, A., Desharnais, J., Lesterhuis, A., Londeix, B., Meli, R., Morris, P., Oligny, S., O'Neil, M., Rollo, T., Rule, G., Santillo, L., Symons, C., Toivonen, H.: The COSMIC Functional Size Measurement Method, version 3.0 (2007)
3. Albrecht, A.: Measuring Application Development Productivity. In: IBM Applications Development Symposium, pp. 83–92 (1979)
4. Condori-Fernández, N.A., Abrah, S., Pastor, O.: Towards a Functional Size Measure for Object-Oriented Systems from Requirements Specifications. In: 4th IEEE International Conference on Quality Software (QSIC), pp. 94-101 (2004)
5. Conradi, R., Mohagheghi, P., Arif, T., Hegde, L.C., Bunde, G.A., Pedersen, A.: Object-Oriented Reading Techniques for Inspection of UML Models – An Industrial Experiment. In: Cardelli, L. (ed.) ECOOP 2003. LNCS, vol. 2743, pp. 483–501. Springer, Heidelberg (2003)
6. Dedene, G., Snoeck, M.: M.E.R.O.DE.: A Model-driven Entity-Relationship Object-oriented Development Method. ACM SIGSOFT Software Engineering Notes 19(3), 51–61 (1994)
7. Diab, H., Frappier, M., St-Denis, R.: Formalizing COSMIC-FFP Using ROOM. In: ACS/IEEE Int. Conf. on Computer Systems and Applications, AICCSA (2001)
8. Fenton, N.E., Neil, M.: A Critique of Software Defect Prediction Models. IEEE Transactions on Software Engineering 25(5), 675–689 (1999)
9. IEEE: IEEE Std 1044-1993 Standard Classification for Software Anomalies (1993)
10. ISO: ISO Standard 9000-2000: Quality Management Systems: Fundamentals and Vocabulary (2000)
11. ISO: ISO/IEC 14143-1 – Information Technology – Software Measurement – Functional Size Measurement – Part 1: Definition of Concepts (1998)
12. ISO: ISO/IEC 14143-2 – Information Technology – Software Measurement – Functional Size Measurement – Part 2: Conformity Evaluation of Software Size Measurement Methods to ISO/IEC 14143-1:1998 (2002)
13. ISO/IEC: ISO/IEC 9126-1, Software Eng. – Product Quality – Part 1: Quality model (2001)
14. ISO/IEC: ISO/IEC 9126-2, Soft. Eng. – Product Quality – Part 2: External metrics (2003)
15. ISO/IEC: ISO/IEC 9126-3, Soft. Eng. – Product Quality – Part 3: Internal metrics (2003)
16. ISO/IEC: ISO/IEC 9126-4, Soft. Eng. – Prod. Qual. – Part 4: Quality-in-Use metrics (2004)
17. ISO/IEC: ISO/IEC 19761, Software Engineering – COSMIC-FFP – A Functional Size Measurement Method (2003)

18. ISO/IEC: ISO/IEC 20926, Software Engineering – IFPUG 4.1 Unadjusted Functional Size Measurement Method – Counting Practices Manual (2003)
19. ISO/IEC: ISO/IEC 20968, Software Engineering – Mk II Function Point Analysis – Counting Practices Manual (2002)
20. ISO/IEC: ISO/IEC 24570, Software Engineering – NESMA Functional Size Measurement Method version 2.1 – Definitions and Counting Guidelines for the application of Function Point Analysis (2005)
21. Marín, B., Condori-Fernández, N., Pastor, O.: Calidad en Modelos Conceptuales: Un Análisis Multidimensional de Modelos Cuantitativos basados en la ISO 9126. In: Revista de Procesos y Métricas de las Tecnologías de la Información. AEMES, vol. 4, pp. 153–167 (2007)
22. Marín, B., Condori-Fernández, N., Pastor, O.: Design of a Functional Size Measurement Procedure for a Model-Driven Software Development Method. In: 3rd Workshop on Quality in Modeling (QiM) of MODELS, pp. 1–15 (2008)
23. Marín, B., Condori-Fernández, N., Pastor, O., Abran, A.: Measuring the Functional Size of Conceptual Models in an MDA Environment. In: Forum at the CAiSE 2008 Conference, pp. 33-36 (2008)
24. Marín, B., Giachetti, G., Pastor, O.: Automating the Measurement of Functional Size of Conceptual Models in an MDA Environment. In: Jedlitschka, A., Salo, O. (eds.) PROFES 2008. LNCS, vol. 5089, pp. 215–229. Springer, Heidelberg (2008)
25. Marín, B., Giachetti, G., Pastor, O.: Measurement of Functional Size in Conceptual Models: A Survey of Measurement Procedures Based on COSMIC. In: Dumke, R.R., Braungarten, R., Büren, G., Abran, A., Cuadrado-Gallego, J.J. (eds.) IWSM 2008. LNCS, vol. 5338, pp. 170–183. Springer, Heidelberg (2008)
26. Meli, R., Abran, A., Ho Vinh, T., Oligny, S.: On the Applicability of COSMIC-FFP for Measuring Software Throughout its Life Cycle. In: 11th European Software Control and Metrics Conference (2000)
27. Meyer, B.: Object Oriented Software Construction (2000)
28. Molina, P.: Especificación de interfaz de usuario: De los requisitos a la generación automática. Universidad Politécnica de Valencia, Valencia, España (2003)
29. Moody, D.L.: Theoretical and practical issues in evaluating the quality of conceptual models: current state and future directions. Data & Knowledge Engineering 55(3), 243–276 (2005)
30. Panach, I., Condori-Fernández, N., Valverde, F., Aquino, N., Pastor, O.: Towards an Early Usability Evaluation for Web Applications. In: Cuadrado-Gallego, J.J., Braungarten, R., Dumke, R.R., Abran, A. (eds.) IWSM-Mensura 2007. LNCS, vol. 4895, pp. 32–45. Springer, Heidelberg (2008)
31. Pastor, O., Gómez, J., Insfrán, E., Pelechano, V.: The OO-Method Approach for Information Systems Modelling: From Object-Oriented Conceptual Modeling to Automated Programming. Information Systems 26(7), 507–534 (2001)
32. Pastor, O., Molina, J.C.: Model-Driven Architecture in Practice: A Software Production Environment Based on Conceptual Modeling. Springer, New York (2007)
33. Poels, G.: A Functional Size Measurement Method for Event-Based Object-oriented Enterprise Models. In: Int. Conf. on Enterprise Inf. Systems (ICEIS), pp. 667–675 (2002)
34. Selic, B.: The Pragmatics of Model-Driven Development. IEEE Software 20(5), 19–25 (2003)
35. Selic, B., Gullekson, G., Ward, P.T.: Real-time Object Oriented Modelling. Wiley, Chichester (1994)
36. Trudel, S., Abran, A.: Improving Quality of Functional Requirements by Measuring Their Functional Size. In: Dumke, R.R., Braungarten, R., Büren, G., Abran, A., Cuadrado-Gallego, J.J. (eds.) IWSM 2008. LNCS, vol. 5338, pp. 287–301. Springer, Heidelberg (2008)

Sustainable Service Innovation Model: A Standardized IT Service Management Process Assessment Framework

Béatrix Barafort and Anne Rousseau

Centre de Recherche Public Henri Tudor
29, avenue John F. Kennedy
L-1855 Luxembourg
{beatrix.barafort,anne.rousseau}@tudor.lu

Abstract. This paper presents the Sustainable Service Innovation Framework that is used in the Public Research Centre Henri Tudor in Luxembourg as a generic framework supporting innovation, and promoting multi disciplinary activities It is demonstrated with the Tudor's IT Service Management Process Assessment (TIPA)'s case: the Tudor's IT Service Management Process Assessment, with the value, design, promotion, management and capitalization of TIPA's services.

Keywords: Process assessment, service innovation, IT service management, process models, standardization, sustainable service innovation process.

1 Introduction

As confirmed by leading institutions, services play a key role in economies. Representing more than 70 percent of gross value added in the European countries in 2006 [1], services also account for almost all employment growth in the OECD (Organization for Economic Cooperation and Development) countries and are the major contributor to productivity growth [2]. Recent figures for Luxembourg indicate that the service sector accounts for above 85% percent of total value added in 2006, granting Luxembourg with the first place in the European landscape. Within the service sector, the financial sector, with more than 150 banks populating the country, is a major component of Gross Domestic Product (GDP) and GDP growth and is an extensive user and provider of so-called knowledge intensive services. With increased competition, accelerated changes in markets needs and technology evolution, organizations have to continuously generate new services and to succeed in their commercialization [3][4][5]. This innovative capability is also considered as a vector of competitiveness.

In this service context of Luxembourg, and in the multi-disciplinary approach featuring Services Science, the Public Research Centre Henri Tudor (CRPHT) has developed a Sustainable Service Innovation Process (S2IP), providing a framework for services managed in a living lab, and then all facilities for several interacting disciplines. This paper firstly presents this service innovation design model called S2IP

R.V. O'Connor et al. (Eds.): EuroSPI 2009, CCIS 42, pp. 69–80, 2009.

and secondly illustrates it by the case of a specific Assessment and Improvement integrated Approach developed by CRPHT. A particular attention is paid on standardization aspects in Luxembourg and at an international level.

In fact, in 2003, a research project (AIDA, standing for Assessment and Improvement integrated Approach) was defined in order to develop an IT Service Management (ITSM) framework for assessing ITSM processes. The innovative ideas of the project were born from many issues in companies where the need for improving ITSM processes appeared but there was a lack of an objective and repeatable approach for assessing processes and a lack of a very structured improvement path. Moreover, similar approaches combining the improvement of software development processes and ITSM ones were missing. In CRPHT, the ISO/IEC 15504 standard has been studied and used since the mid-nineties for assessing software processes (and using the assessment results for improvement programmes). From the year 2003, the ISO/IEC 15504 [6] has been revised as a generic process assessment standard [7]. It was then possible to assess any kind of process, in any company whatever the activity sector. At the same time the IT Infrastructure Library (ITIL®) de facto standard was developing quickly and rising more and more interest in the Grand Duchy of Luxembourg. Then the combined use of both standards became a research objective. The AIDA research project aimed at developing a common approach for IT process assessment and improvement [8][9][10]. From now on the AIDA research framework has been renamed as TIPA: Tudor's IT service management Process Assessment. We will now describe our service innovation design process before to illustrate it by this specific innovation.

2   A Service Innovation Management Model

Based on its practices (mainly action researches, further developed in [11]) the Centre for IT Innovation (CITI) department of CRPHT has developed and is now using a global sustainable service innovation process to support the management of innovation processes: the "Sustainable Service Innovation Process" (S2IP). It is based on a participatory and collaborative innovation approach in order to sustain deep involvement of the network's actors in the development of innovation services. Those services are dedicated to businesses (i.e. process-oriented such as e.g. security management services), to IT-oriented services (such as e.g. tourist information geo-localized mobile access services) and to Human Resources IT-related skills (such as e.g. consultancy services in SME). The overall structure of S2IP is depicted on the figure 1.

Although the figure may suggest that the S2IP is lifecycle oriented, the reality is that each box corresponds to a process by itself that has to be performed and may be pursued in parallel with other processes in a non strict sequence. In accordance with Van de Ven & al (1999) [12], we apprehend innovation in a process perspective as a non-linear dynamic system, which implies several sense-making activities. Our research on the definition of actors, activities, skills and competences mobilized in the S2IP is directly contributing to the body of knowledge developed in the new research domain of Service Science [13].

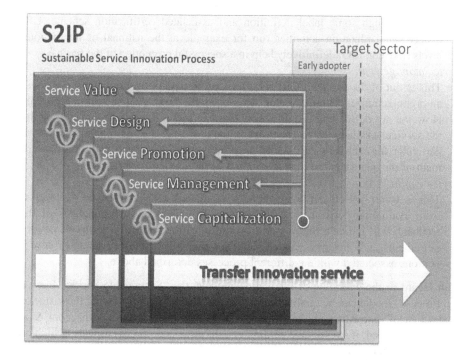

Fig. 1. Sustainable Service Innovation Process

Service value:

- This process covers the activities associated with the identification of an opportunity for a new service innovation. They cover a study of the technological feasibility of the service (which can require the building of a prototype) as well as a preliminary identification of the business model associated with the value (both expressed in terms of tangible financial elements and of intangible assets).

Service design:

- This process is associated with the definition of the service not only in terms of its business functional objectives but also in terms of all its required qualities. These activities required to elicit the strategies of the different early-adopters stakeholders involved in the final acceptance of the service as well as to understand the constraints associated with the environment (like specific regulations associated with the domain). From this initial elicitation, requirements have to be formally expressed in terms of properties of the services that can be organized in terms of a service contract (or a service level agreement).

Service promotion:

- Once early adopters have validated the service contract, we have seen that it is important to promote the service to other potentially interested parties. This can be done within an organization through some marketing regarding the socio-economical sustainability of the service. In a network of organizations or for a sector, this promotion can also include initiatives regarding the branding of the new service through some label definition and associated certification scheme. Ultimately standardization activities run for example at the national or international levels (like e.g. ISO) definitively help in a successful promotion of the service.

Service management:

- This is out of the scope of CRPHT's mission to deploy by itself the service with an organization or within a sector. This is where the market should play its role. However we define and provide tools that can be used by those that will deploy the service for checking and measuring the correctness of its implementation. In particular for each new service we propose metrics associated with the measurement of the quality of the implementation of the services contract.

Service capitalization:

- This is where we collect the feedbacks associated with the measures as well as from evaluation performed with the services end-users. The analysis of this feedback will indicate the possible evolution of the service in terms of new requirements, new business model, etc. Thus this will be the beginning of new iterations associated with the different processes described above.

With regard to the overview of innovation models, the "Sustainable Service Innovation Process "model can be qualified as a 5th generation model following the historical perspective of innovation models proposed by Rothwell [14] (see Bernacconi & al. 2008 [15]). Indeed, it stresses the continuous, iterative and process aspects, which are typical of this generation.

In addition, it highlights the influence of the intensive networking, including the cross-functional collaboration within the organization and further emphasizes the downstream alliances with key beneficiaries and end-users of the generated innovations. In turn, these strong ties with users foster the sustainability of the innovation and through the capitalization phase, it is the innovation process itself that may be considered as sustainable, provided that all the capitalization mechanisms are actually put in place. Finally, this model captures the knowledge-intensiveness characteristic, which is also a common point with the 5th generation models.

We will now describe a S2IP instance regarding the definition of a service innovation related to an Assessment and Improvement integrated Approach. This illustration will highlight the strengths and weaknesses of the followed approach and can thus be helpful to any service innovation definition process.

The applied methodology is based on participant observation in the context of an action research project, coupled with an "external" view to increase the objectivity of the interpretation.

3 TIPA's S2IP Instance

After having introduced the S2IP framework this section is presenting its in the TIPA's context. We can consider here a first iteration where the S2IP framework has been deployed.

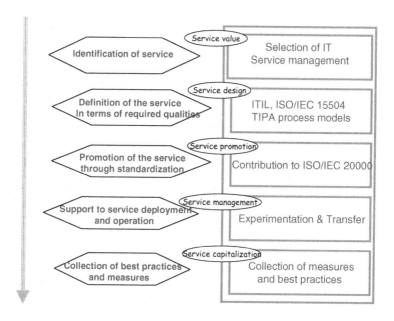

Fig. 2. TIPA's S2IP instance

3.1 Service Value of the TIPAs Framework

In the S2IP framework, the identification of the service value for the potential stakeholders consists in activities such as the development of a business model related to the service innovation. The added value service built around our assessment methodology under the name TIPA (standing for Tudor's IT Service Management Process Assessment), was designed as a solution to reduce the cost for assessing ITSM processes and for companies aiming at improving them. This solution was mainly based on a methodological framework (process models; assessment methodology and associated tools such as questionnaires, templates and case study examples; training courses for assessors) enabling the assessment of ITSM processes. The ITIL de facto standard was selected as the input for deriving process models [16] [17], according to the ISO/IEC 15504 process assessment requirements [6].

At that time, there was no business plan developed for the future use of the TIPA's framework in a commercial perspective, even if Intellectual Property Rights were studied for CRPHT, and tackled for ITIL trademark and ISO standards use. Globally speaking, the identification of the services to be provided by the TIPA's framework was weak.

3.2 Service Design of the TIPAs Framework

Before the AIDA R&D Project, there were already existing process assessment models such as ISO/IEC 15504-5 and CMM, and more recently CMMI [18]. But there were not many initiatives linking assessment purposes and ITSM. So an ITSM

Process Reference Model (PRM) and its associated Process Assessment Model (PAM) [8][9][10] were developed.

ITSM focuses on delivering and supporting IT services that are appropriate to the organisation's business requirements, whatever its type or size. ITIL® provides a comprehensive, consistent and coherent set of best practices for ITSM processes, promoting a quality approach to achieving business effectiveness and efficiency in the use of information systems. Developed in the late 1980s, ITIL® has become the worldwide de facto standard in Service Management.

OGC, the British Office of Government Commerce, defined ten processes for ITSM in the two well-known ITIL® books "Best Practices for Service Support" and "Best Practices for Service Delivery" [16][17].

The TIPA® model was inspired by ITIL® best practices, with the goal to enable objective ITSM capability assessments. The references used to create the PRM and PAM were the Service Support and Service Delivery books published by OGC. These inputs are considered as implementation best practices, and can be seen as a Process Implementation Model (PIM) to start with. The purpose of the PRM was to define, at a high level of abstraction (i.e. in term of Process purpose and Process outcomes), a set of processes that can be used as the process dimension for a PAM in the IT Service Management area. According to the maturity of the definition of these processes, the process list of the PRM was directly derived from the Service Support and Service Delivery ones. The ten processes from Service Support and Service Delivery were then selected without adding or removing any of them.

Using ITIL® best practices, CRPHT developed a Process Reference Model and a Process Assessment Model, by using Goal-oriented Requirement Engineering techniques [19]. Several steps were followed to derive the models.

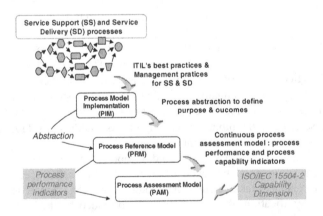

Fig. 3. Deriving the IT Service Management Process models

If we consider the TIPAs framework from the S2IP's perspective, the "Service Design" Process has been tackled in this section on its particular functional features, with a special attention paid on inputs standards. Non-functional ones were neglected. The definition of the TIPA's services in terms of required qualities were just tackling the methodological aspects, without using ITIL® principles themselves for featuring the TIPAS's services, in terms of Service Level Agreements for instance. Nevertheless, there were early adopters of the models through experimentations that contributed to validate the models.

3.3 Service Promotion of the TIPAs Framework

The main component of the TIPA's framework is the set composed of the TIPA's Process Reference Model and Process Assessment Model. These models were build in meeting ISO/IEC 15504 requirements, and were similar as exemplar ones in ISO standards (i.e. the ISO/IEC 12207 PRM [20] and ISO/IEC 15504-5 [21] which is the PAM based on the ISO/IEC 12207 PRM).

The British Standardization Institute drove in the International standardization Organization (ISO) the publication of the ISO/IEC 20000 IT Service Management standard [22][23]. It is aiming at certifying a service provider with a management system for IT Service Management Processes. The ISO/IEC 20000-1 [22] standard, titled "Specification" promotes the adoption of an integrated process approach to effectively deliver managed services to meet the business and customer requirements. On the other hand, ISO/IEC 20000-2 [23], named "Code of practice" provides guidance and recommendations.

From 2005 up to now, Luxembourg played a critical part in ISO international meetings by letting people know how advanced Luxembourg's works were. The International standardization community recognized the benefits of using complementary approaches between audits and Process Assessment [24][25]. TIPAS's works were presented in international meetings, but because ITIL trademark use was not resolved between in 2006, TIPA's PRM and PAM were not ceased to ISO working groups, but it was definitely a fundamental promotion of the TIPA's services.

3.4 Service Management of the TIPAs Framework

As mentioned in the generic description of the S2IP framework, it is out of the scope of the CRPHT's mission to deploy a service. But CRPHT has the duty to transfer R&D results to the market, and then services developed in research projects. So CRPHT can assist companies to deploy services to be transferred of newly transferred services.

In the case of TIPA, there were early adopters that experimented the process models and methods for assessing IT Service Management processes. The way the TIPA services were transferred can be featured in two processes of the S2IP framework: service design (first use of TIPA's framework in a company [26][27]) and service management (TIPA's deployed service in a company, after its transfer). Actually CPRHT engineers were leading first experimentations with a trained TIPA's assessor, without experience. For a second experimentation, these TIPA's assessor was coached by CRPHT experienced assessors but was gaining autonomy. Gradually, TIPA's team also developed some methodological support tools for easing the assessment running, such as questionnaires and templates for reporting assessment results. This contributes to the professionalization of TIPA's services, for a better adoption by the market.

3.5 Service Capitalization of the TIPAs Framework

Some feedbacks were collected from the early adopters of the TIPA's framework, from people but also from our team in order to improve the service design on the functional aspects.

In order to structure the methodology leading to the construction of a PRM-PAM and to organize components, a process model has been drafted, aiming at engineering process models [19]. The purpose of this model is to design and manage an ISO/IEC 15504 compliant process model (validation and traceability) fulfilling the stakeholders' requirements and needs, and to provide a knowledge base supporting uses of the model. This draft Model provides the framework for the overall methodology. By using a rigorous and systematic approach for developing PRMs and PAMs, it provides a very structured and trusted basis for process improvement. Then it can be valuable inputs for combining process modeling and assessment with the help of a support tool, within an improvement approach contextualized to an organization.

In the context of TIPA, the use of this systematic approach for developing process models based on ITIL V2 in a first time, and later on ISO/IEC 20000-1 was very useful and helped to gain structured feedback on the quality of the models. This theoretical feedback is completed by companies using the TIPA's framework, and by CRP Henri Tudor engineers participating in ISO standardization works.

4 Luxembourg Standardization Part

The Luxembourg Institute for Standardization, Accreditation, Security and quality of products and services [28] (ILNAS - Institut Luxembourgeois de la Normalisation, de l'Accréditation, de la Sécurité et qualité des produits et services) is under the administrative supervision of the Minister of economy. The law from May 20th, 2008 was the basis for the creation of ILNAS and its activities started in June 2008.

For complementarity reasons, efficiency, and transparency and in the context of administrative simplification, ILNAS gathers several administrative and technical missions. ILNAS is a network of competences serving competitiveness and consumer protection.

Before it was encompassed within ILNAS, the Luxembourg National Body did not play a very active part in Luxembourg's standardization efforts. It is now evolving with the government strong will to develop digital trust, and determine clear Luxembourg economic advantages in following up some IT standards. Then, in February 2009, Luxembourg became a Permanent member of the Joint Technical Committee 1 covering IT standards.

Moreover, with the support of the Luxembourg government, ILNAS and CPRHT have joined their forces in a collaborative research project in order to connect innovation, research and standardization, with a twofold focus: IT standardization and financial sector potential national standard. So this project is aiming at:

– investigating and developing digital trust domains where standards are innovation and competitive vectors at the national level;
– developing a normative knowledge economy;
– supporting and developing (IT) standardization activities in Luxembourg;

- investigating the opportunity of creating national standards for the financial sector;
- federating all the stakeholders of the financial sector in order to develop a standardization strategy.

This project contributes in the support of standardization in Luxembourg, more particularly in IT, and the development of a two-way communication and exchanges between market and National Body (representing economic interests of Luxembourg). As previously mentioned, special attention is paid by ILNAS on national standard opportunities.

In a more global perspective, a partnership programme is planned between CRP Henri Tudor and ILNAS. It will gather several standardization-oriented collaborative projects, targeting several sectors such as construction, finance, SMEs...

5 Discussion

Considering the TIPA's approach, the S2IP framework has been derived with two iterations. The second one is currently active, and weaknesses that were issued during the first one are on the track to be corrected. As an innovation framework, the 5 identified processes (service value, service design, service promotion, service management and service capitalization) were not deployed with the same maturity, depending on several factors such as the resources and priorities in the Centre.

The Service value of the TIPA's framework had not been identified and prospected right from the beginning of the TIPA's initiative. Some work has still to be performed, in order to finalize a business plan for the exploitation of the TIPA's services, and to determine the exact scope of the proposed services. Some TIPA's focus groups were organized a few months ago, in order to collect market needs, and align TIPA's services to them. Even if this process of the S2IP framework is performed quite late in the context of the TIPA's framework, it still demonstrates the value of the TIPA services, their innovation role and benefits for the market [29]. A certification scheme is also targeted.

The *Service Design* was partially performed, because most of the considered aspects were "only" functional, with methodological and standardization aspects. The contracts aspects of the TIPA's framework have to be more investigated and developed further. TIPA's service level agreements could be derived. But according to the high interest of IT departments in companies on service providers, new methodological developments are considered (ITIL V3 based PRM and PAM development).

About the *Service Promotion*, if we consider globally the S2IP framework, standardization activities and roles played highly promoted TIPA's services at national as well as international level. Thus there is an acknowledgement of CRP Henri Tudor expertise in the standardization domain for the IT Service Management and Process Assessment fields, and also for the corresponding innovation and scientific communities. Having said this, there is a gap still to cover, in order to develop the TIPA's service promotion on the market. Then some new activities are already planned and currently implemented in order to develop a branding, a valorization strategy, some professional partnership for certifications and selling of a TIPA's book describing the TIPA's methodology and tools.

The *Service Management* for TIPA's has to be enhanced with an important deployment in terms of number of uses of TIPA's, and a spreading worldwide. There are also some more R&D works to perform in order to develop measures of the quality of TIPA's services. As for the TIPA's assessment, a very structured approach could enable benchmarking and provide statistics on the TIPA's deployment and quality of service.

About *Service Capitalization*, some more analysis is necessary for deriving real trends from all TIPA's experimentations. An impact analysis is on its way, in order to demonstrate quantitatively as well as qualitatively the added value and return on investment of the TIPA's approach.

6 Conclusion

This paper presents the Sustainable Service Innovation Process that is used in CRP Henri Tudor as a generic framework supporting innovation, and promoting multi disciplinary activities throughout our research teams. Moreover, the S2IP's framework can be instantiated to any service line resulting from our research works. This derivation has been illustrated with the TIPA's framework aiming at proposing IT Service Management Process Assessment services. There are several instances of the S2IP for the TIPA's case. We saw that some improvements have to be made for the TIPA's framework regarding S2IP, which is then used as a tool to see gaps in the innovation process. In this context of research-action, CRP Henri Tudor gains maturity in the Service Science with a multi-disciplinary approach, and targets to use the S2IP framework as a process innovation management governance model. Other services frameworks have been studied on the same way as the TIPA's one (i.e. in the construction sector, in the financial one [30] and for SMEs). It demonstrates how the model works, with strengths and weaknesses. This gives us perspectives for improving innovation approaches, capitalizing and refining the model.

References

[1] Website: http://epp.eurostat.ec.europa.eu/
[2] OCDE. Intellectual Assets and Value Creation – Implications for Corporate Reporting (2006)
[3] de Brentani, U.: New industrial service development: Scenarios for success and failure. Journal of Business Research 32(2), 93–103 (1995)
[4] Cooper, R.G., Easingwood, C.J., Edgett, S., Kleinschmidt, E.J., Storey, C.: What distinguishes the top performing new products in financial services? Journal of Product Innovation Management 11(4), 281–299 (1994)
[5] Voss, C.A., Johnston, R., Silvestro, R., Fitzgerald, L., Brignall, T.J.: Measurement of innovation and design performance in services. Design Management Journal 3, 40–46 (Winter 1992)
[6] ISO, ISO/IEC 15504-2: Information technology - Process assessment - Part 2: Performing an assessment (2003)

[7] Rout, T.P., El Emam, K., Fusani, M., Goldenson, D., Jung, H.-W.: SPICE in retrospect: Developing a standard for process assessment. Journal of Systems and Software 80(9), 1483–1493 (2007)

[8] Barafort, B., Di Renzo, B., Merlan, O.: Benefits resulting from the combined use of ISO/IEC 15504 with the Information Technology Infrastructure Library (ITIL). In: Oivo, M., Komi-Sirviö, S. (eds.) PROFES 2002. LNCS, vol. 2559, pp. 314–325. Springer, Heidelberg (2002)

[9] Barafort, B., Di Renzo, B.: Assessment and improvement integrated approach: combined use of the ISO/IEC 15504 (SPICE) and the Information Technology Infrastructure Library (ITIL). In: Proceedings of the National Conference SPIRAL 2004, Luxembourg (2004)

[10] Barafort, B., Di Renzo, B., Lejeune, V., Simon, J.-M.: ITIL Based Service Management measurement and ISO/IEC 15504 process assessment: a win – win opportunity. In: Proceedings of the 5th International SPICE Conference on Process Assessment and Improvement, Klagenfurt, Austria (2005)

[11] Barlatier, P.-J., Dumont, V., Johannsen, L., Rousseau, A.: The co-conception process of innovation network management tools:Evidence from the TINIS experience. In: Proceedings of the 24th EGOS Colloquium (2008)

[12] Van de Ven, A.H., Polley, D.E., Garud, R., Venkataraman, S.: The Innovation Journey. Oxford University Press, Oxford (1999)

[13] Chesbrough, H., Spohrer, J.: A research manifesto for service science. Communications of the ACM 49(7), 35–40 (2006)

[14] Rothwell, R.: Industrial innovation: success, strategy, trends. In: Dogson, M., Rothwell, R. (eds.) The Handbook of Industrial Innovation. Edward Elgar, United Kingdom (1994)

[15] Bernacconi, J.C., Mention, A.L., Rousseau, A.: Knowledge-based innovation in a service economy: An innovation management process governance model in a RTO. In: 1st Symposium ISPIM, Singapore (2008)

[16] IT Infrastructure Library – Service Delivery, The Stationery Office Edition (2001) ISBN 011 3308930

[17] IT Infrastructure Library – Service Support, The Stationery Office Edition (2000) ISBN 011 3308671

[18] CMMI product team "CMMI(for development, Version 1.2: Improving processes for better products", Carnegie Mellon, Software Engineering Institute (August 2006)

[19] Rifaut, A.: Goal-Driven Requirements Engineering for supporting the ISO 15504 Assessment Process. In: Richardson, I., Abrahamsson, P., Messnarz, R. (eds.) EuroSPI 2005. LNCS, vol. 3792, pp. 151–162. Springer, Heidelberg (2005)

[20] ISO, ISO/IEC 12207: Information technology - Software Life Cycle Processes (2008)

[21] ISO, ISO/IEC 15504-5: Information technology - Software Process Assessment - Part 5: An exemplar process assessment model (2006)

[22] ISO, ISO/IEC 20000-1: Information technology – Service management – Part 1: Specification (2005)

[23] ISO, ISO/IEC 20000-2: Information technology – Service management – Part 2: Code of practice (2005)

[24] ISO, ISO/IEC JTC1/SC7 3797, NWI Proposal - Information Technology - Service Management Process Reference Model (2007)

[25] ISO, ISO/IEC JTC1/SC7 3798, NWI Proposal - Information Technology - Process assessment - Part 8: An exemplar process assessment model for IT service management

[26] Hilbert, R., Renault, A.: Assessing IT Service Management Processes with AIDA – Experience Feedback. In: Proceedings of the 14th European Conference for Software Process Improvement EuroSPI, Potsdam, Germany (2007)

[27] Barafort, B., Jezek, D., Mäkinen, T., Stolfa, S., Varkoi, T., Vondrak, I.: Modeling and Assessment in IT Service Process Improvement. In: Proceedings of the 15th European Conference for Software Process Improvement EuroSPI, Dublin, Ireland (2008)

[28] Website: http://www.ilnas.public.lu/

[29] Marc, S.-J., Anne-Laure, M.: How to evaluate benefits of Tudor's ITSM Process Assessment. In: Proceedings of the SPICE 2009 Conference, Turku, Finland (2009)

[30] Mention, A.-L., Barafort, B.: An Open Innovation Framework for Services Process Improvement and Capability Determination in the Banking and Financial Sector Based on ISO/IEC 15504. In: Proceedings of the International Conference SPICE 2008, Nuremberg, Germany (2008)

How Can Agile Practices Minimize Global Software Development Co-ordination Risks?

Emam Hossain[1], Muhammad Ali Babar[2], and June Verner[3]

[1] UNSW- NICTA, Australian Technology Park
Sydney, Australia
Emam.Hossain@nicta.com.au
[2] Lero, University of Limerick
Castletroy, Limerick, Ireland
malibaba@lero.ie
[3] UNSW, Sydney, Australia
June.Verner@gmail.com

Abstract. The distribution of project stakeholders in Global Software Development (GSD) projects provides significant risks related to project communication, coordination and control processes. There is growing interest in applying agile practices in GSD projects in order to leverage the advantages of both approaches. In some cases, GSD project managers use agile practices to reduce project distribution challenges. We use an existing coordination framework to identify GSD coordination problems due to temporal, geographical and socio-cultural distances. An industry-based case study is used to describe, explore and explain the use of agile practices to reduce development coordination challenges.

Keywords: Agile, Global Software Development, Coordinating Mechanisms.

1 Introduction

Rapid advances in computer networks, telecommunications and internet technologies have provided an infrastructure that supports Global Software Development (GSD) as a new software development paradigm. GSD has gained significant popularity; it is promoted as a means of reducing time to market, increasing productivity, improving quality and gaining cost effectiveness and efficiency [1]. Despite the expected benefits of GSD, there are a number of challenges in practice [2]. In particular GSD is normally characterized by stakeholders with different national and organizational cultures, located in separate geographic locations and time zones, using information and communication technologies to collaborate. Such conditions usually result in major risks in relation to team communication, coordination, control, infrastructure incompatibility, conflicting expectations, and difficulty in building trust [3]. Thus, a GSD project manager needs a number of risk mitigation strategies to assist in managing such a project.

Agile Software Development (ASD) has gained significant popularity because it promises to handle requirements changes throughout the development life cycle, promotes extensive collaboration between customers and developers, and supports

R.V. O'Connor et al. (Eds.): EuroSPI 2009, CCIS 42, pp. 81–92, 2009.

early and frequent delivery of a product [4]. A major reason for the success of agile methods is the physical collocation of development team members [4]. Some project managers are however, using agile practices to minimize GSD challenges or risks [5, 9-11], even though researchers note that agile practices are difficult to scale up to support distributed arrangements [6]. Although project stakeholder distribution creates challenges to using agile practices, we found some instances of success in the literature when agile practices were used with distributed teams [7].

However, current research provides limited evidence of the effective use of agile practices in minimizing risks of GSD processes. To address this research gap, our research focuses on GSD coordination processes. To understand GSD coordination difficulties, we use an existing widely known coordination framework called the Mintzberg Work Coordination Framework [14]. In addition we conduct an industry-based GSD case study in order to investigate the impact of using agile practices to reduce coordination risks. The results of this case study are expected to contribute to the body of knowledge regarding the usefulness of agile practices in minimizing coordination difficulties in GSD projects.

We begin by providing the background to our research and our motivation. Section 3 briefly discusses coordination processes in software development. This section also presents the Mintzberg framework [14] and provides a summary of GSD risks that may impact on project coordination processes. We describe our research methodology in section 4. In section 5 we present results from an industry case study. Section 6 discusses the limitations of the case study. We conclude with section 7, which discusses future research.

2 Background and Motivation

In this section, we briefly discuss agile approaches in GSD and summarize the effectiveness of agile practices in reducing GSD risks based on existing research.

2.1 Agile Approaches in GSD

Though both ASD and GSD appear to share several objectives such as reduced delivery time and cost, and increased quality, there are certain differences that are expected to pose serious problems in any effort to introduce agile practices in distributed teams. For example, agile methods emphasize frequent interaction and communication within collocated teams and pay less attention to upfront detailed design and heavy documentation [4]. Hence the agile community advocates the importance of close proximity and relationships between development team members, continuously turning-out working software, customer-developer collaboration, and quick response to requirements changes [1]. Such agile method requirements are difficult to satisfy in a geographically distributed project. Our Systematic Literature Review (SLR), which was concerned with the use of Scrum in GSD projects, identified a number of risks when using agile practices [29]. Despite the risks, there is a growing interest in assessing the viability of using agile practices for GSD projects [7]. Our SLR also identified that GSD project managers are using several processes to reduce risk factors when using Scrum in GSD [29]. The

SLR also identified that the use of agile practices in GSD provides a number of benefits including increased project communication, improved project management, improved productivity, increased trust, increased team motivation, increased project visibility, increased team morale, improved knowledge sharing, and improved customer focus etc [29].

2.2 Research Context

Communication, coordination, and collaboration processes are at the heart of much software development [10]. Temporal, geographical and socio-cultural distances can however, make GSD communication, coordination and control processes difficult [15] and research is needed to provide strategies to deal with these challenges [3]. Some project managers have attempted to use agile practices to reduce GSD risks that impact on project communication, coordination and collaboration processes [23]. Xiaohu [5] mentions that the use of agile practices can minimize GSD communication delays and increase communication quality. Holmstrom et al [3] claim that using agile practices enhances GSD project communication and, as a consequence, reduces geographical, temporal and socio-cultural distances. Mak and Krutchen [10] claim that agile practices improve the efficiency and quality of GSD task coordination by encouraging frequent, lightweight informal communication in addition to formal communication. Holmstrom et al [3] note that the main challenge of a GSD project is to maintain good communication, and that, the careful incorporation of some agile practices can enhance project communication and reduce GSD risks that impact communication, coordination and control processes. Despite some discussion of the benefits of using agile methods in GSD, there is no clear description or understanding of how the use of agile practices can reduce GSD risks and improve project communication, coordination or collaboration processes. To address this research challenge, the broad objective of our research is to explore how the effective use of agile practices can reduce some GSD challenges and improve project coordination processes.

3   Coordination

Coordination is considered to be a key organizational activity in any software development. A traditional co-located software development team usually builds up the coordination of their different tasks in a number of ways. A highly idealized traditional co-located development team has a shared view of work processes and coordination is achieved either because of shared defined processes, or by acquiring a common set of habits and vocabulary over time [12]. Herbsleb [12] suggests that through frequent formal and informal interactions, co-located team members have a clear idea of who has what sort of expertise, and how responsibilities are allocated throughout the development team. The development team uses informal communication along with formal instructions throughout the development process. But geographical, temporal and socio-cultural distances make GSD communication, coordination and control process difficult and they require more development time than their co-located development counterpart [13, 15]. Herbsleb et al [13] comment that a distributed environment changes the communication context away from an ideal face-to-face setting to a more complex technology-mediated environment. Therefore, a fundamental GSD problem is that many of the mechanisms that function to coordinate work in a co-located setting are absent or disrupted [12].

3.1   Coordination Framework

In this section we discuss a work coordination framework considered to be stable and flexible enough to describe coordination issues; this is the widely known Mintzberg work coordination model. Although Mintzberg's work coordination framework may not be entirely suitable for investigating the use of agile methods in GSD, we use this framework for a better understanding of the impact of GSD risks in project coordination process.   Mintzberg [14] argues that there are three basic coordinating mechanisms that describe the fundamental ways in which organizations coordinate their work. These are:

Mutual adjustment: Mutual adjustment ensures that a software development project can achieve a suitable degree of coordination by the simple process of informal communication among project stakeholders. For example, work can be coordinated when two software developers informally discuss a particular task.

Direct supervision: With direct supervision, coordination can be achieved through one person issuing orders and instructions to several other people whose work is interrelated. For example, when a team leader tells other team members what is to be done, one step at a time.

Standardization: Standardization can be categorized as coordination by programme, where coordination is effected through instructions and plans generated beforehand [26]. Mintzberg [14] notes that there are four types of standardization: 1) work processes, 2) output, 3) skills (as well as knowledge) and 4) norms. Work process standards usually specify how development team members carry out their interrelated tasks. Standardization of output usually specifies the expected results for various development tasks. Standardization of skills ensures that the team has a set of skills that are enough to carry out the development tasks. Standardization of norms, within a software development project, ensures that everyone functions according to the same set of organizational beliefs.

3.2   GSD Challenges and Coordinating Mechanisms

To investigate the impact of GSD challenges on different coordinating mechanisms, we review, from the literature, a number of GSD projects. In Table 1 we summarize the key risks due to the temporal, geographical and socio-cultural distances while using the three different coordinating mechanisms, standardization, direct supervision and mutual adjustment. In this table, for simplicity, we note the problem encountered, even though project context, for example, size, number of distributed teams, complexity, criticality, and project domain etc., can further exacerbate the problem. In a later section, we discuss how the use of agile practices can reduce some of the major identified difficulties.

Table 1. Key Risks for using coordinating mechanisms in GSD

	Standardization	**Direct Supervision**	**Mutual Adjustment**
Temporal Distance	• Management of project artifacts may be subject to delays [15] • Misunderstanding of different work processes [16] • Lack of standardization of: definitions, common tools, norms, work process and practices [17]	• Reduced synchronous communication [3, 15] • Coordination complexity/breakdown [11,15- 16] • Lack of project visibility [16]	• Reduced overlap times [11,15] • Miscommunication, confusion and delays [2-3,16,19-20] • Lack of shared understanding, reduced trust [16, 18]
Geographic Distance	• Lack of standard artefacts [17] • Reduced trust because of: disparity in work practices, outputs, skills and norms [20] • Conflicts due to a lack of common coding, tools, work process and norms, and development practice standards [18]	• Difficulty in conveying vision and strategy [15] • Management coordination overhead [3,11,18] • Management dependency on ICT/tools [15]	• Reduced informal contact due to diffculties of face to face meeting [15] • Lack of group awareness [3, 17,19] • Communication dependency on ICT tools [15]
Socio-cultural Distance	• Misinterpretations of different project standards [9, 12] • Task conflicts [7] • Lack of shared understanding [9]	• Different expectations regarding leadership practices [11,20] • Problems with management due to differing frames of reference [11] • Problems with project managers in adapting to distributed team norms and work culture [9]	• Misunderstandings, miscommunication, confusion and silence [15] • Challenges in creating mutual understanding [21] • Reduced trust [22,23]

4   Research Methodology

In this section, we report on the findings of an exploratory industry-based case study that used agile practices in a globally distributed project. The case study is considered a robust research method with a range of appropriate data collection approaches when a holistic in-depth investigation of a social phenomenon in its real life context is required [24]. To carry out our case study we carefully followed the guidelines suggested in [27]. In this research, we do not provide formal hypothesis testing or draw any general conclusions as GSD has many forms depending on project contextual factors (for example: size, collaboration modes, number of distributed sites etc.). However, in our case study, we consider the research question, "how can the effective use of agile practices reduce coordination risks in GSD?" Thus the finding of this single case study is expected to provide some useful insights into the effectiveness of agile practices to reduce GSD coordination risks.

Our primary data collection approaches were interviews, detailed inspection and analysis of project documentation, onsite demonstrations of software and informal conversations face-to-face and email-based communication with key project staff and some customers. Instead of interviewing several people for a shorter duration, we decided to do in-depth interviews with one representative from each side (i.e., project manager and an actively involved customer). We carried out semi-structured interviews; each interview lasted about two hours. We provided the interviewees with a brief research outline before the interview session. We asked our respondents about the facts of the matter, as well as gaining their opinions about the events that occurred. We had already inspected the project artefacts, such as documentation, before the interviews. The documents made available to the research team included system specifications, project plans, testing scripts and the completed software. Documentary information was also used to corroborate and augment evidence found from the interviews and discussions that focussed in the use of agile practices to reduce coordination risks. A qualitative content analysis technique was used to extract the agile practices that reduced coordination risks from the interview data. Data analysis was done by the key author who coded both interviews, and developed separate codes for addressing each of the practices that reduce GSD coordination risks. Our data analysis aim was to identify, describe and make sense of how agile practices were used to reduce GSD risks that impact coordination processes. To improve the quality of our interpretation, we reported our initial findings back to both the customer and project manager. Both then provided feedback that identified any omissions and rectified misunderstandings in our analysis.

4.1 Project Description

This section describes the case study project. The organization, individuals and product developed are referred to by fictitious names in order to maintain the anonymity of the organizations concerned. "Alpha" is an Australian-based software development company that develops a range of software products using agile software development methodologies. For some time the company has had developers in Australia and Malaysia. The project we investigated is "Alpha-Global". It is a service-based graphical software engineering tool to be used commercially with external customers and it was developed by a distributed team. The project was relatively stable as regards to requirements changes although there were a several initial changes due to very complex graphical requirements.

4.2 Team Description

The project had a team that was distributed to two countries, Australia and Malaysia. The customer was based in Australia and was actively involved in the development. The project manager was also based in Sydney. The Sydney part of the team consisted of two full time developers and one part time test engineer. The Malaysian operation involved around 25 developers with one local development lead. The number of involved developers in the Malaysian site varied during the course of the project and usually 3-5 developers were involved throughout the development life cycle. The engagement of the Malaysian developers varied. They were mostly involved in back end development work, while the Sydney developers implemented the user interfaces. The Malaysian developers' work was assigned based on skills and availability, as they were also involved in several other projects at the same time. All the project team members had previous distributed project development experience although this project was their first experience of using agile approaches in a distributed setting. To support the agile practices in to globally distributed sites the project manager ensured a number of tools were available, including communication, collaboration, and project management and testing tools. Email, Instant Messaging (IM), video conferencing, phone, VOIP (for example: skype) were commonly used as communication tools. Project team members also used a project wiki as a collaboration tool for project members to post their various queries and comments. The project wiki also served as a key project documentation repository. The project manager also used a tool named "Jira" as an issue tracker, bug tracker and also as a project management tool.

As the project stakeholders were distributed in Australia and Malaysia, the project involved geographical, temporal and socio-cultural distances. There is a two hours time difference (three hours in summer) between Sydney and Malaysia. This ensured a number of overlap hours between distributed sites. Hence we can argue that the project had a low temporal distance. Again, Malaysia and Australia are relatively closely located and there are convenient air links and regular flights between the two countries. But the flight cost is relatively high and flight time is almost eight hours. Thus considering ease and travel time, necessity for visas and permits, we can argue that the project had a moderate geographical distance. To understand the socio-cultural distances involved in the project we used Hofstede's [28] definitions of cultural dimensions for Australia and Malaysia to identify national cultural differences. Hofstede's study provides an index of power distance, individualism, masculinity, and uncertainty avoidance. The index range varies from 1-120. Based on this index we found the power distance and individualism are significantly different in the two countries and there are also some differences in masculinity and uncertainty avoidance. In addition, the project customer and project manager mentioned the differences between the Malaysian and Sydney team members in their organizational-national culture, language, politics, individual motivation, work ethics, religious values etc. Thus considering Hofstede's indexes and customer and project manager views, we can claim that the project involved significant socio-cultural distances.

5 Result

Although the project faced several challenges mainly caused by the project team member's distribution, both customer and company considered the project was successful. One of the main reasons for this was that the project was delivered on time and within budget. The project manager used some agile practices in this globally distributed project. The project manager did not use any agile methodology completely; rather he used some XP development practices and some Scrum practices for project management. In the following sections, we will discuss how the use of these agile practices appears to have helped reduce GSD risks and improved project coordination processes. We discuss our findings, based on Table 1 which identifies key risks that impact on the three coordinating mechanisms standardization, direct supervision and mutual adjustment.

Standardization: The use of the coordinating mechanism "standardization" is seriously affected by project temporal, geographical and socio-cultural distance. GSD project temporal distance reduces overlapping work hours and synchronous communication between distributed teams. Thus, because of temporal distance, project stakeholders may misunderstand distributed team work processes, norms, practices and tools [15-17]. Geographical distance may also impact on the management of standard project artefacts and may reduce trust and commitment. Geographical distance can also create conflict if different teams have different standards for work processes, norms, skills and outputs. Socio-cultural distance may also poses challenges by introducing misunderstandings, misinterpretation of the project standards desired by the project manager, and this may lead to task conflict and lack of shared understanding among distributed project stakeholders [7, 9-12]. Hence from the literature we conclude that maintaining a common standard definition of work process, skills, norms and outputs is difficult in a GSD project due to geographical, temporal and socio-cultural distances. However, our case study reveals that some agile practices helped distributed project stakeholders to maintain a common set of standards throughout the development. These were:

- The **"Sprint planning meeting"** which provided close interaction among distributed project stakeholders that helped to minimize misunderstanding and misinterpretations about project standards. The communication tool, video conferencing, was used in this meeting which lasted for up to two hours.
- **"Retrospective meeting"** scheduled to assess teamwork in the completed sprints, helped to maintain a shared understanding of different project standards among distributed project stakeholders. The customer was actively involved in the retrospective meeting sessions with the project management team including the Malaysian based development lead.
- **"Coding standards"** provided coding rules which were followed at both sites; this also helped to maintain common standards.
- **"Test Driven Development** (TDD)" also helped to maintain a shared standard development view, facilitating a better understanding of what functionality was required from the client perspective.
- **"Refactoring"** which restructures the system by removing duplication, improving communication, simplifying and adding flexibility, provided both teams with a better understanding of project outputs.

Direct Supervision: The use of the coordinating mechanism "direct supervision" is also affected by project temporal, geographical and socio-cultural distance. Temporal distance reduces opportunities for synchronous communication and increases coordination overhead (for example: a project manager cannot provide urgent instructions) [3, 11, 15-16]. Geographical distance may also limit frequency of visits to distributed team sites by the project manager. Thus it may be difficult to convey project vision and strategy to distributed sites [15]. Geographical distance also creates coordination overhead and project managers are heavily reliant on different tools for project coordination [3, 11, 15, 18]. Socio-cultural distances may also add some extra challenges to the direct supervision coordinating mechanism. The differences in work culture may introduce different expectations regarding leadership practices, frames of reference, different perceptions of authority/hierarchy, and norms etc [9, 11, 20]. Our case study reveals that some agile practices can help to minimize GSD risks that impact on the use of the coordinating mechanism "direct supervision". These were:

- The agile practice "**Daily stand up meetings**" with participation by distributed team members through Skype helped to minimize the possibility of coordination breakdown caused by temporal and geographical distance. In these meetings the project team members were informed what had been done thus far, and what needed to be done; any existing problems were also covered in these meetings. The meetings also helped to minimize some socio-cultural issues such as different perceptions of authority/hierarchy, different frames of references etc., and also conveyed vision and strategy to the project stakeholders as well as the development teams.
- "**Sprint review meeting**" attended by the project stakeholders increased project visibility and transparency and helped the project manager with more efficient project supervision.

Mutual Adjustment: Reduced opportunities for synchronous communication due to temporal distance may also impact on the use of the coordinating mechanism "mutual adjustment" in GSD projects. Temporal distance may introduce response delay [15], and as a result, distributed team members may misunderstand and become confused [2-3, 16, 19-20]. Geographical distance may also limit face-to-face meetings; thus distributed project stakeholder communication is dependent on tools, and team members feel a lack of group awareness or "teamness" [3, 17, 19]. In addition, socio-cultural distances may create difficulties in information exchange [21] which creates barriers to building mutual understanding among distributed team members [23]. As a result, project stakeholders suffer misunderstandings, miscommunication and confusion [15] which ultimately reduces trust and commitment, and increases fear in distributed team members [23]. Our case study reveals that some agile practices helped to reduce the challenges of using the coordinating mechanism "mutual adjustment" in GSD projects. These were:

- The "**Daily stand up meetings**" with participation by both sites provided the opportunity to establish mutual adjustment and build trust and increase "teamness" between the Sydney and Malaysian team members.
- The "**Sprint planning meeting**" with participation by all team members reduced misunderstandings and confusion among project stakeholders through collaboration and helped to build mutual adjustment.
- The "**Sprint review meeting**" attended by project stakeholders also helped to increase project communication and build relationships.
- "**Retrospective meeting**" scheduled to assess the teamwork in completed sprints also helped to build mutual understanding among project stakeholders including the business user.
- "**Code Refactoring**" restructured the system by removing duplication, and facilitated improved communication and better understanding among distributed team members by providing communication through the coding environment.

6 Case Study Limitations

The design of this case study is based upon the four criteria for judging the quality of research design recommended by Yin [24]. Construct validity, which involves establishing correct operational measures for the concepts being studied, was not a limitation in our study. We developed a sufficient operational set of measures for data collection. As our case study is exploratory in nature, not explanatory or causal, we need not consider internal validity. Our study is also not concerned with external validity as our study findings are not generalized to other GSD projects. Our single case study initiates an exploration of the use of agile strategies in a GSD project. In this case study, we must consider reliability; data was collected based on the risks identified in the literature that impact the coordinating mechanisms, standardization, direct supervision and mutual adjustment due to project stakeholder distribution. However we cannot exclude bias on the part of our interviewees who reported what they thought happened. However, we did use multiple sources of evidence (documentation, discussion, interaction etc) to help us ensure sufficient reliability.

7 Conclusions and Future Research

Our initial case findings reveal that the use of some agile practices did help to reduce some GSD risks and improve project coordination processes. In particular we found that:

- The **"Daily stand up meeting"** with participation by both the Sydney and Malaysian team members helped to minimize some risks that impact on the use of the coordinating mechanisms direct supervision and mutual adjustment. Project coordination overhead was minimized as the project manager could discuss with both teams what had been done, and what needed to be done; existing problems were also covered. Daily stand up meetings with the aid of various communication tools ensures a synchronous communication environment and helps to build mutual understanding among distributed project stakeholders.
- Similarly, the **"Sprint planning meetings"** and **"Retrospective meetings"** with participation by distributed project stakeholders helped to maintain project standards, and better project coordination; communication among project stakeholders was also facilitated.
- The practice **"Sprint review meeting"** attended by team members from both sites also helped to increase project visibility and helped the project manager to minimize the challenges impacting on the coordinating mechanisms "direct supervision" and "mutual adjustment".
- The practices **"Test driven development"**, **"Coding standards"**, and **"Refactoring"** also helped to maintain project standards and increased project communication as these practices usually support communication through the code.

Our research provides only a single case study and we do not expect these findings to be generalizable to all GSD projects as GSD projects have many forms as noted earlier. A series of case studies can, however, provide insight into the use of agile practices that can help to reduce GSD risks and improve project co-ordination processes.

We plan to carry out a set of case studies that will start to set up a body of knowledge to help us identify effective agile practices able to assist in minimizing GSD work coordination challenges. In addition to conducting the case studies, we also plan to carry out a large scale survey among experienced GSD project managers and practitioners to investigate the effectiveness of agile practices in reducing GSD risks to project communication, coordination and collaboration processes. Our survey will mainly focus on the effectiveness of using XP and Scrum practices in reducing GSD risks. Some important project contextual factors will also be explored to help us understand the characteristics of GSD projects able to successfully use agile practices. We expect that the findings from the new case studies and the survey will enable us to empirically confirm the findings from the literature. While the case studies will provide more data about the potential impact of agile practices on coordination challenges in GSD projects.

Acknowledgments. M. Ali Babar's research is partially supported by Science foundation Ireland under grant number 03/CE2/I303-1. We also acknowledge the contribution of Nils Brede Moe, SINTEF ICT, Norway and Darja Smite, Blekinge Institute of Technology, Sweden in this paper.

References

1. Herbsleb, J., Moitra, D.: Global Software Development. IEEE Software, 16–20 (March/April 2001)
2. Conchuir, E.O., Holmstrom, H., Agerfalk, P.J., Fitzgerald, B.: Exploring the Assumed Benefits of Global Software Development. In: 2nd IEEE International Conference on Global Software Engineering, pp. 159–168. IEEE Press, New York (2006)
3. Holmstrom, H., Fitzgerald, B., Agerfalk, P.J., Conchuir, E.O.: Agile Practices Reduce Distance in Global Software Development. Information Systems Management, 7–26 (Summer 2006)
4. Abrahamsson, P., Salo, O., Ronkainen, J., Warsta, J.: Agile software development methods - Review and analysis, VTT Electronics (ed.). VTT Publications (2002)
5. Xiaohu, Y., Bin, X., Zhijun, H., Maddineni, S.R.: Extreme Programming in Global Software Development. In: Canadian Conference on Electrical and Computer Engineering, pp. 1845–1848 (2004)
6. Turk, D., France, R., Rumpe, B.: Limitations of Agile Software Processes. In: Extreme Programming and Agile Methods- XP/Agile Universe, pp. 43–46 (2002)
7. Taylor, P.S., Greer, D., Sage, P., Coleman, G., McDaid, K., Keenan, F.: Do agile GSD experience reports help the practitioner? In: Global Software Development, pp. 87–93 (2006)
8. Williams, L., Kerbs, W., Layman, L., Anton, A.I., Abrahamsson, P.: Toward a Framework for Evaluating Extreme Programming. In: 8th International Conference on Empirical Assessment in Software Engineering, pp. 11–20 (2004)
9. Agerfalk, P., Fitzgerald, B.: Flexible and Distributed software processes: Old Petunias in new bowls? Communications of the ACM 49, 41–46 (2006)
10. Mak, D.K.M., Kruchten, P.B.: Task coordination in an agile distributed software development environment. In: Canadian Conference on Electrical and Computer Engineering, pp. 1845–1848 (2006)
11. Carmel, E.: Global software teams: collaborating across borders and time zones. Prentice-Hall, Englewood Cliffs (1999)

12. Herbsleb, J.D.: Global Software Engineering: The Future of Socio- technical Coordination. In: International Conference on Future of Software Engineering, pp. 188–298 (2007)
13. Herbsleb, J.D., Mockus, A., Finholt, T.A., Grinter, R.E.: Distance, dependencies, and Delay in a Global Collaboration. In: ACM Conference on Computer Supported Cooperative Work, pp. 319–327 (2000)
14. Mintzberg, H.: Mintzberg on Management: Inside Our Strange World of Organizations. Free Press, New York (1989)
15. Ågerfalk, P.J., Fitzgerald, B., Holmström, H., Lings, B., Lundell, B., O'Conchuir, E.: A Framework for Considering Opportunities and Threats in Distributed Software Development. In: International Workshop on Distributed Software Development 2005, pp. 47–61 (2005)
16. Šmite, D., Moe, N.B., Torkar, R.: Pitfalls in Remote Team Coordination: Lessons Learned from a Case Study. In: 9th International Conference on Product Focused Software Process Improvement, pp. 345–359 (2008)
17. Prikladnicki, R., Audy, J.L.N., Damian, D., Oliveria, T.C.: Distributed Software Development: Practices and Challenges in different business strategies of Offshoring and Onshoing. In: 2nd IEEE International Conference on Global Software Engineering, pp. 262–264 (2007)
18. Karolak, D.W.J.: Global software development. Wiley InterScience, Chichester (1998)
19. Damian, D., Zowghi, D.: Requirements Engineering Challenges in Multi-site Software Development Organizations. Requirements Engineering Journal 8, 149–160 (2003)
20. Carmel, E., Agarwal, R.: Tactical Approaches for Alleviating Distance in Global Software Development. IEEE Software, 22–29 (March/April 2001)
21. Prikladnicki, R., Audy, J., Evaristo, R.: Distributed Software Development: Toward an Understanding of the relationship between project team, users and customers. In: 5th International Conference on Enterprise Information Systems, pp. 417–423 (2003)
22. Kotlarsky, J., Oshri, I.: Social ties, knowledge sharing and Successful collaboration in globally distributed system development projects. European Journal of Information Systems 14, 37–48 (2005)
23. Moe, N.B., Šmite, D.: Understanding a Lack of Trust in Global Software Teams: A Multiple-Case Study. Software Process Improvement and Practice 13(3), 217–231 (2008)
24. Yin, R.K.: Case Study Research. Sage Publications, Thousand Oaks (1994)
25. Geert, H., Gert, H.: Cultures and organizations: software of the mind, Revised and expanded 2nd edn. McGraw-Hill, New York (2005)
26. Groth, L.: Future Organizational Design: The Scope for the IT-based Enterprise. John Wiley & Sons, New York (1999)
27. Verner, J., Sampson, J., Tosic, V., Bakar, N., Kitchenham, B.: Guidelines for Industrially-based Multiple Case Studies in Software Engineering. In: 3rd IEEE International Conference on Research Challenges in Information Science, pp. 347–358 (2009)
28. Geert Hofstede™ Cultural Dimensions, http://www.geert-hofstede.com/
29. Hossain, E., Babar, M.A., Paik, H.: Using Agile Practices in Global Software Development: A Systematic Review. UNSW CSE Technical Report, TR 904 (2009)

Mapping CMMI Level 2 to Scrum Practices: An Experience Report

Jessica Diaz[1], Juan Garbajosa[1], and Jose A. Calvo-Manzano[2]

[1] Systems & Software Technology Group (SYST), E.U. Informática
[2] Dpto. LSIIS, Facultad de Informática,
Technical University of Madrid (UPM), Madrid, Spain
yesica.diaz@upm.es, jgs@eui.upm.es, jacalvo@fi.upm.es

Abstract. CMMI has been adopted advantageously in large companies for improvements in software quality, budget fulfilling, and customer satisfaction. However SPI strategies based on CMMI-DEV require heavy software development processes and large investments in terms of cost and time that medium/small companies do not deal with. The so-called light software development processes, such as Agile Software Development (ASD), deal with these challenges. ASD welcomes changing requirements and stresses the importance of adaptive planning, simplicity and continuous delivery of valuable software by short time-framed iterations. ASD is becoming convenient in a more and more global, and changing software market. It would be greatly useful to be able to introduce agile methods such as Scrum in compliance with CMMI process model. This paper intends to increase the understanding of the relationship between ASD and CMMI-DEV reporting empirical results that confirm theoretical comparisons between ASD practices and CMMI level2.

Keywords: CMMI, Agile Software Development, Scrum.

1 Introduction

A wide range of large organizations rely on the Capability Maturity Model Integration (CMMI) as indicator for organizational maturity and they enforce that all their processes are a certain capability level of compliance. The reason is that improvements in software quality, budget and milestones fulfilling, and customer satisfaction usually have been associated with higher levels of CMMI compliance [1] [2]. These improvements have been reported for example by Galin et al. [3] who analyzed more than 400 projects during the 1990s about plan-driven software development methods where continuous CMMI-based SPI (Software Process Improvement) strategies were applied. However, medium and small organizations, usually featured by sparse resources, have a lot of difficulties to apply CMMI [4] [5] [6]. Some reported data prove that over 77 percent of process improvements have taken longer than expected, and over 68 percent have cost more than expected too [7].

At the same time organizations look for the improvement of their processes and they must respond continually to changing environments in a global market.

R.V. O'Connor et al. (Eds.): EuroSPI 2009, CCIS 42, pp. 93–104, 2009.
© Springer-Verlag Berlin Heidelberg 2009

The rapid change increases frustration to the heavyweight plans, specifications, and other documentation imposed by plan-driven software development with maturity model compliance criteria [8]. Some authors assert even CMMI is not applicable to turbulent and volatile business environments [9] concluding that processes not only must respond to change but embrace it [10].

The competitiveness and evolution of the software market has led software companies to avoid heavy software development methodologies and to follow light software development methodologies, which are open for new changes. From these needs, Agile Software Development (ASD) [11, 12] emerged with the definition of the Agile Manifesto [13]. The Agile Manifesto is a statement of the principles that underpin agile software development, some of them are continuous delivery of valuable software, simplicity, on-site customer, and welcome changing requirements. ASD is mainly based on the improvement of the software development productivity, the human relationships of the development team, the tacit knowledge processes with little ware, adaptive planning, and lightweight. These values are preserved by introducing the customer as another member of the development team and by doing short time-framed software development iterations. These short iterations allow the checking of partial results of the work product and the introduction of new changes in a simple way. As a result, software development is more effective and adaptable; so agile methodologies have proved its effectiveness in projects with very changing requirements [14] [15]. ASD is growing mature for large projects, and this is demonstrated by its increasing put into practice at the industry [16, 17, 18], even for outsourcing projects [19]. In fact, the data reported in [16] show that over 69 percent of analyzed organizations are putting into practice agile practices on their projects.

But, what about CMMI compliant organizations that need to introduce light software development methods for adapting to turbulent markets? And, what about agile organizations whose clients require a certain CMMI level of compliance? These issues lead to the challenge for embracing CMMI-based SPI strategies and agile principles, as well as understanding the relationship between both approaches. This challenge may be addressed through an effort to stretch agile to fit CMMI analyzing the interrelations, constraints, and adjustments between agile and CMMI. Comparisons between CMMI and ASD have often been criticized comparing them like oil and water [20]. However the literature has summarized that CMMI and agile are compatible [20, 10] because agile methods are development process descriptions and CMMI is a reference process model that it is used for appraisals and improvements [21]. This means, CMMI tells us what to do, while agile methods tells us how to do it.

The primary purpose of this paper is to increase the understanding of the relationship between ASD and CMMI-DEV [22]. This paper reports empirical results that confirm the theoretical comparisons [23, 24, 25, 26, 27] between agile practices (in particular Scrum method) and three processes related to CMMI capability level 2. The paper is organized as follows. Section 2 analyzes background and related work. A mapping between CMMI specific practices and agile practices is described in section 3. Section 4 presents an internal CMMI appraisal in a software development process in which agile practices are used. Finally, some conclusions and future work are presented in section 5.

2   Background

2.1   CMMI Overview: CMMI v1.2

CMMI for Development [22] is a reference model that consists of best practices that address development and maintenance activities applied to products and services. CMMI-DEV contains practices that cover project management, process management, systems engineering, hardware engineering, software engineering, and other supporting processes used in development and maintenance.

2.2   ASD Overview: Scrum

Agile methodologies provide the infrastructure (i) to evaluate the state of the product, (ii) to identify new changes in the development process, and (iii) to incorporate them in the final product by means of continuous integration. There are different agile methodologies such as Scrum [28] or eXtreme Programming (XP) [29]. Each one of them defines their own techniques for planning, estimating, or reviewing, but all of them are based on the same values defined by Agile Manifesto. Even, some of them share some practices, for example requirements in agile are captured as User Stories (US) [30]. The US objective is to reduce the cost of the requirement elicitation and management by means of scenarios written by customers without techno-syntax versus conventional methodologies based on formal requirements specification documents. These previous guidelines have offered a general vision of agile methodologies but this work has been focused on the Scrum methodology. Following Scrum is described in detail.

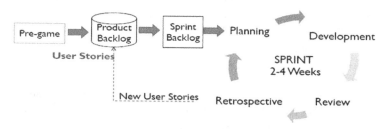

Fig. 1. Scrum Lifecycle

Scrum implements an iterative, incremental life cycle (see Figure 1) which involves three stakeholders: the *Product Owner*, the *Team*, and the *ScrumMaster* [28]; all together make up the *Scrum Team*. The Scrum life cycle defines a pre-game phase at the project beginning; planning, review, and retrospective meetings in an iterative way; and daily meetings during the whole iteration. The *pre-game phase* consists in a light planning process where representative customers and members of the Scrum Team capture requirements as US; the result is the *product backlog*, a list of known US. Then US are prioritized and divided into short time-framed iterations called *sprints*. A sprint is a 2-4 weeks period of development time. Each sprint has a sprint *planning meeting* at the sprint beginning where the Product Owner and Team plan together about what to be done for the next sprint; the result is the *sprint backlog*, a list of US and tasks that must be performed to achieve the *sprint goal*, i.e., to deliver an increment valuable functionality of the final product. During the execution of each sprint, the team meets *daily in 15-minute meetings* to track the work progress answering three questions [28]: *What have I done since the last Scrum meeting?, What will I do before the next Scrum meeting?, What prevents me from performing my work as efficiently as possible?*

Anything that prevents a team member from performing his work as efficiently as possible is an impediment. The ScrumMaster is in charge of ensuring *impediments* get resolved; for it project adjustments could be necessary. At the end of the sprint, in the sprint *review meeting*, the Team asks the Product Owner whether the goals were met, the Product Owner could change US, add US, etc. Finally a *retrospective meeting* is held between the Team and ScrumMaster to discuss what was well and what could be improved for the next sprint; this is an estimate and tracking activity to achieve continuous improvement; i.e., retrospective meetings provide feedback to apply needed changes and adjustments for the next sprint.

2.3   Related Work

Existing literature has summarized that CMMI and agile are compatible [10,20, 31,23,24,25,26,27,32,33,34,35], even that hybrid approaches that combine both agile methods and methods based on the CMM[1] are feasible and necessary [36].

Only few works show how to achieve CMMI levels with agile practices, some of them are high level, theoretical and difficult to implement in a general full software product life cycle, and often do not provide specific details and examples. Theoretical comparisons between XP and CMM claim that XP does not fulfill CMM requirements but it may be possible to construct a process that fulfills CMM level 2 and 3 by adding sound practices to XP [34,23,33]. Vriens suggests that it is possible to achieve CMM levels 2 process areas using a combination of XP and Scrum as the base for the software development process [24]. Kähkönen and Abrahamsson [35] have reported empirical evidences when CMMI is used for assessing software development processes where XP practices are used. Afterward, some works haver assert that CMMI level 5 may be possible [32, 27]. Fritzsche and Keil [25], in turn, state that level 4 or 5 are not feasible under the current specifications of CMMI and XP, and describe the limitations of CMMI in an agile environment. Pikkarainen and Mäntyniemi [21] propose an approach for agile software development assessment and improvement strategies using CMMI;

---

[1] Some studies are related to the previous version of CMMI.

this approach is based on a mapping between CMMI specific goals and agile practices and supported by empirical evidences. However only two process areas are supported (Project Planning and Requirements Management) and only from a CMMI goal (not specific practice). Marcal et. al [26] describe a more detail mapping between CMMI Project Management Process Area to Scrum practices but do not provide empirical evidences.

Unlike these researches, our work tries to increase the detail of previous mappings between Scrum and CMMI, and to illustrate this mapping with a case study providing empirical evidences of the obtained results.

3 Mapping between CMMI Specific Practices and Scrum Practices

Software requirements elicitation, budgeting, and scheduling are very relevant process areas in software development. For it Project Planning (PP), Project Monitoring and Control (PMC) and Requirements Management (REQM) CMMI process areas were mapped with SCRUM practices.

3.1 Project Planning (PP)

According to CMMI-DEV, the aim of PP is to establish and maintain plans that define project activities. PP has 3 specific goals (SG) that enclose 14 specific practices (SP). A detailed description is carried out below:

- *SP1.1 Estimate the Scope of the Project.* Basically it consists in the identification of work packages in sufficient detail to specify estimates of project tasks, roles, responsibilities, and schedule. It is covered by the Scrum pregame phase where the product backlog and the sprints are defined; both items provide the resources for estimate the scope of the project.
- *SP1.2 Establish Estimates of Work Product and Task Attributes.* Estimate is carried out in two levels: product level and sprint level. So, Scrum establishes a first estimation in the pre-game phase and an iterative estimate in the sprint beginning (planning meeting). Estimates usually are based on size or complexity attributes. Some agile practices recommend the *Planning Poker*[2] estimation technique; it is based on the consensus of the participants (similar to Wideband Delphi) for estimating relative size of US. Some units might include story points [37] or function points.
- *SP1.3 Define Project Lifecycle.* This specific practice is fully addressed by Scrum because it defines the lifecycle shown in Figure 1.
- *SP1.4 Determine Estimates of Effort and Cost.* Again estimation is carried out in two levels: product level and sprint level. Product estimates are high level and less accurate and sprint estimates are low level and more accurate than the first ones. Scrum practitioners estimate the US effort in ideal

---

[2] http://www.planningpoker.com/

engineering days based on previous sprints (historical base of sprint back-logs), previous projects (historical base of product backlogs), capacity for the forthcoming sprint and the relative US complexity required to deliver the sprint goal. Burndown and Burnup models [37] facilitating the effort estimate.

- *SP2.1 Establish the Budget and Schedule.* During pre-game phase initial milestones (sprint goals), schedule (sprints), constraints and budget are setup according to the initial product backlog. Additional milestones or budget may be assigned to the project in each sprint during its planning. Corrective action criteria are identified during retrospective meeting. The Product Owner is an outstanding figure to implement these practices in a successful way.
- *SP2.2 Identify Project Risks.* In Scrum risks are captured as impediments (list of impediments). Their identification is not carried out in the initial plan or in a systematic manner. But this practice is partially satisfied in an iterative way, during daily meetings, and impediments are revised in retrospective meeting. The ScrumMaster is the outstanding figure in this identification process.
- *SP2.3 Plan for Data Management.* Any data generated by the project is stored in public folders or white-boards available to everyone [28], but there is no formal data management plan or procedure to collect this data [26]. Privacy and security are another weaknesses.
- *SP2.4 Plan for Project Resources.* During pre-game phase the staffing requirements and equipment list are defined. As the result the Scrum Team is established. During the sprints execution, the ScrumMaster is in charge of providing new resources it should be necessary.
- *SP2.5 Plan for Needed Knowledge and Skills.* Knowledge and skills needs are identified during pre-game phase, however the definition of mechanisms to provide knowledge and skills not found in the organization are considered as impediments and resolved during daily and retrospectives meetings.
- *SP2.6 Plan Stakeholder Involvement.* Scrum defines roles, responsibilities, and involvement of the stakeholders at the beginning and end or each sprint. This involvement is monitored by the ScrumMaster who is in charge of assuring the fulfilling of Scrum practices by all stakeholders.
- *SP2.7 Establish the Project Plan.* To start a Scrum project a vision and a product backlog are the basis for the project plan [28].
- *SP3.1 Review Plans That Affect the Project.* Plans reviews are carried out during planning and retrospectives meetings.
- *SP3.2 Reconcile Work and Resource Levels.* Work reconciliation occurs during planning meetings because product backlog is dynamic, so new estimations or schedules are possible.
- *SP3.3 Obtain Plan Commitment.* The commitment is obtained in an iterative way during face to face planning meetings in which stakeholders are involved.

3.2   Project Monitoring and Control (PMC)

According to CMMI-DEV, the aim of PMC is to establish and maintain plans that define project activities. PMC has 2 specific goals (SG) that enclose 10 specific practices (SP). The mapping described in Table 1 was carried out.

3.3   Requirements Management (REQM)

According to CMMI-DEV, the aim of REQM is to manage the requirements of the projects products. REQM has 1 specific goal (SG) that encloses 5 specific practices (SP). The mapping described in Table 2 was carried out.

Table 1. Mapping between PMC specific practices and Scrum practices

PMC specific practices	Scrum practices
SP1.1 Monitor Project Planning Parameters	
SP1.2 Monitor Commitments	
SP1.3 Monitor Project Risks	Daily and Retrospective meetings
SP1.4 Monitor Data Management	Not supported
SP1.5 Monitor Stakeholder Involvement	Retrospective meetings
SP1.6 Conduct Progress Reviews	Review meetings. Burndown and Burnup graphs
SP1.7 Conduct Milestone Reviews	Review meetings
SP2.1 Analyze Issues	Daily and Retrospective meetings
SP2.2 Take Corrective Action	Review meetings
SP2.3 Manage Corrective Action	Retrospective meetings

Table 2. Mapping between REQM specific practices and Scrum practices

REQM specific practices	Scrum practices
SP1.1 Obtain an Understanding of Requirements	User Stories (US) in an iterative way (sprints)
SP1.2 Obtain Commitment to Requirements	Planning meetings. Backlogs
SP1.3 Manage Requirements Changes	Planning and Review meetings
SP1.4 Maintain Bidirectional Traceability of Requirements	User Stories (US)
SP1.5 Identify Inconsistencies Between Project Work and Requirements	Pre-game and Planning meetings

4   An Experience Report: An Internal CMMI Appraisal

Once theoretical comparisons between Scrum and CMMI (level 2 for PP, PMC and REQM) were established, an internal assessment was carried out to confirm these hypotheses. An internal assessment against a CMMI reference model provided evidences about good agile practices, strengths and weaknesses for achieving a CMMI level 2 in agile contexts.

4.1 Case Study Description

The assessed project consisted in a software evolution of a product called Test and OPeration Environment (TOPEN) [38]. TOPEN is an acceptance testing tool built in-house that provides mechanisms for the definition and execution of operation and test cases through a domain specific language. The product evolution consisted in adapting TOPEN to test a biogas plant. The product evolution was developed following Scrum method in 6 sprints and 15 weeks. The Scrum Team was composed of 8 engineers: a Product Owner, a ScrumMaster, and a Team of six developers. An internal proxy customer was taken into account too. The Scrum methodology was applied as it is described following.

During the pre-game phase, US were first captured, together with the proxy customer, which formed a product backlog. The US were grouped in sprints of two weeks approximately. A planning meeting was established for every sprint. During the planning meeting, the sprint ending date is defined and the initial US are further elaborated together with the Product Owner and the Team in by means of a *planning game*. The planning game is technique that guides the estimating of the US involving all the Scrum Team. However, the developers found that the US estimations were too optimistic in the first planning games, which made several deviations during the first sprints. Through sprints developers learned more about Scrum practices, the needs of the customer and the product under development. As a consequence, the US estimations became more precise. After the planning game, the sprint backlog is formed. Product backlog and sprint backlogs were stored and managed through a tool named Rally[3]. Rally is a web based tool for managing user stories, tasks, backlogs, plan, releases, test cases, and defects.

During the sprint, daily meetings solved small problems in an agile way making technical decisions by themselves (self organizing teams). At the end of the sprint, a progress report was elaborated in the review meeting. The customer representatives validated the work products (documents, releases, or other artefacts), and thus the inconsistencies between their needs, plans and project work were continuously followed. Changes in the client needs were discussed, and the product backlog was updated correspondingly. Finally a retrospective meeting was established at the end of every sprint for analyzing strengths, weaknesses, problems, and improvements of the methods, the team and the project. The feedback obtained was applied to the following sprints.

4.2 A CMMI Appraisal Process Approach

Once the empirical case project has been described, the next step is the appraisal process description. We are selected the appraisal process defined by [21]. It is characterized by (i) appraisal teams of 3-4 members, (ii) appraisal time of 2-3 weeks, (iii) require considerable resources, (iv) medium intrusiveness, and (v) medium reliability and validity of the appraisal results.

---

[3] http://www.rallydev.com/

Three participants in the appraisal have scored each subpractice related to CMMI on a questionnaire; this questionnaire is supported by interviews with participants and reviews of the project documentation.

4.3   Results

Figure 2 and Figure 3 and Figure 4 show the results of the appraisal for some PP, PMC and REQM specific goals. Figure 2 shows the results of the appraisal for PP process area. Subpractices for SG1 are satisfied for this case study where Scrum method was applied. This process area is a challenge for the team because this case study was the first contact with Scrum method. However, since planning is an iterative process repeated at the beginning of the sprints, the team had the chance to improve the process practices in each sprint. So, the iterative planning enabled development teams to estimate more accuracy and answer to

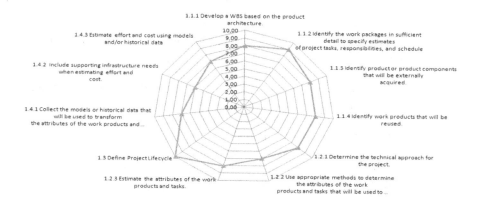

Fig. 2. PP - SG1 Establish Estimates

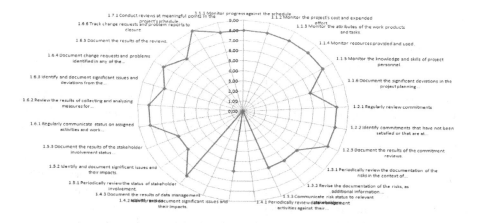

Fig. 3. PMC - SG1 Monitor Project Against Plan

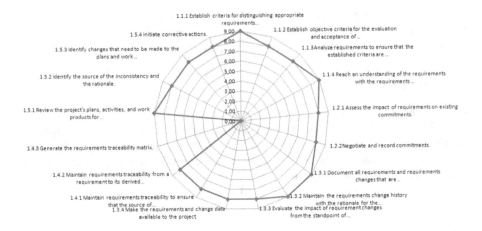

Fig. 4. REQM - SG1 Manage Requirements

changes quickly. As the project progressive, historical data of previous sprints were collected and used in order to estimate effort and cost.

Figure 3 shows the results of the appraisal for PMC process area. Subpractices for SG1 are largely satisfied because the Scrum lifecycle defines explicitly times for monitoring and control through daily, review, and retrospective meetings. Finally Figure 4 shows the results of the appraisal for REQM process area. Subpractices for SG1 are largely satisfied. Customers must not specify most of the requirement at the project beginning, so understanding of requirements is easier through iterative sprints and requirements change processes are flexible and largely supported by Scrum method.

5   Conclusions and Further Work

Agile methodologies are associated commonly to informal and lightweight documentation that do not emphasize process definition or measurement to the degree that models such as the CMMI do. However the literature has proved that CMMI model can be applied in a lightweight manner without incurring in excessive documentation. In particular, this paper has proved that Scrum processes can be considered valid under the CMMI paradigm. So, the appraisal has provided evidences that those process areas related to CMMI-DEV level 2 were largely covered. These results will be used for learning and selecting practices for the following agile projects.

The conclusion is that agile methodologies provide many good engineering practices, and together with CMMI, both approaches can achieve very positive synergies. Since Scrum method provides criteria to identify a minimum set of good practices to achieve CMMI capability level 2, small-medium organizations can take advantage of more flexible and lightweight methods to achieve a certain CMMI level compliance.

Acknowledgment

The work reported here has been partially sponsored by the OVAL/PM TIC2006-14840 project, the FLEXI FIT-340005-2007-37 (ITEA2 6022) project and UPM under their Researcher Training program.

References

1. Herbsleb, J., Carleton, A., Rozum, J., Siegel, J., Zubrow, D.: Benefits of cmm-based software process improvement: Initial results. Technical report, CMU/SEI-94-TR-013, Software Engineering Institute (1994)
2. Goldenson, D.R., Gibson, D.L.: Demonstrating the impact and benefits of cmmi: An update and preliminary results. Technical report, CMU/SEI-2003-SR-009, Software Engineering Institute (2003)
3. Galin, D., Avrahami, M.: Are cmm program investments beneficial? analyzing past studies. IEEE Software 23(6), 81–87 (2006)
4. Paulk, M.: Using the software cmm in small organizations. In: Proc. Joint 16th Pacific Northwest Software Quality Conf. and 8th Int'l Conf. Software Quality, Washington, DC, USA, pp. 350–360. IEEE Computer Society, Los Alamitos (1998)
5. Staples, M., Niazi, M., Jeffery, R., Abrahams, A., Byatt, P., Murphy, R.: An exploratory study of why organizations do not adopt cmmi. Journal of Systems and Software 80(6), 883–895 (2007)
6. Pino, F.J., García, F., Piattini, M.: Software process improvement in small and medium software enterprises: a systematic review. Software Quality Control 16(2), 237–261 (2008)
7. Goldenson, D.R., Herbsleb, J.D.: After the appraisal: A systematic survey of process improvement, its benefits, and factors that influence success. Technical report, CMU/SEI-95-TR-009, Software Engineering Institute (1995)
8. Boehm, B.: A view of 20th and 21st century software engineering. In: ICSE 2006: Proceedings of the 28th international conference on Software engineering, pp. 12–29. ACM, New York (2006)
9. Lebsanft, K.: Process improvement in turbulent times – is cmm still an answer? Product Focused Software Process Improvement, 78–85 (2001)
10. Cohen, D., Lindvall, M., Costa, P.: An introduction to agile methods. Advances in Computers 62, 2–67 (2004)
11. Cockburn, A.: Agile Software Development: The Cooperative Game, 2nd edn. Addison-Wesley Professional, Reading (2006)
12. Abrahamsson, P.: Agile software development methods review and analysis. Technical report, VTT Electronics, 112 (2002)
13. K. Beck et al.: The agile manifesto, www.agilemanifesto.org (accessed, February 2009)
14. Dingsoyr, T., Dybå, T., Abrahamsson, P.: A preliminary roadmap for empirical research on agile software development. In: AGILE 2008: Proceedings of the Agile 2008, Washington, DC, USA, pp. 83–94. IEEE Computer Society, Los Alamitos (2008)
15. Dybå, T., Dingsoyr, T.: Empirical studies of agile software development: A systematic review. Inf. Softw. Technol. 50(9-10), 833–859 (2008)
16. Ambysoft: Agile adoption rate survey (February 2008), http://www.ambysoft.com/surveys/agileFebruary2008.html

17. Ambler, S.W.: Has agile peaked? let's look at the numbers (May 2008),
    http://www.ddj.com/architect/207600615?pgno=1
18. Flexi research project: Flexi newsletter (February 2008) ISBN 978-951-42-8586-8
19. Fowler, M.: Using an agile software process with offshore development (July 2006),
    http://www.martinfowler.com/articles/agileOffshore.html
20. Turner, R., Jain, A.: Agile meets cmmi: Culture clash or common cause? In: Proceedings of the Second XP Universe and First Agile Universe Conference on Extreme Programming and Agile Methods - XP/Agile Universe 2002, London, UK, pp. 153–165. Springer, Heidelberg (2002)
21. Pikkarainen, M., Mäntyniemi, A.: An approach for using cmmi in agile software development assessments: Experiences from three case studies. In: Proceedings of SPICE 2006 (2006)
22. CMMI Product Team: Cmmi for development, version 1.2. Technical report, CMU/SEI-2006-TR-008, ESC-TR-2006-008, Software Engineering Institute (2006)
23. Paulk, M.C.: Agile methodologies and process discipline. The Journal of Defence Software Engineering (October 2002)
24. Vriens, C.: Certifying for cmm level 2 and is09001 with xp@scrum. In: Proceedings of the Agile Development Conference. ADC 2003, June 2003, pp. 120–124 (2003)
25. Fritzsche, M., Keil, P.: Agile methods and cmmi: Compatibility or conflict? e-Informatica Software Engineering Journal 1(1) (2007)
26. Marcal, A.S.C., Soares, F.S.F., Belchior, A.D.: Mapping cmmi project management process areas to scrum practices. In: SEW 2007: Proceedings of the 31st IEEE Software Engineering Workshop, Washington, DC, USA, pp. 13–22. IEEE Computer Society, Los Alamitos (2007)
27. Sutherland, J., Jakobsen, C., Johnson, K.: Scrum and cmmi level 5: The magic potion for code warriors. In: AGILE 2007, August 2007, pp. 272–278 (2007)
28. Schwaber, K., Beedle, M.: Agile Software Development with Scrum. Prentice-Hall, Englewood Cliffs (2002)
29. Beck, K.: Extreme Programming Explained: Embrace Change. Addison-Wesley, Reading (1999)
30. Cohen, M.: User Stories Applied for Agile Software Development. The Addison-Wesley Signature Series (2004)
31. Paulk, M.C.: Extreme programming from a cmm perspective. IEEE Software 18(6), 1–8 (2001)
32. Anderson, D.J.: Stretching agile to fit cmmi level 3 - the story of creating msf for cmmi®process improvement at microsoft corporation. In: ADC 2005: Proceedings of the Agile Development Conference, pp. 193–201. IEEE Computer Society, Los Alamitos (2005)
33. Glazer, H.: Dispelling the process myth: Having a process does not mean sacrificing agility or creativity. The Journal of Defence Software Engineering (November 2001)
34. Martinsson, J.: Maturing xp through the cmm. In: Extreme Programming and Agile Processes in Software Engineering (2003)
35. Kähkönen, T., Abrahamsson, P.: Achieving CMMI level 2 with enhanced extreme programming approach. In: Bomarius, F., Iida, H. (eds.) PROFES 2004. LNCS, vol. 3009, pp. 378–392. Springer, Heidelberg (2004)
36. Barry, B.: Get ready for agile methods, with care. Computer 35(1), 64–69 (2002)
37. Buglione, L., Abran, A.: Improving estimations in agile projects: issues and avenues. In: Proceedings of the 4th Software Measurement European Forum (SMEF 2007), May 9-11, pp. 265–274 (2007)
38. Magro, B., Garbajosa, J., Perez-Benedi, J.: A software product line definition for validation environments. In: Software Product Lines Conference, SPLC (2008)

The QualOSS Process Evaluation:
Initial Experiences with Assessing Open Source Processes

Martín Soto and Marcus Ciolkowski

Fraunhofer Institute for Experimental Software Engineering
Fraunhofer-Platz 1
67663 Kaiserslautern, Germany
{soto,ciolkows}@iese.fraunhofer.de

Abstract. For traditional software development, process maturity models (CMMI, SPICE) have long been used to assess expected product quality and project predictability. For the case of OSS, however, these models are generally perceived as inadequate. In practice, though, many OSS communities are well-organized, and there is evidence of varying levels of process maturity in OSS projects. This paper presents work in progress—performed as part of the EU project QualOSS—on developing a process evaluation framework specifically aimed at OSS projects. We present a first version of our evaluation procedures, and discuss some lessons learned during its preliminary application to a small number of OSS projects.

Keywords: Software process, Open Source Software, OSS, process assessment, process evaluation, QualOSS, software quality.

1 Introduction

Since the introduction of the Capability Maturity Model (CMM) in the early 1980s, maturity-oriented process assessment models have become a fundamental tool for determining the extent to which an organization can deliver software on time and with an acceptable level of quality. Currently, the most prominent examples of such process assessment models are CMMI-DEV (Capability Maturity Model® Integration for Development [10]) and SPICE (Software Process Improvement and Capability dEtermination [4]).

The growing popularity of Open Source Software (OSS) constitutes a big challenge to software process assessment, since, at first sight, maturity-oriented models appear very difficult to apply to OSS development. On the one hand, they seem to expect an organizational structure that is not present in most OSS communities, and, on the other hand, it is a widespread belief that OSS communities operate in an essentially chaotic way, and that, for this reason, no systematic development processes can be taking place during OSS development. Consequently, most casual observers would regard traditional maturity models as completely inappropriate for OSS software.

We disagree with this vision. The main assumption underlying process assessment approaches is that mature processes consistently lead to higher-quality products,

R.V. O'Connor et al. (Eds.): EuroSPI 2009, CCIS 42, pp. 105–116, 2009.

whereas for an organization with immature processes, the capacity to deliver high-quality products is unreliable and cannot be predicted. There is no reason to believe that this assumption is not valid for OSS. Concretely, we expect that a higher level of process maturity will lead to better products and more sustainable communities, and that successful OSS communities often owe a good portion of their success to the introduction of sound software processes.

Indeed, many OSS communities have been able to consistently produce software of adequate quality, making regular releases over the years. There is evidence that this consistency does not stem from some mysterious property of OSS development that makes it work against all odds, or from the sheer talent of individual developers, but that it could be the result of good software development practices being applied and enforced by OSS communities in a disciplined fashion [7]. For this reason, the EU project QualOSS—which is generally concerned with the overall quality of OSS products, as well as with the sustainability of the communities around them—decided to add a process evaluation framework to its quality model, which is aimed at determining the ability of an OSS community to consistently deliver adequate products over time.

In this paper, we describe the first version of this process evaluation framework, and discuss our preliminary experience with applying it to a small number of OSS projects. In order to provide some background to the reader, Section 2 briefly describes the overall quality model defined by the QualOSS project. After a short discussion of related work in Section 3, Section 4 presents the QualOSS process evaluation in detail. Our initial experience with the process evaluation is discussed in Section 5. We close with some general conclusions and a brief discussion of future work in Section 6.

2 The QualOSS Quality Model

The process evaluation framework we describe in this paper is one component of the comprehensive quality model developed for the *Quality of Open Source Software* (QualOSS) project. Since the process evaluation framework was designed from the ground up to contribute to the overall QualOSS model, we start by describing it briefly.

The QualOSS quality model (or, simply, "QualOSS model" for short) is intended to support the quality evaluation of OSS projects, with a focus on evolvability and robustness. One central, underlying assumption while defining the model has been that the quality of a software product is not only related to the product itself (code, documentation, etc.), but also to the way the product is developed and distributed. For this reason, and since the development of OSS products is the responsibility of an open community, the QualOSS model takes both product- and community-related issues into account on an equal basis, and as comprehensively as possible.

The QualOSS model is composed of three types of interrelated elements: quality characteristics, metrics, and indicators. Quality characteristics correspond to the concrete attributes of a product or community that we consider relevant for evaluation (see below for an explanation of how these characteristics were chosen). Metrics correspond to concrete aspects we can measure on a product or on its associated community assets that we expect to be correlated with our targeted quality characteristics. Finally, indicators define how to aggregate and evaluate the measurement values resulting from applying metrics to a product or community in order to obtain a consolidated value that can be readily used by decision makers when performing an evaluation.

The quality characteristics in the model are organized in a hierarchy of two levels that we call characteristics and subcharacteristics for reasons of simplicity. The subcharacteristics are considered to contribute in one way or another to the main characteristic they belong to. For defining our hierarchy of quality characteristics, we relied mainly on three sources: (1) related work on OSS quality models, (2) general standards for software quality, such as ISO 9126 [6], and (3) expert opinion. For the third source, we conducted interviews among industry stakeholders to derive relevant criteria for the QualOSS model.

Given our emphasis on covering not only OSS products but also the communities behind them, we have grouped the quality characteristics into two groups: those that relate to the product, and those that relate to the community. On the product side, the QualOSS model covers the following top-level quality characteristics:

- *Maintainability:* The degree to which the software product can be modified. Modifications may include corrections, improvements, or adaptation of the software to changes in the environment, and in requirements and functional specifications.
- *Reliability:* The degree to which the software product can maintain a specified level of performance when used under specified conditions.
- *Transferability (Portability):* The degree to which the software product can be transferred from one environment to another.
- *Operability:* The degree to which the software product can be understood, learned, used and is attractive to the user, when used under specified conditions.
- *Performance:* The degree to which the software product provides appropriate performance, relative to the amount of resources used, under stated conditions.
- *Functional Suitability:* The degree to which the software product provides functions that meet stated and implied needs when the software is used under specified conditions.
- *Security:* The ability of system items to protect themselves from accidental or malicious access, use, modification, destruction, or disclosure.
- *Compatibility:* The ability of two or more systems or components to exchange information and/or to perform their required functions while sharing the same hardware or software environment.

The community side of the model, in turn, covers the following characteristics:

- *Maintenance capacity:* The ability of a community to provide the resources necessary for maintaining its product(s) (e.g., implement changes, remove defects, provide support) over a certain period of time.
- *Sustainability:* The likelihood that an OSS community remains capable of maintaining the product or products it develops over an extended period of time.
- *Process Maturity:* The ability of a developer community to consistently achieve development-related goals (e.g., quality goals) by following established processes. Additionally, the level to which the processes followed by a development community are able to guarantee that certain desired product characteristics will be present in the product.

The QualOSS process evaluation framework is aimed at covering the last characteristic mentioned, namely, process maturity. In what follows, we describe this framework in more detail.

3 Related Work: OSS Assessment

In recent years, Open Source Software has often been used as the target of quantitative analyses of code quality, mostly due to the fact that large code repositories are available for analysis. Many publications exist on (semi-)automatic analysis of code, mailing lists, bug tracking, and versioning systems. Contrary to what happens with code and repository analysis, few publications have addressed OSS processes so far. A paper by Michlmayr [7] is one notable exception, providing evidence of disciplined processes in OSS projects and relating it with project success.

As a reaction to the insight that software quality is not restricted to code aspects, assessment models for OSS projects have emerged whose aim is to support potential OSS users in making decisions regarding the selection of OSS products. The most prominent examples are the *Qualification and Selection of Open Source Software* (QSOS) model [9], two different models called *Open Source Maturity Model* (OSMM)—one from CapGemini [2] and one from Navica [8]—and the *Open Business Readiness Rating* (OpenBRR) model [1]. Although these models take the OSS product into account (i.e., code, documentation), as well as the community that produces it, they only have a rudimentary process perspective, if any. For example, QSOS considers two process criteria: quality assurance processes (with levels none, informal, supported by tools), and bug/feature request tools (none, standard tools, active use of tools), which, in our opinion, are far from covering the wide variety of quality-relevant processes typically observed in OSS development. This lack of coverage for the process perspective constitutes one of our main motivations for proposing the more comprehensive approach discussed here.

4 Towards a Process Maturity Model for OSS

As discussed in the introduction, the idea of assessing an OSS community in order to determine which good practices it follows, as well as how established these practices are, is perfectly reasonable. Still, it is true that existing process assessment models cannot generally be applied directly to OSS, as they include too many elements that are specific to companies and other conventional development organizations. In this section, we describe our process evaluation framework, which is directly aimed at OSS development. This model reuses a number of the ideas present in existing maturity models, but adapts them in order to make them more directly applicable in an OSS context.

4.1 Maturity Models as a Basis for Open Source Process Assessment

In order to create an assessment model for OSS process maturity, we started by reviewing existing maturity models with the purpose of extracting, and, where necessary, adapting some of their elements to the specifics of OSS. Concretely, we used the *Capability Maturity Model for Software Development* (CMMI-DEV) as a starting point. Released in 2006, the current CMMI-DEV model is the latest version in a series of maturity models started in the 1980s by Humphrey's Capability Maturity Model (CMM). CMMI-DEV covers 22 process areas, ranging from process improvement practices to specific development practices. Each process area is subdivided into a number of goals, which, in turn, are structured as sets of practices. Goals and practices are associated to process maturity levels (also called *capability levels* when they are related to a single process area). In order to be classified at a particular maturity level, an organization must have implemented all practices required by that level.

Given how comprehensive CMMI-DEV is, reaching its highest capability levels represents a serious challenge for any software development organization. Clearly, OSS communities are not an exception in this respect, and, in addition, the vast majority of them are not involved in any explicit process improvement efforts. Consequently, most, if not all, OSS communities are still quite far from reaching the levels of process discipline required by the higher levels of CMMI-DEV.

This last fact notwithstanding, there is evidence of good practices being applied in an established and disciplined fashion by a variety of OSS communities and with regard to different areas of the software development process. We think that many of these practices correspond to the spirit, if not directly to the letter, of the practices and goals specified by CMMI-DEV.

Some examples of such disciplined good practices, observed in prominent OSS communities, are:

- *Version/Configuration Management:* Many OSS projects rely on advanced versioning tools for managing their source code. In most cases, access to such systems will be carefully regulated, and the processes for creating new versions are well established and enforced.
- *Release Management:* The GNOME Desktop project, as well as the popular GNU/Linux distribution Ubuntu, both have strict 6-month release cycles that have been successfully operating for years. The complex coordination process required for each such cycle is well documented and carefully supervised and enforced by an established release board.
- *Requirements Management:* The community behind the Python programming language has a well-documented requirements elicitation and management process as represented by the so-called *Python Improvement Proposals* (PIPs). Proposals for language enhancements are presented by community members and thoroughly refined through feedback from the community until they are considered ready for implementation. The process is conducted in the open and actively enforced by the community.

Many other similar examples can be found by directly observing the dynamics of OSS communities. This led us to believe that, despite the inviability of applying a full-fledged process maturity model to OSS, a process evaluation model for OSS is not only viable, but potentially very useful in order to gauge the ability of OSS communities to consistently deliver software of appropriate quality. This belief constitutes the main motivation for the QualOSS process evaluation framework described here.

4.2 The Generic QualOSS Process Evaluation

In its current form, our Open Source process evaluation framework covers a number of basic software development tasks (described in more detail in the next subsection).

Each of these tasks is evaluated with respect to five main questions, which constitute a simplified form of the sort of assessment a standard maturity model would require:

1. Is there a documented process for the task?
2. Is there an established process for the task?
3. If there is an established process, is it executed consistently?
4. If both an established, consistent process, and a documented process could be found, do they match?
5. Is the process adequate for its intended purpose?

In order to produce assessment results that allow for comparison of a project's performance in different areas, the answers to these questions are encoded in a predefined, normalized form. These basic results, in turn, are used to compute indicators that are integrated into the QualOSS model, and that, similar to other QualOSS metrics, are intended to contribute to an overall view of an OSS project's quality.

In order to address these questions for each of our selected tasks, we have already defined simple evaluation procedures. In the following, we outline these procedures.

Question 1 is concerned with process documentation. Although process documentation is seldom found under that name for Open Source projects, many projects have indeed documented procedures for a variety of development tasks. The reasons for providing documentation are often related with making it easier for external contributors to perform certain tasks (e.g., submit a problem report or a so-called *patch file* with a correction), as well as with making certain tasks more reliable (release processes are a typical case). Our procedure for finding documentation for a task is based on searching through the Internet resources made available by a given project for the relevant information as follows:

1. Check project resources for documentation regarding the task. Perform an Internet search if necessary. Acceptable documentation are explicit documents (Web/Wiki pages, archived mail/forum messages) that contain direct instructions about performing the task. In some cases, these are presented as templates, or as a set of examples.
2. If no explicit documentation was found, check if a tool is being used to support the task. If this is the case, check if the tool can be used in a self-explanatory manner. If this is the case, this can be accepted as documentation.
3. If 30 minutes of search do not yield any positive results, stop searching.

The final step confines the evaluation to a time box. This is important because, in fact, we can never be sure that there is no documentation about a task, only that it could not be found with reasonable search effort.

The second question is concerned with how established a process is. Notice that this question is, to a large extent, independent from the first one, because undocumented processes can nonetheless be well established, and documented processes may not be followed as prescribed. In order to check for established processes, standard maturity models use the fact that such processes leave a *paper trail* behind them that can be used to observe them in a very reliable manner. If such a trail cannot be found, the odds are very high that the process is not established, e.g., not followed at all, or not followed in a consistent manner. Strictly speaking, of course, a paper trail cannot be found for OSS processes, but a data trail is often seen when looking at the diverse data repositories that belong to a project, such as:

- Internetbased tools, if the process is supported by a tool. For example, such processes as defect reporting and issue management can be analyzed by looking at the discussions stored in a project's bug/issue tracking system.
- Mailing lists, forums, Wikis, etc, used by community members to collaborate while performing the process. These repositories are useful, for instance, to track decision-related processes such as release planning, or to follow the interaction between developers and testers in preparation for a release.
- Internet-based repositories used to publish the results of a process, such as versioning repositories or download servers.

The procedure used to evaluate how established a process is consists of identifying specific instances of process execution in the potential process trail:

1. Determine the period of time the process has been/was active, by looking at the dates for the identified instances.
2. Identify instances where the process was successfully completed.
3. Identify instances where the process was not successfully completed/was left unfinished.
4. Identify currently running instances.
5. Use the identified instances to classify the process (see below).
6. If the number of instances available is large, the analysis can be performed by randomly sampling a smaller number of them.

The outcome of this evaluation should be one of the following four possible results:

1. *No established process:* no data trail found, or too few instances to be representative.
2. *Dead process:* tried at some point, but no evidence of continued use, no instances currently active.
3. *Young/immature process:* introduced recently, few actual instances, but instances appear active.
4. *Established process:* many successful completed instances, significant number of active instances.

The third question, which is subordinated to the previous one, refers to the consistency with which a process is executed over time. Clearly, this question can also be answered by looking at the process trail in order to sample instances of the established process for consistency. The purpose of this inspection is to look for potential significant variations in the way individual instances are executed. The evaluation should result in one of the following values:

1. *Not applicable:* no established process.
2. *Low consistency:* instances vary strongly in the way they are executed.
3. *High consistency:* relatively few variations between instances.

The fourth question has to do with the degree of coincidence between the documented process and the process that is actually executed. It is the last question of those concerned with the process maturity in itself, and depends on the previous ones being answered in a positive way. The evaluation procedure, of course, consists of comparing a representative number of instances of the process with the identified process documentation. Possible results for this evaluation are:

1. *Not applicable:* no documented process, no consistent process.
2. *Low agreement:* low agreement between documentation and established practice.
3. *High agreement:* high agreement between documentation and established practice.

The fifth and final question is concerned with how adequate the process is for the task it is intended for. This is, of course, a difficult question, not only because it is specific to each particular task, but because experts often disagree regarding the practices that are appropriate for a certain task. Our approach to handling this problem is to provide a list of additional questions that address the specificities of every task. These questions are normally not comprehensive, but provide a minimum checklist that helps to make sure that essential aspects of the corresponding process are being taken into account. We see these questions only as complementary to the first four assessment questions, because, clearly, if a process is established in the sense defined above, it is probably adequate to a certain measure, given how pragmatic OSS communities usually are.

4.3   Process Areas Currently Covered by QualOSS

As already mentioned, the QualOSS process evaluation covers a number of software development related tasks that are usually important for the success of an OSS project. The following table lists the tasks that are currently covered (left column) and provides a brief description for each of them, together with some information about where their process data trail could be found (right column). This is just an initial selection of tasks, which we are likely to extend as we gain experience with the process evaluation.

Task	*Description and Evidence Sources*
Change submission	Submit changes (e.g., defect corrections, enhancements), typically in the form of so-called patch files, to the project for potential inclusion. This task is restricted to changes proposed by community members who do not have commit rights to the main project versioning repository, and thus cannot change the project's code directly. Common methods used to submit changes include sending them to a mailing list, putting them in an issue tracking system, or, more recently, publishing modified code using a distributed version control system. After identifying the method used by a project, individual change submission instances can be studied using the generic evaluation procedure.
Review changes submitted by the community	This task is complementary to the previous task, namely, changes submitted by community members must be reviewed and either rejected with an appropriate justification, or accepted and integrated into the project's main code repository. This task can be analyzed in a way similar to the previous task.

Task	Description and Evidence Sources
Promote actively contributing members of the community to committers	Community members who provide valuable contributions to the project over a period of time often receive rights to contribute directly to a project's code repository. Instances of this process can sometimes be seen on a project's development mailing lists.
Review changes by committers	In some projects, changes proposed by developers with direct commit rights are also subject to review by other community members. This type of peer reviews can significantly contribute to code quality. This process can be evaluated by looking at the project's change log files or at the log messages written when committing changes to the code repository.
Propose significant enhancements	Some projects have disciplined processes that allow community members to formally propose enhancements for discussion by the community. Enhancement proposals may take many forms, including web pages, Wiki pages, and messages submitted to a mailing list or forum.
Report and handle issues with the product	For obvious reasons, this process is present in almost all Open Source projects in some form or another. Except for very small projects, this task is normally supported by an issue tracking system, in which case process instances correspond to the reports in the system, as well as their accompanying discussions. Small projects may handle this through a mailing list, in which case instances are the messages reporting the problem and the discussions following it.
Test the program or programs produced by the project	Most projects doing repeatable testing do it by defining an automated test suite. If no test suite is available, there may be explicitly defined manual test cases, but this is much less likely to happen. Test suites and defined test cases are normally part of the source code and can be found in the code repository. Instances of this process are test reports, either created automatically by running the test suite or manually.
Decide at which point in time a release will be made.	Either releases are done on a time-based fashion or based on a feature "road map". Instances of any of these two documents can often be found as part of a project's web or Wiki pages, or, occasionally, as messages to a certain mailing list or forum.

Task	Description and Evidence Sources
Release new versions of the product	Release processes in Open Source often include the creation of a number of alpha, beta and release-candidate versions that are delivered by the developers in order to obtain feedback from the community (active users of an OSS system are often willing to test these versions and report about problems they may find). Release processes also often include running a test suite or performing other forms of formal testing. This process can be followed by looking at release announcements for preliminary versions in a project's mailing lists or forums. Actual releases can be easily found in software download repositories.
Backport corrections in the current release to previous stable releases	When a stable and an unstable (development) branch of a project are maintained simultaneously, so-called *backports* are often necessary that move corrections or selected improvements made to the development branch into the stable branch. Backports are often announced in project mailing lists or forums.

5 Initial Experience with the QualOSS Process Evaluation

To this date, our experience with the QualOSS process evaluation is still quite limited, since we have applied it to only a handful of projects so far. A larger number of full QualOSS OSS assessments—which include the process assessment—is planned for the final, evaluation phase of the QualOSS project. We expect this effort to result in significant adjustments to the process assessment framework, as we better understand its limitations and improve it accordingly.

Nonetheless, our current experience has already taught us some valuable lessons:

– In its current form, the QualOSS process evaluation can be applied to small to medium OSS projects in about six hours of work. This makes its costs reasonable for a number of purposes, including comparison when selecting between OSS alternatives. A caveat here is that, so far, evaluations have been conducted exclusively by an OSS and process expert. We still have to evaluate our approach when applied by other assessors who may lack this expertise. This includes, among other aspects, studying inter-rater reliability in this context.
– The time box limitation of 30 minutes of searching may lead to important information being missed. One alternative for handling the collection of information about a task would be to ask the community directly, for example, by writing to an appropriate mailing list. This would not only make this aspect of the process evaluation fairer, but would potentially create opportunities for the community to learn from the evaluation and improve based upon it.

- In some cases, the number of instances of a particular task is too high for manual inspection. For example, some projects have databases of reported issues that have been operating for years and contain thousands of reports. So far, we have analyzed such data repositories by manually choosing a small number of instances "at random", but this method is clearly unsatisfactory due to the high risk of introducing biases. Ideally, we should be able to guarantee that we did a fair, random sample, and that the number of instances observed is representative. We still have to do more research in appropriate methods for this purpose, and, potentially, provide software tools to assist this procedure.

- The importance of some of the tasks listed in the previous section may vary depending on the size of the evaluated project. For instance, many small OSS projects have a single maintainer who is the only person with access to the main versioning repository. Such projects will rarely, if ever, accept new permanent contributors, and thus having a defined process for this purpose would be simply unnecessary. On the other hand, large projects with tens or even hundreds of official developers definitely require an explicit process for accepting new members. For this reason, we are considering the idea of giving variable importance to different tasks depending on such characteristics of a project as its number of active contributors or its code size.

Future versions of the QualOSS process evaluation framework are likely to incorporate enhancements based on the previous observations.

6   Conclusions and Future Work

The purpose of the QualOSS project is to produce a comprehensive quality model for assessing OSS projects. In this paper, we have presented a small portion of this work, namely, a process evaluation framework aimed at OSS. We expect OSS process evaluation to provide a better foundation for judging a community's ability to deliver high-quality software, as well as its long-term sustainability ("will this project exist in 10 years?"). Indeed, sustainability of suppliers is critical to many stakeholders, and is also a problem with commercial software. For example, the European defense consortium EADS decided to turn a critical piece of software into OSS in order to become independent of specific suppliers [11].

Moreover, highly regulated industries, such as the automotive, medical, or pharmaceutical industries, have established standards for evaluating software, which include assessment of the supplier [3] [5]. These industries often find it problematic to use OSS, because there is little support for the assessments required by their quality standards. Consequently, we believe that OSS assessment models that include a process assessment may help to increase the adoption of OSS in these industries.

As mentioned in Section 5, our experience with applying the QualOSS process assessment is still very limited. The final, evaluation phase of the QualOSS project will provide us with a valuable opportunity to introduce some initial improvements—such as those suggested in Section 5—as well as to collect more experience with using the process evaluation framework. We expect this experience to allow us to produce a much more robust and reliable framework during the next few months.

Acknowledgments

This work was supported in part by the EU QualOSS project (grant number: 033547, IST-2005-2.5.5). We would like to thank Sonnhild Namingha, from Fraunhofer IESE, for proofreading this paper.

References

[1]   Business Readiness Rating, http://www.openbrr.org/ (last check March 9, 2009)
[2]   Cap Gemini: OSS Partner Portal. Internet address,
      http://www.osspartner.com/ (last check March 9, 2009)
[3]   International Society for Pharmaceutical Engineering (ISPE): Good Automated Manufacturing Practice (GAMP-4) Supplier Guide for Validation of Automated Systems in Pharmaceutical Manufacture (1995)
[4]   ISO/IEC 15504-5:2006, Software Process Improvement and Capability Determination, Part 5
[5]   ISO/IEC 61508:1998, Functional safety of electrical/electronic/programmable electronic safety-related systems
[6]   ISO/IEC 9126 International Standard, Software engineering – Product quality, Part 1: Quality model (2001)
[7]   Michlmayr, M.: Software Process Maturity and the Success of Free Software Projects. In: Zieliński, K., Szmuc, T. (eds.) Software Engineering: Evolution and Emerging Technologies
[8]   Navica Software Web Site, http://www.navicasoft.com/ (last check March 9, 2009)
[9]   Qualification and Selection of Open Source software (QSOS) Web Site,
      http://www.qsos.org/ (last check March 9, 2009)
[10] Software Engineering Institute (SEI): Capability Maturity Model Integration (CMMI) for Development, Version 1.2 (2006)
[11] TOPCASED: Toolkit in Open Source for Critical Applications & Systems Development,
      http://www.topcased.org/ (last check March 13, 2009)

Innovation Process Design: A Change Management and Innovation Dimension Perspective

Thomas Peisl[1], Veronika Reger[1], and Juergen Schmied[2]

[1] University of Applied Sciences Muenchen, Department of Business Administration,
Am Stadtpark 20, 81243 Munich, Germany
tpeisl@hm.edu, vreger@hm.edu
[2] Anywhere.24 GmbH, Lindberghstr. 11, 82178 Puchheim, Germany
j.schmied@anywhere24.com

Abstract. The authors propose an innovative approach to the management of innovation integrating business, process, and maturity dimensions. Core element of the concept is the adaptation of ISO/IEC 15504 to the innovation process including 14 innovation drivers. Two managerial models are applied to conceptualize and visualize the respective innovation strategies, the Balanced Scorecard and a Barriers in Change Processes Model. An illustrative case study shows a practical implementation process.

Keywords: Innovation management, Innovation Processes, Change Management, Maturity Models, Organizational Maturity, CMMI, ICE, ISO/IEC 15504.

1 Introduction

Most organizations face an inherent structural conflict between holistic strategy and functional organizational design. A successfully linked strategic planning and budgeting process depends not only on integrating all the entities of an enterprise, but also on reconciling long-term goals with short-term realities. A potential solution is using strategic themes to identify a portfolio of strategic innovation initiatives and, based on a dynamic quantitative and qualitative process analysis, creating a separate new class of innovation centred initiatives. Immelt (2006) launched a GE corporate initiative to drive growth through innovation called 'imagination breakthroughs'. Davenport (2007) argues that "the frontier for using data to make decisions has shifted dramatically". High-performing organizations are starting to build their competitive strategies around data-driven insights that will in turn generate impressive business results. They identified analytics as key for superior performance through sophisticated quantitative and statistical analysis as well as predictive modelling. Sawhney, Wolcott & Arroniz (2006, p.76) propose a holistic definition of business innovation as "the creation of substantial new value for customers and the firm [and, implicitly, the stakeholders] by creatively changing one or more dimensions of the business system". The quest for new value is confirmed by Kim & Mauborgne (2005, p. 17): "Value innovation requires companies to orient the whole system toward achieving a leap in value for both buyers and themselves." In this context, value innovation is about driving costs down while creating surplus on value for customers and stakeholders.

R.V. O'Connor et al. (Eds.): EuroSPI 2009, CCIS 42, pp. 117–127, 2009.

The concept of connecting innovation and process capability combines both, the challenge of developing competitive strategies by introducing innovative value propositions as well as innovation process measurements by visualizing innovation capability. The objective of this research is to illuminate how to leverage the power of analytics in measuring capability in innovation processes.

In general, improvements in innovation processes have been sought through either increasing the budget for R&D or the implementation of best practices. Dooley, Subra & Anderson (2001, p. 25) define a "best practice as a tactic or method [chosen to perform a particular task, and/or to meet a particular objective] that has been shown through real life implementation to be successful". Booz Allen Hamilton confirmed in their 2006 study on Global Innovation 1000 that "higher investments in R&D do not automatically lead to an increase in corporate performance, and a high number of patents do not necessarily lead to higher profits". Research studies and management thinkers have developed a large number of best practices, either via description or prescription that could be used in organizations to improve the innovation process. The recognized challenge in importing best practices for any organization is the fact that in order to successfully implement an innovation strategy it is not only the practice but also the issues of capability and diffusion. The authors hypothesize that well performed practices and processes that are widely and continuously applied in the organization lead to a higher rate of successful innovations.

It is the objective of this research paper to propose a holistic Innovation Capability dEtermination Model based on the ISO/IEC 15504 that integrates the change management dimension.

This paper includes:

- Extension of ISO/IEC 15504 to innovation
- Application of a model of barriers in change management processes
- Design of an integrated design of a process reference model to determine the innovation capability of organization.
- Introduction to and an overview of the Innovation Capability dEtermination (ICE) model for improvements in innovation.
- Adaptation of the Balanced Scorecard Approach of Connected Innovation Driver Processes.
- Proposal of an Applied Research Framework.

2   Concept

2.1   Idea to Extend ISO/IEC 15504 to Innovation

The ISO/IEC 15504 capability construct has proven to have good validity in predicting process performance in various industries, like Automotive Spice, Coso Spice, etc. The authors argue that it is reasonable to use the capability dimension and propose a new process reference model for innovation. The application of a new reference model to the existing capability construct can be used to facilitate the latent conflict of interest between technical innovation and controlling by proposing a joint communication platform. The ISO framework is a widely used and accepted method in the software engineering domain (one of the drivers for technological innovation), whereas the methods and tools of strategic management (the base practices to assess process capability) are usually the domain of business strategists. The result of our research about applying the concept of ISO/IEC 15504 to innovation management was first published in Peisl, Schmied (2007 and 2008) and is further detailed in this paper (see figure 1).

PRIMARY Life Cycle Processes	ORGANIZATIONAL Life Cycle Processes
Idea to Innovation Process Group (IIP) IIP.1 Idea Generation Process IIP.2 Concept Evaluation Process IIP.3 Concept Implementation Process IIP.4 Innovation Piloting Process IIP.5 Innovation Diffusion Process	**Innovation Objective Analysis and Decision Process Group (IAD)** IAD.1 Innovation System Objectives Analysis Process IAD.2 Innovation System Improvement Process IAD.3 Innovation System Controlling Process
Connected Innovation Driver Process Group (CID) **Customer Innovation Drivers** CID.1 Product or Service Innovation Process CID.2 Solution Innovation Process CID.3 Customer and Market Innovation Process CID.4 Brand and Marketing Innovation Process CID.5 Value Capture Innovation Process CID.6 Customer Experience Innovation Process	**Innovation Management Process Group (IMA)** IMA.1 New Venture Management Process IMA.2 Management of Innovation projects Process IMA.3 Conflict Management Process IMA.4 Market research Process IMA.5 Customer Relationship Process
Financial Innovation Drivers CID.7 Balance Sheet Innovation Process	**Human Resource Process Group (HRP)** HRP.1 Knowledge Management Process HRP.2 Skills Management Process HRP.3 Motivation Management Process HRP.4 Distributed Team Management Process HRP.5 Team communication Process HRP.6 Learning culture Management Process
Business Innovation Drivers CID.8 Value Chain Innovation Process CID.9 Process Innovation Process CID.10 Distribution Innovation Process CID.11 Business Design Innovation Process	
Learning and growth Innovation Drivers CID.12 Platform Innovation Process CID.13 Networking Innovation Process CID.14 Human Resource Innovation Process	**BUSINESS RESOURCE Processes (BRP)** BRP.1 Analytical Tools BRP.2 Implementation Tools

Fig. 1. ICE Process Reference Model

2.2   Application of a Model of Barriers in Change Management Processes

Any change process creates barriers because of the human behavior to resist change. Any innovation process results in organizational change and, therefore, creates barriers. The understanding of successful innovation process design requires a holistic approach to change management, i.e. the proposed model of barriers in transformation processes, as well as an integrated view on innovation dimensions. More than ever before, organizations need to innovate to sustain growth. Despite a long history of extensive discussions in academia and business innovation is all too often accidental rather than intentional. Research shows that organizations do not lack ideas to drive new product or service introductions but structured ways to allocate resources on the right innovation initiative.

The authors build their concept on a model defining three dimensions of barriers, i.e. structural, performance, and value perspectives explaining why change processes within organizations may fail (Peisl, 1995; Hopfenbeck, Peisl, Müller, 2001). Key findings of this model include (see also figure 2):

- Structured processes and well defined metrics are essential to create an innovative organizational culture.
- Successful implementation of innovation processes requires two perspectives: An organizational and an individual perspective.
- The individual dimension includes human resource capability and motivation leading to creativity.
- The organizational dimension includes processes, metrics and value systems leading to an open innovation organizational culture.

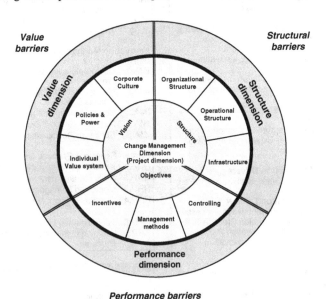

Fig. 2. Three dimensions of barriers in change processes

The purpose of this paper is to link the change management (i.e. business) challenge to reduce or eliminate barriers in transformation processes with the innovation capability perspective to create an effective innovation process design. In order to achieve the objectives the authors generalize the concept of capability in SPICE beyond the software and systems engineering domain and propose a process reference model for evaluating the innovation capability of organizations. The authors define the concept of capability as the degree to which a process is performed, managed, established, predicted, and continuously optimized (ISO/IEC 15504-2). In a second stage the Innovation Capability dEtermination (ICE) model provides an organizational innovation maturity concept based on ISO/IEC 15504-7. It provides a framework to identify, prioritize, and describe the status quo as well as necessary changes to develop an organization's innovation capabilities and to develop better products and services and so to achieve the best market position and business success.

The generic innovation process from idea generation to innovation diffusion (IIP), i.e. the successful – and profitable – positioning of new products and services in the market, includes five steps:

1. idea generation,
2. concept evaluation,
3. concept implementation,
4. innovation piloting, and
5. innovation diffusion

The Analysis of organizational objectives generates the initial input for IIP, combined with a consequent process improvement across all steps and a system controlling (IAD). The authors integrate a filter, including 14 innovation dimensions (CIDs), previous to the idea generation process, to match the organizational objectives with the innovation dimensions and therefore to focus the idea generation process on selected areas (for a complete overview of the process reference model see figure 1).

The CIDs are based on the dimensions of the model of barriers in transformation processes and further literature research, and are structured according to the perspectives of the balanced scorecard (see figure 4):

- financial,
- customer,
- business process, and
- learning and growth perspective.

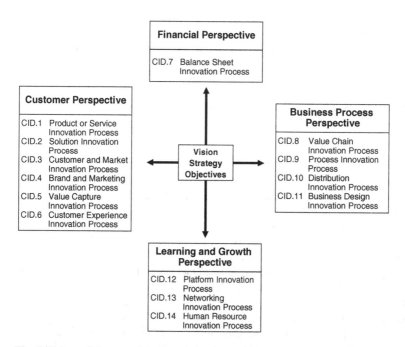

Fig. 3. Balanced Scorecard Approach for Connected Innovation Driver Processes

In conjunction with innovation management, human resource processes, and analytical and implementation tools from the business area a holistic innovation process design is established.

The ICE Model can support organizations to prioritize innovation possibilities by the use of an Innovation opportunity matrix which illustrates the strategic attractiveness of the innovation and the ROCE (return on capital employed). Thus an ideal allocation of scarce resources to the most promising innovation opportunities can be facilitated (see figure 4).

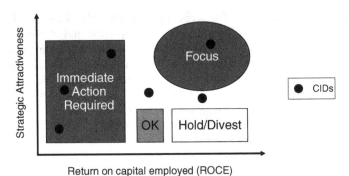

Fig. 4. Innovation Opportunity Matrix

In the following chapter we will demonstrate the benefit of the ICE model exemplified with the virtual organization FindYourWay AG taken from Schmied, Wentzel, Gerdom, Hehn, 2008.

In further research projects the ICE model will be implemented in various industries with representative small and medium-sized enterprises.

3   Applied Research Framework

3.1   The FindYourWay AG

The FindYourWay AG is a medium-sized organization founded in the 50s. At the beginning the organization was focused on electronic developments, the most important products were radios and televisions. Today the software development became an important part of the product development portfolio. The organization is focused on radios and navigation systems in the automotive industry and therefore generates the main turnover with these products. Worldwide FindYourWay AG employs more than 1000 people at various locations globally.

Core product development takes place in Germany. However, manufacturing locations exist in Portugal and China. In the main target markets like the USA, France, and Japan Sales and Service locations have been established.

Recently FindYourWay AG relocated parts of the applied research and development to Eastern Europe and set-up a location in Estonia. This new unit is focusing on the development of software tools and tests. Furthermore the relocation of development of reusable software libraries is planed for the near future. For the development additional services of external employees and partners are needed.

In the past FindYourWay AG had some major difficulties with the accurate implementation of projects. For example, an important customer, the Alemannischer Lastwagen Verbund (ALV), canceled an order for the development of a new generation of navigation systems. The key reasons were among others:

- customer requirements were partly not or partly too late considered
- the effort to realize important functions was underestimated
- the performance of the system was insufficient
- the stability of the navigation was insufficient.

The cancelation of this project caused a financial loss for FindYourWay AG and especially a massive loss of confidence on the part of ALV. In order to sustain the collaboration with FindYourWay AG ALV requires a process improvement project and medium-term a companywide CMMI Capability Level 2 for all process areas with CMMI Maturity Level 2 and some selected processes on CMMI Maturity Level 3. In particular ALV challenged FindYourWay management with the concept of Open Innovation and demanded a clear innovation concept.

The following organizations, projects, persons, and tools are involved in the project improvement project:

Organizations:
- Alemannischer Lastwagen Verbund (ALV)
  (Key customer of FindYourWay AG)
- FindYourWay AG
  (In the organization the process improvement project is conducted)
- process!park (external consulting organization)

Tools:
- Capability Maturity Model Integration for Development (CMMI-Dev)
- Innovation Capability dEtermination model
- Balanced Scorecard

In the meanwhile the initial assessment, the CMMI based improvement project and the final CMMI Scampi Appraisal was conducted by the external consulting company process!park (for further information please see: Schmied et. al. 2008).

Faced with the prospects of slow growth, commoditization and global competition, FindYourWay AG has now emphasized innovation as critical to their future success. Therefore the ICE model is applied in addition to CMMI for Development for innovation process improvement. In the following chapters the authors describe the implementation of the Idea to Innovation processes (IIP) (see figure 3).

3.2 Innovation Capability dEtermination

3.2.1 Vision, Mission and Objectives

First of all FindYourWay AG needs to define their organizational vision, mission and objectives. A clear and consequent definition of the objectives is the prerequisite of any innovation process.

Vision of FindYourWay AG:

- Advantage through integrated intelligent communication

Mission of the FindYourWay AG:

- Providing essential solutions for mobility

Objectives of the FindYourWay AG:

- The organizational objectives are allocated to the four dimensions of the balanced scorecard; financial, customer, process, and leaning and growth dimension (Figure 5 shows an excerpt of the organizational objectives).

Based on the organization objectives (see figure 6) FindYourWay AG has to derive innovation objectives. The Connected Innovation Driver Process Group includes 14 drivers of innovation and can be used for prioritization of innovation objectives (Remark: The prioritization of the innovation objectives will be done in the Concept Evaluation process).

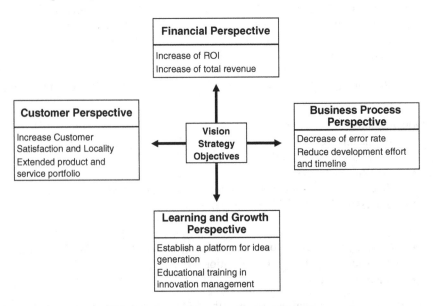

Fig. 5. Excerpt of the organizational objectives

Within a brainstorming session of the strategic business team (CEO, Head of product management, head of product development, head of sales management) the following four Connected Innovation Driver Processes were identified:

1. CID.1 Product and Service Innovation Process (→ Extended product and service portfolio)
2. CID.3 Customer and Market Innovation Process (→ Extended product and service portfolio)
3. CID.9 Process Innovation Process (→ Decrease of error rate, → Reduce development effort and timeline)
4. CID.14 Human Resource Innovation Process (→ Educational training in innovation management)

3.2.2 Idea Generation

The Idea Generation process (see figure 6) can only be efficient if you use the CID processes as a strategic filter to focus the idea generation process on selected areas.

FindYourWay AG: A brainstorming session together with the CEO, Head of product management, Head of product development, Head of sales management and representatives of the main customer ALV is carried out to generate ideas within the defined innovation dimensions (CID.1, CID.3, CID.9, CID.14).

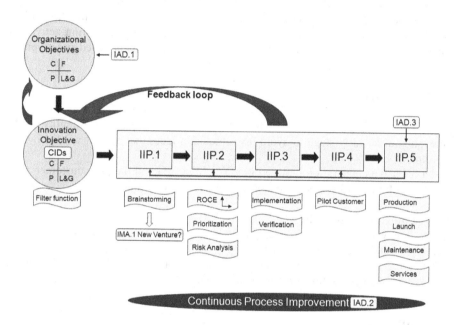

Fig. 6. Innovation Process (FindYourWay AG)

As an example the main results for CID.1 Product and Service Innovation Process are:

- Next generation of navigation system:
    - Geo Business Intelligence: Connection between meta data about geographical objects (e.g. sights) and the navigation system
- Enhancement of navigation system to a holistic logistic solution:
    - E.g. localization of commercial vehicles, optimization of routing (e.g. distance) and capacity and availability management

If ideas don't fit into the current innovation objectives the organization should consider about a new venture (see IMA.1 New Venture Management).

3.2.3 Concept Evaluation

The main focus of Concept Evaluation (see figure 6) is a prioritization of the ideas. Criteria for prioritization could be e.g.

- a detailed analysis of the Return-On-Capital-Employed
- technical feasibility
- risk analysis in legal and administrative aspects

According to the Concept Evaluation FindYourWay AG will currently focus their innovation processes on the development of a holistic logistic solution.

3.2.4 Concept Implementation

FindYourWay AG realizes the holistic logistic solution according to the system life-cycle model (requirements analysis, design, implementation, verification activities), which was defined formerly within the CMMI for Development based improvement project.

3.2.5 Innovation Piloting

Within the Innovation Piloting Process e.g. a prototype of the idea is evaluated together with the piloting customer. It is important to ensure the profitability of the innovation at an early stage to avoid investments in ideas that are not needed by any customer.

An intensive cooperation between FindYourWay AG and the pilot customer ALV is the basis for an early piloting and objective oriented investments.

3.2.6 Innovation Diffusion

For the Innovation Diffusion a detailed market introduction plan including marketing and sales strategy has to be formulated.

Therefore FindYourWay AG needs to allocate resources (e.g. financial and human resources) to launch the holistic logistic solution.

4 Summary

In this research paper the authors propose an integrated view on innovation based on business tools, change management, and process maturity and capability. The brief case study provides an initial understanding on how to implement and visualize innovation initiatives in an open innovation context. The need to innovation and continuously create value to customers and stakeholders is based on the understanding that processes and process measurements shape culture and innovative behavior in all organizational dimensions. In applying change management models, the balanced scorecard, and ISO/IEC 15504 the authors integrate well-known instruments and design a new concept that still needs verification across industries. This paper is a work in process documentation and we would like to invite interested organizations to join in our applied research project.

References

Booz Allen Hamilton: The Customer Connection: The Global Innovation 1,000 (2007), http://www.boozallen.com/news/2007Innovation1000
Davenport, Harris: Competing on Analytics: The New Science of Winning. HBS Press Book (2007)

Dooley, Subra, Anderson: Maturity and its impact on new product development project performance. Research in Engineering Design 13(1) (August 2001)

Hopfenbeck, Peisl, Müller: Wissensbasiertes Management, Managementkonzepte in der Internet Ökonomie. MI Verlag (2001)

Immelt: Growth as a Process. Harvard Business Review, 69 (June 2006)

ISO/IEC 15504-2:2003: "Information technology – Process assessment – Part 2: Performing an Assessment"

ISO/IEC TR 15504-7:2008: "Information technology – Process assessment – Part 7: Assessment of Organizational Maturity"

Kim, Mauborgne: Blue Ocean Strategy. How to create uncontested market space and make the competition irrelevant. Harvard Business School Publishing Corporation, Boston (2005)

Kaplan, Norton: The balanced Scorecard. Translating Strategy into Action. HBS (1996)

Peisl: Barrieren in Veränderungsprozessen. In: Ein Erklärungsmodell für das Scheitern von Veränderungsprozessen in Mittel- und Großunternehmen. Dissertationsschrift (1995)

Peisl, Schmied: Connected Innovation: Innovation Capability dEtermination (ICE). In: International SPICE Days, Frankfurt/Main (2007)

Peisl, Schmied: Improvement through Innovation. In: International SPICE Days, Prag (2008)

Sawhney, Wolcott, Arroniz: The 12 Different Ways for Companies to Innovate. MIT Sloan Management Review 47(3), 75–81 (2006)

Schmied, Wentzel, Gerdom, Hehn: Mit CMMI Prozesse verbessern, dpunkt (2008)

Discovering Changes of the Change Control Board Process during a Software Development Project Using Process Mining

Jana Šamalíková, Jos J.M. Trienekens, Rob J. Kusters, and A.J.M.M. (Ton) Weijters

University of Technology Eindhoven
Department of Industrial Engineering & Innovation Sciences
P.O. Box 513, 5600 MB Eindhoven, NL
{J.Samalikova,J.J.M.Trienekens,R.J.Kusters,
A.J.M.M.Weijters}@tue.nl

Abstract. During a software process improvement program, the current state of software development processes is being assessed and improvement actions are being determined. However, these improvement actions are based on process models obtained during interviews and document studies, e.g. quality manuals. Such improvements are scarcely based on the practical way of working in an organization; they do not take into account shortcuts made due to e.g. time pressure. Becoming conscious about the presence of such deviations and understanding their causes and impacts, consequences for particular software process improvement activities in a particular organization could be proposed. This paper reports on the application of process mining techniques to discover shortcomings in the Change Control Board process in an organization during the different lifecycle phases and to determine improvement activities.

Keywords: Process mining, performance analysis, software process improvement.

1 Introduction

The quality of software can currently be accomplished through various approaches and techniques. One of the main quality improvement approaches focuses on the assessment and subsequent improvement of the software development process (e.g. CMMI). The assumption is that a structured way of developing software products prevents injecting errors and defects into software. Software process improvement models focus on improving development processes which are obtained e.g. during interviews and the study of document, such as quality manuals. However, such processes descriptions are often different from the real practice within an organization, for example due to the lack of discipline or time pressure. Analyzing information stored in a software project database or repository could reveal the "real" processes that developers are following, their deviations from a documented process model and also the causes and impacts of such deviations. Becoming conscious about the presence of the deviations and understanding their causes and impacts, consequences for particular software process improvement activities in a particular organization could be proposed.

R.V. O'Connor et al. (Eds.): EuroSPI 2009, CCIS 42, pp. 128–136, 2009.

The aim of this paper is to use process mining techniques to analyze the Change Control Board (CCB) process based on real data. We attempt to find whether the real executions of a CCB process in a particular organization deviate from the documented process as the project progresses. Knowing the "real" process and its differences from the documented process, we investigate what the possible implications are, and what type of advices can be given on the basis of the results, with respect to software process improvement.

2 Previous Research

During software development various kinds of data are recorded. Developers and managers are making use of these data in order to estimate and predict the results of the software development, to plan software development activities [8] and to steer the development process. In this project, we try to use this data as input for process mining techniques to get a better understanding what is really happening during software development.

Process mining is strongly related to the more general field data mining. The main difference between the two areas is the strong focus of process mining on processes. Process mining has already been applied in several case studies in different professional domains, e.g. in energy supply companies[5]. Regarding the software industry Cook et al. started to analyze the behavior of processes in software engineering from a theoretical point of view[2]. In [3] process mining approaches and techniques are presented in a framework for software development processes. A complete overview of recent research in the process mining area is beyond the scope of this paper, therefore we refer to [6] and http://www.processmining.org for additional information on the subject.

In a previous paper [4] we showed the possibility of applying process mining to a software development process. The process models were derived from data on actual 'real-practice' activities that are taking place. The case study revealed that although people tend to believe that specified and well-documented processes are followed, the real practice is different. The main finding was that a particular process, as specified in a Quality Manual, was not followed in 70% of the cases. In the case study in this paper, we analyze the process further in order to understand common patterns or circumstances, under which the development team makes shortcuts in the CCB process. More in particular we investigate the way the CCB process changes, i.e. deviates from the 'standard', during the subsequent phases in the software development life cycle.

3 Case Study

Projects under study are middleware embedded-software projects of a company X in the Netherlands. The company develops software components for consumer electronic devices. Over the past years the company reached level 3 of the Capability Maturity Model Integration (CMMI)[1]. This means that the organization is capable to define their software development processes and interrelated activities. As such, the environment offers opportunities for the application of process mining techniques.

The software development in company X follows a modified V-model (Figure 1). The V-model is a sequential software development model with emphasis on testing activities. Company X modified the model such that it is possible to the phases might start simultaneously or in the middle of progress of the previous phase. A permanent link between the phases is provided by *Architectural support*, which interrelates phases in order to provide information and support of one phase to the others.

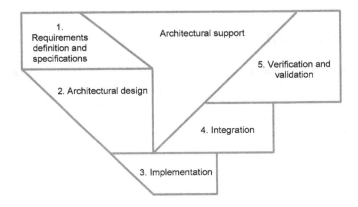

Fig. 1. Software development lifecycle in the company X

In this case study we analyzed the Change Control Board process of company X. The Change Control Board (CCB) process coordinates changes made to deliverables. The CCB tracks and records the status of each change request from its entry until its exit of the CCB process. The change requests are further referred to as defects.

The structure of the CCB process is sequential with possible rework in case of failing a task. The tasks are not executed in parallel, and each task is completed before the next task starts.

The flow of tasks of the CCB process is as follows:

Task 1.   The CI' defect is detected and submitted. The tester assigns attributes to the defect (e.g. priority, severity). Based on the importance, the defect is either:

        A.   further evaluated by the CCB board (Task 2),

        B.   or the defect will directly start with the *Analysis* task (Task 3).

Task 2.   The CCB board analyzes the defect and sends it to the required task depending on the need (*Analysis, Resolution, Evaluation*, or *Concluded* task), with the following possibilities:

        C.   The CI' defect is redirected to the *Concluded* task in case the defect is found duplicated, expected to be fixed in next release or out of the scope of the functionality required;

        D.   The defect is redirected to tasks *Analysis, Resolution*, or *Evaluation* depending on the need.

Task 3.   The task, i.e. either *Analysis, Resolution*, or *Evaluation*, starts to handle the CI's. When the task is completed, one of the four possibilities is chosen:

E. If the task's execution is successful then an important defect is directed to the CCB, and it waits to be redirected again to the next task, (it returns to Task 2)

F. If the task's execution is successful then a less important defect continues with the next logical task, for instance after *Analysis* it can be *Resolution*.

G. If the task was not successfully executed then an important defect is returned to the CCB for a re-evaluation (Task 2).

H. If the task was not successfully executed then a less important defect is handled again by the same task (Task 3)

Task 4.   Once all the tasks of the CCB process have been successfully carried out, the case of the defect is closed.

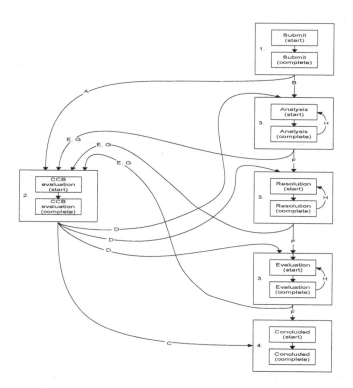

Fig. 2. CCB process model as described in the Quality Manual

Although the analysis is based on four projects, we selected one, project P, to illustrate the analysis process. In order to be able to control the development process of project P and to predict its outcome, the development team collects data about software defects. A consultant makes a copy of such database each week. Using this data, we attempted to retrieve non-trivial information that provides a useful insight into the CCB process. Having the insight that is based on the real behavior within the process, the organization could improve its CCB process.

4 Process Mining

Process mining has proven to be a valuable approach that provides new and objective insights into the way processes are actually carried out within organizations [7]. Taking a set of real executions (a so-called "event-log") as a starting point, these techniques attempt to extract non-trivial and useful information about the "real" process. The central object in process mining is a particular operational process, such as a review or change control process in a software development organization. Control over these processes is often supported by information systems that help to coordinate the steps that need to be performed in the course of the process. Examples of these information systems are Document and/or Version Management Systems.

The process mining of the CCB process as a whole (i.e. 6870 cases) revealed that in most of the cases (70%) *Analysis* task is skipped and the cases are being directly resolved [4]. We assumed that people tend to make such shortcuts in order to save time. As the project progresses, people feel time pressure because of the approaching deadline Our hypothesis is then that they decide to skip the *Analysis* task in order to save some time. We expected that the number of the cases skipping the *Analysis* increases towards the end of the project. In order to prove this hypothesis, we analyzed each lifecycle phase separately. Table 1 shows the number of cases per each lifecycle phase.

Table 1. Number of cases per lifecycle phase

	Number of cases	Number of cases skipping the Analysis	
Specification	543	408	75.14 %
Design	477	368	77.15 %
Implementation	1282	998	77.85 %
Component testing	470	371	78.94 %
Integration testing	862	531	61.60 %
System testing	1759	861	48.95 %
Customer testing	81	48	59.26 %
Consumer use	33	20	60.61 %
Not Applicable	1363	1173	86.06 %

Although, we expected the number of cases that are not handled according to the documented process increases towards the end of the project, the results of our analysis do not prove that. The number of such cases is similar from the Specification phase till the *Component testing*. A significant decrease is observed during the *System testing*. *Customer testing* and *Consumer use* contain both too little cases for any conclusions to be made.

5 Task Duration

In our case study, we focused on the time aspect of the CCB process. Namely, we analyzed the throughput time of the process and the duration of tasks per lifecycle phase. We compared the duration of the three tasks *Analysis, Resolution* and *Evaluation*. These tasks are described in detail by their *Start* and *End* events directly in the project database. We calculated the average duration of the tasks as the time elapsed between these two events. First, we considered all cases in the event-log. Figure 3 shows a graphical overview of the task duration for each of the lifecycle phases.

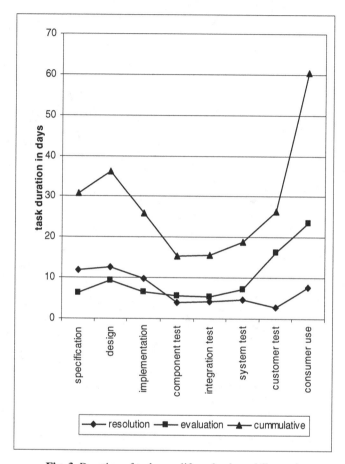

Fig. 3. Duration of tasks per lifecycle phase (all cases)

As we discovered in previous case study [4], majority of the cases does not conform to the specified process model by skipping the *Analysis* task. We were interested in the impact this deviation made on performance characteristics of the process, hence we examined such cases (as not analyzed cases) separately. Figure 4 shows a graphical overview of the results. The duration of the tasks *Resolution* and *Evaluation* is slightly longer than the average duration when considering all cases.

5.1 Different Durations of Tasks

Figure 3 shows that during the *Specification* and *Design* phase, the *Resolution* tasks take a large amount of time. A possible explanation to this could be that the product is not clearly defined and structured in the beginning of the project. Therefore, the *Analysis* could be more difficult and, as a result, not much executed.

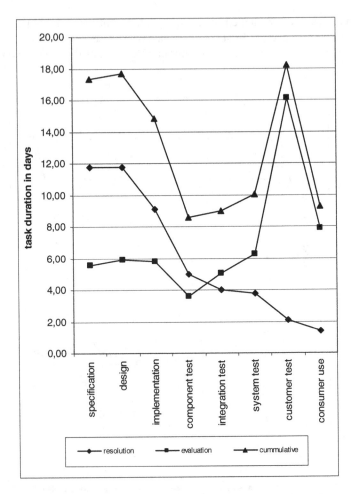

Fig. 4. Duration of tasks per lifecycle phase (not analyzed cases)

5.2 Drop in Duration of Tasks

On the other hand, the duration of the *Resolution* task significantly drops in the *Implementation* and *Component and Integration testing* phases, while the duration of the *Analysis* and *Evaluation* task increases. The decrease of the *Resolution* could be explained by the fact that the project had a fixed deadline. It was not possible to spend more time on the *Resolution* activity because of the fact that more time was simply not available. This hypothesis was also given by the organization that provided us with information prior to our analysis. However, this hypothesis does not explain the increase of the duration of the *Evaluation* task

5.3 Total Throughput Time

Considering the total throughput time of a case, the throughput time is the highest during the *Specification, Design, System testing, Customer testing* and *Consumer use* phases. During these phases, validation activities are being handled by involving external stakeholders. The participation of the external stakeholders requires synchronizing agendas of all involved parties. The external stakeholders' participation is mainly required during the *Analysis* and *Resolution* tasks. The duration of a task is calculated based on the start and end events in the database, hence it also includes the waiting time. The waiting time is then reflected in the increased duration of the tasks. The throughput time drops during the *Implementation, Component testing* and *Integration testing* during which the developers perform verification activities without contribution of the external stakeholders.

5.4 Duration in Other Projects

Besides the project P, we analyzed three other projects: P1 – P3. Each of them had more than 1000 cases. All of the projects P1 – P3 showed similar trend in task duration and the throughput time with respect to the verification and validation activities as observed in the project P.

6 Conclusions

In our case study, we showed that it is possible to use process mining techniques to get more insight into a selected software development process. We compared the duration of tasks and the total throughput time during different lifecycle phases. The results showed that the duration of the validation tasks involving external stakeholders are longer than the verification tasks performed without the external involvement. Possible implications for the software process improvement might be that meetings with the external partners are plan ahead, maybe on the regular basis. The problems with synchronizing different agendas are minimized and the project progresses more smoothly. Project issues are then solved more promptly without any extensive waiting times.

Although, we expected the number of cases that are not handled according to the documented process increases towards the end of the project, the results of our analysis do not prove that. The number of cases that do not comply with the documented model is overall high. This indicates that skipping the *Analysis* task is a structural problem. A decrease is observed during the System testing, possibly due to the fact that more attention to the handling of defects is given during this phase.

In the future projects, we have the intention to use process mining techniques to analyze other important aspects of software development processes.

References

1. CMMI Product Team. CMMI for Development, Version 1.2. CMU/SEI-2006-TR-008 (2006)
2. Cook, J.E., Wolf, A.L.: Discovering Models of Software Processes from Event-Based Data. ACM Transactions on Software Engineering and Methodology 7(3), 215–249 (1998)

3. Rubin, V., Günther, C.W., van der Aalst, W.M.P., Kindler, E., van Dongen, B.F., Schäfer, W.: Process Mining Framework for Software Processes. In: Wang, Q., Pfahl, D., Raffo, D.M. (eds.) ICSP 2007. LNCS, vol. 4470, pp. 169–181. Springer, Heidelberg (2007)
4. Šamalíková, J., Kusters, R., Trienekens, J., Weijters, T., Siemons, P.: Discovering the Change Control Process in a Software Development Environment using Process Mining. Submitted Information and Software technology journal (2008)
5. van Beest, N.R.T., Maruster, L.: A Process Mining Approach to Redesign Business Processes - A Case Study in Gas Industry. In: Proceedings of Proceedings of the Ninth International Symposium on Symbolic and Numeric Algorithms for Scientific Computing, SYNACS, pp. 541–548 (2007)
6. van der Aalst, W.M.P., van Dongen, B.F., Herbst, J., Maruster, L., Schimm, G.: Workflow mining: A survey of issues and approaches. Data & Knowledge Engineering 47(2), 237–267 (2003)
7. Weijters, A.J.M.M., van der Aalst, W.M.P., Alves de Medeiros, A.K.: Process Mining with the Heuristics Miner Algorithm 1. BETA Working Paper Series, WP 166. Eindhoven University of Technology, Eindhoven (2006)
8. Weiss, C., Premraj, R., Zimmermann, T., Zeller, A.: How Long Will It Take to Fix This Bug? In: Proceedings of MSR 2007: Proceedings of the Fourth International Workshop on Mining Software Repositories (2007)

Global Software Development Patterns for Project Management

Antti Välimäki[1], Jukka Kääriäinen[2], and Kai Koskimies[3]

[1] Metso Automation Inc, Tampere, Finland
Antti.Valimaki@metso.com
[2] VTT, Oulu, Finland
Jukka.Kaariainen@vtt.fi
[3] Tampere University of Technology, Tampere, Finland
Kai.Koskimies@tut.fi

Abstract. Global software development with the agile or waterfall development process has been taken into use in many companies. GSD offers benefits but also new challenges without known, documented solutions. The goal of this research is to present current best practices for GSD in the form of process patterns for project management, evaluated by using a scenario-based assessment method. The best practices have been collected from a large company operating in process automation. It is expected that the resulting pattern language helps other companies to improve their GSD processes by incorporating the patterns in the processes.

Keywords: Global Software Development, Agile, Organizational patterns, Process patterns, Assessment.

1 Introduction

Global software development (GSD) is reality in many companies. There are many benefits and motivations for using GSD such as access to the world-wide talent pool, cost savings, advances in infrastructure and software development tools, mergers and acquisitions and the need to be close to a local market [1]. However, there are also different challenges with communication, coordination and co-operation which make GSD more difficult than centralized development [1]. GSD has been widely used with the waterfall development process and, recently, it has been applied to agile development methods as well [2]. The experiences show that agile methods can be applied to GSD [3, 4].

Whether a traditional or an agile process model is used, the problems related to the nature of GSD have to be dealt with. Rather than developing a totally new GSD process that addresses these problems, a more appropriate approach is to try to come up with solutions to specific problems, and present these solutions in such a way that they can be easily integrated with existing processes. An obvious advantage of this approach is that a company need not adopt a new process model, but merely tune the existing process for GSD.

R.V. O'Connor et al. (Eds.): EuroSPI 2009, CCIS 42, pp. 137–148, 2009.

An attractive way to document proven solutions to specific development process problems is to use organizational patterns [5] (or process patterns [6]). A collection of such solutions can be further organized into process pattern languages [7]. A process pattern language need not cover the entire process, but it can concentrate on a certain viewpoint of the software development process. In this work the viewpoint is GSD: we derive a pattern language for project management in GSD (GSD Patterns). The solutions in these patterns have been mined from the practices that have been found to work well in a large company operating in the field of process automation.

In general, patterns represent knowledge that is validated by previous experience. However, if patterns are mined from a limited environment, as in our case, this argument does not hold. In this work we have evaluated the resulting patterns by using a scenario-based technique introduced in [8].

This paper is organised as follows: The next section describes our research approach, and the methods used. Section 3 presents the GSD pattern language. Section 4 discusses the evaluation results of the GSD pattern language. Finally, we discuss related work in Section 5 and conclude the paper in Section 6.

2   Research Approach

This section introduces the research approach which includes both the collection of process patterns and an assessment method for the pattern language.

2.1   Collecting Process Patterns

GSD patterns presented in this paper have been collected from industry and literature during studies [9, 10, and 11] and the pattern evaluation meetings in a large company operating in the sector of the process automation industry. The pattern evaluation meetings have also been organised with other companies. The total number of respondents in these studies has been 32 in questionnaires and 25 in interviews.

Each separate study has been started by choosing a certain software process area in which problems and best practices have been collected from the viewpoint of global software development. The best practices have been presented in the form of GSD patterns. In each study, the collection of case data has been done by using questionnaires and interviews. The framework for data collection is organised based on the concepts, practices or phases of the development process (referred to as framework items in the sequel) depending on the study area. For each framework item there have been three open-formed questions: what is good, what needs improvement and how to improve if there were no restrictions in the implementation. After the questionnaire, key persons were interviewed to get more detailed information about the case. The persons selected for the interviews represented project managers, product managers and project members. The interviewees worked in the company or in its partner companies. The framework was used as a checklist for the interviewer, leaving room for open discussion. Questionnaires and interviews produced raw data for analysis. The raw data has been processed and analysed by organising it based on the framework items. After that, proposed process patterns were created based on processed case data, related literature and workshops in the organization. To ensure that the patterns were feasible the proposed process patterns have been tentatively validated by discussing the patterns with key persons.

2.2 Evaluating Process Patterns

The evaluation technique used here for the pattern language is called Q-PAM [8]. The basic idea of Q-PAM is to use scenarios as test cases which are analyzed against the patterns, in the same way as scenarios have been used in ATAM [12] for assessing the quality attributes of software architecture.

The first step in Q-PAM is to create a quality profile for the process (here, a process pattern language). The quality profile is a set of quality factors considered essential in the assessment of the process. The quality profile thus depends not only on the quality requirements of the process, but also on the purpose of the assessment: the same process may be assessed with different profiles. Quality profiles are assumed to be obtained by extracting them from quality attribute lists available in standards e.g. ISO 9126 [13].

When the quality profile has been constructed, each quality attribute is associated with scenarios that serve as test cases for the quality attribute. A scenario is a concrete desired situation in an imaginary instance of the process where the existence or non-existence of the required quality property can be verified. Scenarios can also be prioritized for more focused processing, if needed.

The next step is the actual quality analysis. Each (possibly prioritized) scenario is analyzed against the process patterns: which patterns (if any) support the realization of the scenario, and which patterns counteract the scenario (if any). A tag is attached to the scenario, characterizing the extent to which the pattern language is considered to pass the scenario test, on the basis of the analysis.

3 GSD Pattern Language

In this section we introduce the GSD pattern language and present the organisation of the GSD patterns based on PRINCE2 which is a project management method [14].

3.1 GSD Patterns

The purpose of the Global Software Development for Project Management Pattern Language is to enhance performance of project management work through improved global software project management practices. The GSD Pattern Language includes 18 process patterns which have been found to be important in the area of project management in GSD. The current version of GSD Pattern Language includes process patterns supporting both traditional waterfall and agile project management.

GSD patterns are presented in Table 1. The first column contains the name of the pattern, the second describes the problem the pattern is supposed to solve, and the last column gives the solution outline of the pattern. An example of a more detailed pattern is in Table 2.

Table 1. GSD Patterns for project management

ID-Name	Problem(s)	Solution outline
01-GSD Strategy	A lack of a company level GSD strategy.	List the reasons and motivation to start GSD based development in a company. Make a short and long term plan about GSD. Find out the competence of different sites and make a SWOT and risk analysis for GSD strategy. Also measure the real costs of GSD.
02-Fuzzy Front End	Unclear how to gather product needs globally from external and internal customers and how to form plans and change requests from these needs.	The needs of different customers will be gathered to a global database. It is also important to have the possibility for global access regardless of time and place as well as have the possibility to use a discussion forum inside the tool. Product managers will go through gathered needs and make decisions about them with e.g. architects. A new feature or requirement will be made if it is accepted in a decision meeting. Product managers will make a Road Map and a Business plan for a product including many features. These features will be realized in development projects.
03-Communicate Early	What is the goal of a GSD project and who are the members of a project? Lack of trust.	Arrange kick-off meeting for all relevant members. Present common goal and motivation of this project and present release plan made by **Divide and Conquer with Iterations**. Also present responsibilities made by **Work Allocation**. Present used **Common Processes** and **Common Repositories and Tools.** Organize leisure activities for teams to improve team spirit.
04-Divide and Conquer with Iterations		See an example below (Table 2).
05-Key Roles in Sites	Difficult to know who to contact in different sites with your questions.	A project manager will have negotiations with site managers or other supervisors about team members before final decisions. Also needed roles will be formed in every site (e.g. Site project Manager, Architect, IT Support, Quality assurance etc.) The main site person is in a leading position and the persons from other sites will help to take care of the issues, tasks and responsibilities in their sites. Publish the whole project organization with roles for every site to improve communication. One person can have many roles in a project.
06-Communication Tools	Lack of communication, communication tools can also vary between sites.	Have reliable and common communication methods and tools in every site. Use different tools at the same time as net meeting to show information and project data, conference phones to have good sound and chat tool to discuss in written form if there are problems to understand e.g. English language used in other sites. Also train and motivate project members to use these tools.
07-Common Repositories and Tools	Separate Excel files are difficult to manage and project data is difficult to find, manage and synchronize between many sites.	Provide a common Application Lifecycle Management (ALM) tools for all project artefacts (documents, source code, bugs, guidelines etc.). ALM provides almost real-time traceability, reporting, visualization and access to needed information etc. for all users in different sites. It can be implemented as a single tool or it can be a group of different tools which has been integrated with each other. ALM tools can include means to support operation according to the organisation's processes and development methods (state models, process templates, workflows). Use different levels (team, project, and program) reports to improve visibility of status of projects.

Table 1. (*continued*)

08-Work Allocation	Work needs to be shared between sites with some criteria.	Find out what the **GSD Strategy** is in your company and check **Competence** information of persons in each site with help of site managers. Make **Architectural Work Allocation** and/or make **Phase- Based Work Allocation** and/or make **Feature Based Work Allocation** and/or other allocation according to some other criteria. Make a decision about division of work between sites according to a company's **GSD Strategy** and the above analysis.
09- Architect- ural Work Allocation	Work needs to be shared between sites with architectural criteria.	Check architectural analysis of your product and plan which site will be responsible for maintaining and increasing knowledge in some architectural area. Architectural area can also be a whole subsystem or part of a subsystem.
10-Phase- Based Work Allocation	Work needs to be shared between sites with phased-based criteria.	Check how phase- based work allocation will be made. Also check which site is possibly responsible for maintaining and increasing knowledge in some phase-based area e.g. testing or requirements engineering in a certain product area.
11-Feature- Based Work Allocation	Work needs to be shared between sites with feature- based criteria.	Check the **GSD Strategy** how feature- based work allocation strategy has been described. Form a group of members from different sites to realize the features, if needed.
12-Use Common Processes	Different processes and templates at different sites make communication inefficient.	Choose common upper level processes and allow local processes if they do not cause problems with upper level processes.
13- Iteration Planning	Persons do not know what kinds of features are needed for a GSD project and what the current goal is.	Project manager will present prioritized features and other tasks. Project members will participate in a planning meeting either personally or by **Communication Tools**. The project members will estimate amount of work for features and tasks. If needed, more detailed discussion can be arranged in sites with participants' mother language. In the end of planning, meeting the list of selected features and tasks is created and is visible by **Common Repositories and Tools.**
14-Multi- Level Daily Meetings	Problems to have a daily common meeting with all members with different time zones. Lack of trust and long feedback loops.	Organize many daily meetings and organize another daily or weekly meeting between project managers from different sites to exchange information about the results of daily meetings. With foreigners, written logs can be one solution to ensure that communication messages are understood correctly in every site. Choose the same working time for meetings in different sites.
15- Iteration Review	It's difficult to know what the status of a project is and the feedback loop is long.	Check the project status by a demo and present results to all relevant members and stakeholders from different sites. Gather comments and exchange requests for further measures for both product and process. Make frequent deliveries to improve visibility of the status of the product.
16- Organize Knowledge Transfer	It's difficult to transfer a huge amount of knowl- edge to new or experienced developers of different sites.	Make sure that there is a product knowledge repository available for project members. Train the product and get members also to use. Specification with use cases will be presented in the **Iteration Planning** meeting or separate meetings. Also earlier customer documentation and demo will be presented in some cases. **Key Roles in Sites** network will be utilized by trying to find solutions for problems. Use frequent or longer visits to enhance knowledge transfer and be sure that there are good communication channels between project members.

Table 1. (*continued*)

17-Manage Compe-tence	It's difficult to know what the competence of each project member is.	Create a competence database for gathering information of members' competence levels at different sites. Otherwise at least site manager and/or project manager knows the competence of team members. Define competence levels and criteria for them. Define the areas of competence you want to monitor. Ask site managers and /or project managers to gather information about their team members.
18-Notice Cultural Differences	Certain methods are appropriate in one nation's culture and might not be appropriate in another.	Raise the awareness of your team nations' culture for team members. Use site visits, ambassadors and liaisons, if possible. Notice cultural differences when you are applying **GSD Strategy** and **Work Allocation**. **Use Common Processes**. Use **Communication Tools** and **Common Repositories and Tools**. Allow local approaches in processes, tools, meeting methods etc. to decrease problems with cultural differences, if they do not disturb common processes etc.

Table 2. An example of GSD pattern

Name:	GSD 04 **Divide and Conquer with Iterations**
Problem:	One big project plan is a risk in distributed development and long feedback loops.
Solution:	Implement the following actions: • Plan many iterations to describe the project plan • Develop new application architecture and module structure during first iterations, if needed • Explore the biggest risks (e.g. new technologies) in the beginning of a project • The length of iteration can be e.g. 2-4 weeks to improve control and visibility. • Main site can have 4 weeks iteration and other sites 2 weeks to improve visibility.
Resulting Context:	• Iterations improve the visibility of a project and motivation of project members • Iterations make it easier to control a project when you split the whole project into many manageable parts • Administration work is increased with many iterations

3.2 Pattern Language Organization with PRINCE2

In this section the pattern language organization is described based on the PRINCE2 project management method [14]. The PRINCE2 (PRojects IN Controlled Environments2) process overview is presented in Figure 1.

PRINCE2 is comprised of eight major processes which are collections of sub-processes. We organize the pattern language by attaching the patterns to the main processes of PRINCE2. In this way, PRINCE2 acts as a structuring device for the pattern language: a project manager can easily identify the patterns applicable for a particular main process in PRINCE2. In Table 3 the eight PRINCE2 major processes are rows and the (numbers of the) GSD patterns are columns. An x-mark in the matrix means that the column pattern is related to the row process.

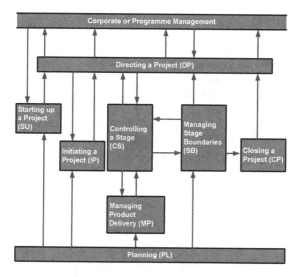

Fig. 1. Process overview of PRINCE2

Table 3. Relations between GSD Patterns and PRINCE2 major processes

	1	2	3	4	5	6	7	8	9	10	11	12	13	14	15	16	17	18
DP	x	x		x	x			x	x	x	x		x		x			
SU	x	x						x	x	x	x	x				x	x	x
IP			x	x	x	x	x					x				x	x	x
CS						x	x					x		x		x		x
MP								x				x		x	x			
SB						x	x					x	x		x	x		x
PL				x	x	x	x	x	x	x	x	x				x		
CP												x				x		

From Table 3 we can see that GSD06 (**Communication Tools**), GSD07 (**Common Repositories and Tools**), GSD12 (**Use Common Processes**), GSD16 (**Organize Knowledge Transfer**), GSD17 (**Manage Competence**) and GSD18 (**Notice Cultural Differences**) have a strong relationship with PRINCE2 processes. GSD06, GSD07 and GSD12 are key issues when implementing an efficient global software environment. GSD16 is also important because often employees in other sites do not possess domain knowledge at all, especially if they are starting the co-operation with the main site. GSD17 is needed in order to know what the competence of each employee is, especially for the planning phase of a project. GSD18 is also a fundamental practice to achieve efficient co-operation with employees from different countries.

4 Assessing a Pattern Language for GSD

In this section we describe how Q-PAM was applied in the evaluation of the GSD Pattern Language and discuss the evaluation results.

4.1 Applying Q-PAM

Three faculty members from Tampere University of Technology and four GSD project mangers from two industrial companies participated in the assessment workshop along with the main author. The author of the pattern language introduced a candidate quality profile in the first evaluation session based on ISO 9126. It was accepted with some changes after discussion. The main part of the first workshop session was used for constructing the scenarios and finally 57 scenarios were defined. Those were prioritized and ten of the most important scenarios were assessed in the second workshop session. As an example, the analysis of one of the resulting scenarios is introduced in Table 4.

Table 4. Example analysis of a scenario

Scenario	S12	An offshore designer decides to decrease the contents of a feature by 50%. In this way, he/she can get the feature to suit one iteration but the problem is that he/she doesn't talk with the product manager. This problem should be visible in two weeks.		
Response		A problem need to be solved in GSD as fast as in centralized development.		
Quality	Main Factor	Accuracy (Functionality), Time Behaviour (Efficiency)		
	Pattern	Analysis of Pattern Application	R	N
	Iteration Review	The pattern ensures that the change can be found at the latest in the next Iteration Review.		N
	Multi-Level Daily Meetings	As a result of using this pattern, a project manager might also notice the change during daily meetings		N
	Common Repositories and Tools	Common repositories and reports will improve visibility of a project between different sites and from repositories it is possible to find task lists and reports e.g about remaining work, in which it is possible to notice the change by this pattern.		N
	Communication Tools	Communication tools make it easier to clarify change when it has been found.		N
	Common Processes	With Common processes, there can be a risk if there isn't specific process guidelines to make a decision about making changes and/or all project members have not been trained well.	R	
Result		**Some Support:** The implementation of the scenario S12 is supported through four patterns in the language and one pattern can have a risk.		

We illustrate the results of the analysis with a scenario-pattern matrix (Table 5) where for each scenario the involved patterns are marked with an N (non-risk) or R (risk).

4.2 Evaluation Indicators

We have computed certain indicator values suggesting problematic scenarios or patterns. These indicators are intended only as hints; the actual conclusions can be made only after studying the seriousness of each risk separately. We have used the following indicators: IR (involvement ratio) = $(N+R)/S$ indicating the potential applicability scope of the pattern with respect to this set of scenarios, RR (risk ratio) = $R/(N+R)$ indicating the total degree of risk of the pattern with respect to the scenario set, and SI (support index) = $(N-R)/P$ indicating the level of support the pattern language provides for a scenario. Here N and R denote the number of N's and R's in a row/

column, respectively, S denotes the number of scenarios and P the number of patterns. If IR is low, the pattern seems to be less relevant for the scenario set, if RR is close to 1, the pattern may cause more problems than benefits, and if SI is negative the pattern language may counteract the scenario.

Table 5. Summary of the analysis of scenarios for GSD patterns

	S12	S3	S22	S16	S25	S31	S17	S19	S24	S28	IR	RR
GSD01												
GSD02		R									0,1	1,0
GSD03			R	N		N	R	N		N	0,6	0,3
GSD04			N								0,1	0,0
GSD05		R		R			R			R	0,4	1,0
GSD06	N	N		N	N	N	N				0,6	0,0
GSD07	N	N	N	R	N		N	N			0,7	0,1
GSD08		R		N	N		N				0,4	0,3
GSD09								N			0,1	0,0
GSD10												
GSD11												
GSD12	R			N		N		N			0,4	0,3
GSD13		N							N		0,2	0,0
GSD14	N	N	N		N	N		N	R		0,7	0,1
GSD15	N		N	N	N						0,4	0,0
GSD16								R			0,1	1,0
GSD17		N	N				R			N	0,4	0,3
GSD18		N	N		N			N	N	N	0,6	0,0
SI	0,2	0,1	0,3	0,1	0,3	0,3	0	0,3	0,1	0,1		

From Table 5 we can see that IR (involvement ratio) was at least 0.6 with the following patterns: GSD03 (**Communicate Early**), GSD06 (**Communication Tools**), GSD07 (**Common Repositories and Tools**), GSD14 (**Multi-Level Daily Meetings**) and GSD18 (**Notice Cultural Differences**). These patterns seem to be the most important ones for GSD and they give some involvement with the set of scenarios used in this assessment.

Suspicious patterns were GSD02, GSD05 and GSD16 in which RR (risk ratio) was 1.0. GSD 02 (**Fuzzy Front End**) has a risk because the pattern did not include a proper change management process. GSD05 (**Key Roles in Sites**) was interesting because it has only risks, but one main problem with this pattern was that deputy persons were not mentioned to ensure communication if the main responsible person is not available and it was required in three scenarios. GSD16 (**Organize Knowledge Transfer**) has a risk because it did not include process knowledge which is also a key area to train, although training of common processes was mentioned in GSD03 (**Communicate Early**).

It can also be noticed that GSD01, GSD10, GSD11 do not have any marks. GSD01 is a GSD strategy pattern which is mainly used before the start of a project. GSD10 and GSD11 as well as GSD09 are patterns for different types of work allocation and the main work allocation pattern was GSD08 which was mainly used instead of GSD09, GSD10 and GSD11 in the assessment.

The third index was SI (support index) and it was from 0 to 0.3 and for five scenarios from ten this index was at least 0.2.

In this case we can conclude that although there are some suspicious patterns (GSD02, GSD05 and GSD16), as a whole the pattern language provides good support for the scenarios. For instance, patterns that relate to the application lifecycle management, especially GSD06 and GSD07, indicate strong support for the selected scenarios.

During the workshop, several improvement possibilities for GSD patterns were found and the analysis resulted in a better understanding of the limits of the GSD Pattern Language. For example, the analysis resulted in the finding that GSD patterns do not include all needed practices in critical fault management or knowledge transfer areas. GSD patterns also assume that the development environment is in very good shape and that the communication network is working at a reasonable level. Some patterns originally intended for the beginning of a project were also found useful during a project.

5 Discussion

Various process or organizational pattern languages have been presented in the literature, concentrating mainly on local development [5,6,15,17]. Social patterns have been presented in [18].

The results obtained from the evaluation of GSD patterns indicate important issues for global software development. One of the issues is secure shared Common Repositories *and Tools* as an ALM (application lifecycle management) solution: electronic connections (e-meetings, teleconferencing, web cameras, chat, wiki) were seen as essential solutions to support a collaborative mode of work. This has also been indicated in other case studies related to global product development, for instance, in [19] and [20] (e.g. intranet data sharing, teleconferencing). The authors have also studied the applicability of ALM to support the management of distributed software development projects [21]. The results showed that ALM supported the operation in a global development environment. The results of Q-PAM analysis presented in this paper support this claim, too. From all GSD process patterns presented in this paper, especially GSD06 (**Communication Tools**) and GSD07 (**Common Repositories and Tools**) are related to ALM. Analysis results indicate that ALM related patterns support the selected scenarios.

The results from earlier work [9,10,11] show that the most successful global software development issues have been improvements in visibility, management of features, communication, and commitment to the goals of the project. The importance of these issues for global software development has also been discussed in [22].

Communication problems have been resolved by utilizing **Multi-Level Daily Meetings, Iteration planning, Iteration review**. These issues have also been discussed both in [23] and [24].

6 Conclusions

An efficient global software development process is very important for companies. Project management is a key process to improve efficiency in distributed development projects. This paper presents GSD patterns for project management, aiming to solve identified problems of distributed project management. The results show that the pattern language provides support for the GSD scenarios derived during the Q-PAM evaluation. In particular, patterns that relate to the Application Lifecycle Management (GSD06 and GSD07) indicate good support for the prioritized scenarios. It also turned out that Q-PAM helps to find improvement ideas and risks for current patterns.

The distributed development of complex products involves several teams and projects, often with hierarchically organized work. The results of this study indicate that information visibility and consistency is needed in this context to support the overall administration of complex product development.

Future research directions include the analysis of experiences with the current patterns in actual development projects, the improvement of the patterns and the creation of new patterns according to the feedback gained from different projects.

Acknowledgements. This work is being supported by the Academy of Finland under grant 130685 and this research is also part of the ITEA project called TWINS (Optimizing HW-SW Co-design flow for software intensive system development). The work is funded by Tekes, Metso Automation and VTT. The authors would like to thank all respondents and interviewees for their assistance and cooperation.

References

1. Carmel, E., Tjia, P.: Offshoring information technology. In: Sourcing and Outsourcing to a Global Workforce. Cambridge University Press, Cambridge (2005)
2. Abrahamsson, P., Salo, O., Ronkainen, J., Warsta, J.: Agile software development methods: Review and Analysis. Espoo, Finland: Technical Research Centre of Finland. VTT Publications 478 (2002)
3. Sutherland, J., Viktorov, A., Blount, J., Puntikov, J.: Distributed Scrum: Agile Project Management with Outsourced Development Teams. In: Proceedings of the 40th Annual Hawaii International Conference on System Sciences, HICSS (2007)
4. Moore, R., Reff, K., Graham, J., Hackerson, B.: Scrum at a Fortune 500 Manufacturing Company. In: AGILE 2007 (2007)
5. Coplien, J.O., Harrison, N.B.: Organizational Patterns of Agile Software Development. Pearson Prentice Hall, London (2005)
6. Ambler, S.: Process Patterns – Building Large-Scale Systems Using Object Technology. Cambridge University Press/SIGS Books (1998)
7. Alexander, C., Ishikawa, S., Silverstein, M., Jacobson, M., Fiksdahl-King, I., Angel, S.: A Pattern Language: Towns, Buildings, Construction. Oxford University Press, New York (1977)
8. Välimäki, A., Vesiluoma, S., Koskimies, K.: Scenario-Based Assessment of Process Pattern Languages. In: 10th International PROFES conference, Oulu, June 15-17 (2009)
9. Välimäki A., Koskimies K.: Mining best practices of project management as patterns in distributed software development. In: EuroSPI 2006 Industrial Proceedings, EuroSPI 2006, Finland, Joensuu, October 2006, pp. 6.27–6.35 (2006)
10. Välimäki, A., Kääriäinen, J.: Product Managers' Requirement Management Practices As Patterns in Distributed Development. In: 8th International PROFES conference, Latvia, July 2-4 (2007)

11. Välimäki, A., Kääriäinen, J.: Patterns for Distributed Scrum – a Case Study. In: Mertins, K., Ruggaber, R., Popplewell, K., Xu, X. (eds.) International Conference on Interoperability of Enterprise, Software and Applications, Enterprise Interoperability III - New Challenges and Industrial Approaches, March 25– 28. Springer, Heidelberg (2008)
12. Clements, P., Kazman, R., Klein, M.: Evaluating Software Architectures: Methods and Case Studies. SEI Series in Software Engineering. Addison-Wesley, Reading (2002)
13. International Organization for Standardization. Software engineering - Product quality - Part 1: Quality model. ISO/IEC 9126-1:2001 (2001)
14. Bentley, C.: The Essence of the Prince2 Project Management Method (2005 Revision), Protec (2005)
15. Coplien, J.: A Generative Development-Process Pattern Language. In: Coplien, J., Schmidt, D. (eds.) Pattern Language of Program Design, pp. 183–237. Addison-Wesley, Reading (1995)
16. Bozheva, T., Gallo, M.E.: Framework of agile patterns. In: Richardson, I., Abrahamsson, P., Messnarz, R. (eds.) EuroSPI 2005. LNCS, vol. 3792, pp. 4–15. Springer, Heidelberg (2005)
17. Elssamadisy, A.: Agile Adoption Patterns. Addison-Wesley, Reading (2009)
18. Biro, M., Messnarz, R., Ivanyos, J.: Managing Multi-Cultural and Multi-Social Projects in SPI. In: Proceeding of EuroSPI 2006, Joensuu, Finland (2006)
19. Battin, R.D., Crocker, R., Kreidler, J., Subramanian, K.: Leveraging resources in global software development. IEEE Software 18(2), 70–77 (2001)
20. Ramesh, B., Cao, L., Mohan, K., Xu, P.: Can distributed software development be agile? Communications of the ACM 49(10) (2006)
21. Kääriäinen, J., Välimäki, A.: Get a Grip on your Distributed Software Development with Application Lifecycle Management. Accepted to be published in International Journal of Computer Applications in Technology, IJCAT (To be publish, 2009)
22. Leffingwell, D.: Scaling Software Agility. Addison-Wesley, Reading (2007)
23. Schwaber, K.: Agile Project Management with Scrum. Microsoft Press, Redmond (2004)
24. Schwaber, K.: Agile The Enterprise and Scrum. Microsoft Press, Redmond (2004)

Applying Application Lifecycle Management for the Development of Complex Systems: Experiences from the Automation Industry

Jukka Kääriäinen[1] and Antti Välimäki[2]

[1] VTT, Oulu, Finland
jukka.kaariainen@vtt.fi
[2] Metso Automation Inc, Tampere, Finland
antti.valimaki@metso.com

Abstract. In this paper we present an industrial study about the history of Application Lifecycle Management (ALM) improvement in a case company. The study is part of broader research with the aim to improve global development in a company. The improvement of ALM started three years ago when the company decided to acquire a commercial ALM solution. Two SW teams developing different kinds of SW products started to pilot the solution and after various steps ended up with fairly different ALM solutions. This paper concludes the history and experiences of ALM improvement and discusses the reasons why two teams ended up with different solutions. The improvement of ALM solutions has been facilitated with the use of an ALM framework.

Keywords: Application Lifecycle Management, Product Lifecycle Management, Configuration Management, Agile, Scrum.

1 Introduction

The ability to produce quality products on time and at competitive costs is important for any industrial organization. Globalisation forces companies to operate in a distributed development environment. Nowadays, companies are seeking systematic and more efficient ways to meet these challenges. One response to these challenges is the rise of so called agile methods, such as XP (Extreme Programming), SCRUM, etc [1]. Originally these methods were intended for local development teams. Recently, the usage of agile methods in a distributed development environment has been under active research, e.g. in [2, 3, 4]. In the literature and among tool vendors, the term Product Lifecycle Management (PLM) has been discussed widely, for instance, in [5, 6]. In Stark's [6] definition, "PLM is the activity of managing a company's products all the way across their lifecycles in the most effective way". A PLM solution can comprise various systems that are used to create and manage product related data, such as requirements management (RM), configuration management (CM), enterprise resource planning (ERP), computer aided software engineering (CASE), etc. Interfaces and application integration may be needed to enable these systems to work together [6]. Abramovici [7] estimates that in the future, PLM should better support the

R.V. O'Connor et al. (Eds.): EuroSPI 2009, CCIS 42, pp. 149–160, 2009.

integration of multi-disciplinary products, not just mechanical or electrical products. The concept "Application Lifecycle Management" (ALM) has emerged to indicate the coordination of activities and the management of artefacts (e.g. requirements, source code, test cases) during the software product's lifecycle. There is a belief that comprehensive well-integrated ALM solutions are targeted for traditional plan-based product development. However, Goth [8] states that recently, the market for ALM tools for agile development is booming. The roots of ALM solutions are in the history of configuration management (CM). CM solutions are usually the foundations of ALM infrastructures providing storage, versioning and traceability between all lifecycle artefacts [9]. In the development of complex multi-disciplinary products, ALM has to fit into a wider frame of PLM. In these products, ALM focuses on the management of the SW portion of the multi-disciplinary product.

This paper presents the results from a study that has been carried out in an automation company. The study is part of broader research with the aim to improve distributed development solutions in a target organization and study the concept of application lifecycle management (ALM). The research has had two focus areas: product management (PM) [10] and application lifecycle management (ALM) [11, 12, 13]. The contribution of this paper is two-fold. Firstly, the aim is to present the history, current state and experiences from the ALM improvement work. Secondly, ALM improvement has been supported with an ALM framework that has been used for documenting and analyzing the ALM solutions of a company. The paper further specifies the ALM framework by introducing the relations of the framework elements.

This paper is organised as follows: the next section discusses the development lifecycle of complex products. Section three presents the industrial context and research process. Then the history and current state of the solutions are presented and lastly, the results are discussed and conclusions are drawn up.

2 Activities of Development Lifecycle

To understand the interfaces and the role of different information management systems during product development, the development lifecycle needs to be studied. The following Figure 1 describes the simplified development processes of a complex system and their related lifecycles [14]. From a product development point of view, PLM should support this whole chain from product ideas to system release. On the other hand, ALM is focused on supporting the management of the SW development portion of this chain.

According to Crnkovic et al. [14], the process is divided into three main activity types. First, the process contains common activities which relate to the system level. These activities produce information that will be used at a subsystem level, such as requirements, change requests and overall system design. Kotonya & Sommerville [15] and Stevens et al. [16] state that after system level requirements specification, architectural design divides and assigns system level requirements into sub-system level entities which are further specified and divided into smaller entities. Sufficient coordination and requirements traceability between these levels is needed to ensure that all requirements flow from the top, through all requirements levels [17]. Second, there are independent activities which relate to the different disciplines (e.g. HW and

SW development). However, there is the need for coordination during these activities. Third, there are integrated activities where information from all processes must be accessible and integrated into common information. Information assets that will be flowed from a sub-system level to system level are final deliverables and refined requirements/design.

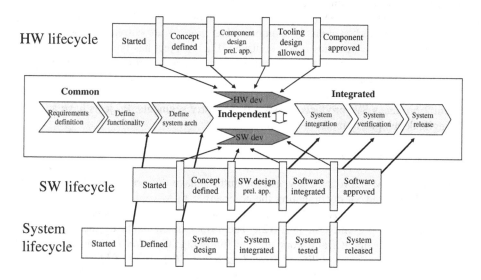

Fig. 1. System development process and lifecycles (adapted based on [14])

The development of multidisciplinary products is supported with various product information management systems, such as Requirements Management tools, ALM tools, PDM (Product Data Management) tools, Document Management tools, etc. The need for integration of various product information management systems has been discussed, e.g. in [14, 18]. One challenge with these tool domains is that often their functionality and managed information overlaps [14, 18]. The same data is duplicated in various applications that complicate the traceability and maintenance of data. Keeping the data consistent would require integrations between existing systems. The technical integration of these tools in itself is not sufficient but also adequate understanding of the development processes and their interrelations in the particular case is required [19]. Therefore, the management of product related data requires a holistic viewpoint, i.e. lifecycle management that contributes to better consistency of product data.

3   Research Approach

This section introduces the industrial context and research process.

3.1   Industrial Context

The case company operates in the field of the automation industry. The company operates in a multi-site environment. Therefore, the challenges of the global development environment need to be resolved. Product development is organized according to product lines. As it is no longer competitive to develop multiple products one at a time, the case company has adopted a product platform approach. Therefore, the product is based on a product platform where the customer-specific features are configured. The company produces complex automation systems where SW is a part of the whole system. The improvement of ALM is focused on two SW teams (referred to as "SW Team 1" and "SW Team 2") each having several SW projects running in parallel. Each team has about 10 members. The projects are currently geographically distributed over several sites (two countries). Each project has typically less than 10 project members as reported the appropriate size for agile projects. Previously, projects have followed a partly iterative development process. SW Team 1 produces a SW product that is one part of the common automation product platform, whereas SW Team 2 produces SW products for specific industry segments. Projects have adopted the agile development method, Scrum.

3.2 Research Process

To support ALM improvement work, the authors have defined the ALM framework that has been used for documenting the company's ALM solutions as well as to find improvement ideas for ALM solutions in company. The development of the framework has been presented in [11, 12]. The principal elements of the Application Lifecycle Management framework are the following: *Creation and management of lifecycle artefacts, Traceability of lifecycle artefacts, Reporting of lifecycle artefacts, Communication, Process support* and *Tool integration*. Figure 2 and 3 present the history of ALM framework development and the history of the case company's ALM improvement.

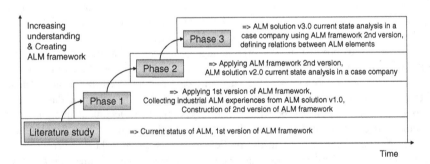

Fig. 2. Phases of ALM framework development and validation

The improvement work in SW teams has been a continuous activity and thus ALM versions indicate the ALM solutions at a certain moment. The notable problem with version 1 & 2 solutions related to the requirements management. The decisions for improvements were made in project meetings or in retrospective meetings. Methods used for data collection during the first and second research phase have covered a questionnaire for SW team members (two teams) and two interview rounds for the project managers of SW teams. In this paper we present the results of the third research phase that produced the current state analysis of ALM solution version 3.0 in a company and further elaborated the ALM framework by defining relations between framework elements. The data for this study has been collected by updating the company's previous ALM description based on information received from the complementary interviews of the project managers (i.e. what has changed and why teams ended up with different solutions). The ALM description, analysis results and conclusions drawn have been reviewed by the project managers.

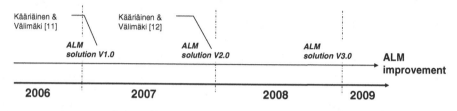

Fig. 3. History of ALM improvement in a company

4   History of ALM Improvement and Current Solution

Previously, the company's ALM solution for distributed development was comprised of several somewhat isolated databases to manage project related data, such as local version control and distributed document management and fault management systems. This caused challenges especially in a global development environment where the consistency and real-time visibility of the information is important. Therefore, the company started to seek more integrated solutions to coordinate distinct project phases and to provide a centralised project database for all project related data. In practice, this meant that the SW teams deployed a commercial ALM tool with the Scrum method.

The documentation and the history of version 1.0 and 2.0 ALM solutions have been reported in [11, 12] (see Figure 3). The teams started from somewhat similar solutions for ALM. The backbone of this solution was a commercial ALM solution called Microsoft's Team Foundation Server (TFS). This solution was configured with a 3rd party Scrum process template. Both teams wanted to keep the changes to the process template to a minimum. After two years, teams ended up with fairly different solutions. The ALM solution of SW team 1 was comprised of several interconnected product information databases, whereas the backbone of the ALM solution of SW Team 2 was a single central global ALM tool, TFS.

Different solutions were due to the different kinds of SW products produced in these teams and organisations' management constraints related to these SW products. SW Team 1 produces a SW product that is one part of an evolving "product platform", whereas SW Team 2 develops industry-specific SW products. Therefore, SW Team 1 had a need to integrate with, for instance, the test document and fault management databases that are also used by other platform projects to maintain consistency with other projects, provide a single channel for accessing information and allow, for instance, test staff to use a single interface for reporting faults that relate to a certain product platform.

Current ALM solutions (referred to as version 3.0 solutions) for two SW teams have been differentiated even more. The biggest difference compared to the version 2.0 ALM solution is that SW Team 1 has started to use a Notes –database for managing Product Backlog Items (PBI) and Sprint Backlog Items (SBI) instead of TFS. Currently, TFS has a strong role in SW Team 2 as a central global project information repository. SW Team 1 uses TFS just for source code control (SCC). If comparing the history of the ALM solutions of both teams it can be noted that SW Team 1 has moved towards a Notes –dominant ALM solution with several interconnected databases, whereas SW Team 2 has moved towards a TFS –dominant central ALM solution. Table 1 summarises SW Team 1 and SW Team 2 ALM solutions.

Table 1. Summary of SW Team 1 and SW Team 2 version 3.0 ALM solutions

	SW Team 1 *Developing SW for a platform product*	SW Team 2 *Developing industry- specific SW*
Creation and management of lifecycle artefacts	Various databases are used to manage project related data: - TFS (SCC). - Feature management DB, System fault management DB, Test document DB and System configuration DB.	MS TFS and SharePoint as a central point for SW product information management. Team uses also System configuration DB to associate SW version with other sub-system versions.
Traceability of lifecycle artefacts	Traceability of lifecycle artefacts that reside in same or different databases (links between Notes documents or databases). SCC traceability in TFS (e.g. SC items, ChangeSets and labels). Label ID is manually copied from TFS to System configuration database (Notes) to ensure traceability from SW baseline to system configuration.	Traceability of lifecycle artefacts (PBIs, SBIs, SCC, SharePoint documents) that reside in TFS and Project Portal (SharePoint). Label ID is manually copied from TFS to System configuration database (Notes) to ensure traceability from SW baseline to system configuration.
Reporting of lifecycle artefacts	Views and reports from Notes databases are used to produce needed information for project reporting.	TFS Scrum predefined and tailored reports are used to produce project reports. Reports are distributed in Visual Studio 2005 user interface or Project Portal. Some reports are exported to Excel.
Communication	Synchronous: Chat, Remote connection (screen sharing) with voice and/or video, Phone. Asynchronous: E-mail, databases (TFS, Notes). Scrum communication practices.	Synchronous: Chat, Remote connection (screen sharing) with voice and/or video, Phone. Asynchronous: E-mail, databases (TFS, Project portal, Notes). Scrum communication practices.
Process support	Notes process guidance is used. TFS SCC policies set for a project. Notes items have state models that support the operation according to defined procedures.	TFS Scrum process template is used to configure project specific features for a project (e.g. TFS items' state models, Scrum reports, etc.). TFS SCC policies set for a project.
Tool integration	TFS is integrated into Visual Studio (SW development and SCC). Point-to-point integrations between Feature management, System fault management, Test document and System configuration databases.	MS TFS and Project Portal provide integrated project environment. MS tools, such as Office (Excel, Project) and Visual Studio, integrate well to this environment.

In SW Team 1, the use of TFS for managing SW requirements and tasks, i.e. PBIs and SBIs, was seen as a solution that creates a gap between system level definitions (product ideas, features/requirements) and SW project level definitions (PBIs/SBIs). In parallel with ALM improvement, the case company has started to pilot a proprietary Notes database for feature management. This solution is comprised of the management of system level product ideas, features and requirements. Now this solution has been extended to also cover the management of SW PBIs and SBIs. The current feature management solution starts from gathering ideas or needs from various sources e.g. from marketing, support, development, customers, etc. The solution proceeds with the feature and requirement definition, analysis and prioritization. Features are related to Sprints and Product Backlog Items and, furthermore, Sprint Backlog Items are defined to assign SW project tasks to realize features and track the implementation of features. The solution establishes a common way to share, combine and analyze the information and therefore provides a common global database for platform projects including product level definitions and SW requirements and tasks. This solution provides a link between system and SW level definitions for SW Team 1 that produces SW for a platform product. However, SW Team 2 uses MS SharePoint to collect features and to store the results of analysis, estimation and prioritization. PBIs are linked to features but in the TFS the link is only a free text comment.

The project managers of both SW Teams stated that it was beneficial to use TFS for managing PBI and SBI when starting to deploy the new working method, Scrum. TFS had the 3rd party process template ready for handling Scrum work items and, therefore, worked as a ready-to-use platform for experimenting with Scrum in a SW project. This facilitated the deployment of the Scrum method. However, in the long run it was more feasible for SW team 1 to work with technology (i.e. Notes) that is also used by other platform projects. It was also stated that the use of existing familiar technology is cost-effective since the infrastructure is in place and the users are familiar with the terminology and basic functions of the technology. On the other hand, for SW Team 2 the single central ALM tool has worked well. In both teams, the solutions support the project management with the management of PBI and SBI and project reporting even though the solutions are based on different technology. Both teams are using TFS for source code control and they reported that it has many advantages compared to their old source code control solution. All databases in both teams (TFS and Notes) are accessible globally that was an essential prerequisite for the databases when the company started to improve the solutions of global development.

5 Discussion

This section discusses issues related to ALM improvement in a case company and the further elaboration of ALM framework.

5.1 ALM Improvement in a Case Company

The improvement history shows that two SW teams ended up with a fairly different solution because of their different characteristics. This adaptation of information management solutions for a development context has been treated in several publications.

E.g. from a configuration management point of view in [20, 21, 22] as well as from a requirements management point of view in [15, 23]. In our case, SW Team 1 produces SW that is part of an evolving platform product whereas SW Team 2 produces industry-specific SW products. This study showed that one ALM solution does not necessarily fit all teams in an organisation. The study showed that SW Team 1 needed a common way to share and access the same type of information with the other platform projects. Therefore, the organization can view and access consistent product platform related information, for instance, faults or test reports, through a single channel based on product structure. In SW Team 1, this meant that it was reasonable for the team to use the same global product information management systems as other platform projects, i.e. a feature management DB, fault management DB and test document management DB. The lack of integration between the commercial ALM tool (TFS) and company's Notes databases caused that TFS could not be used for managing all lifecycle artefacts. The use of consistent practices and tools over related development projects has also been stressed in the telecommunication industry [19]. On the other hand, for SW Team 2 the single central ALM solution has worked well since they do not have strong relations to the platform level. One challenge with several databases is that often their functionality and managed information overlaps [14, 18]. The same data is duplicated in various applications that complicate the traceability and maintenance of data. In this case, this has forced the organisation to build point-to-point integrations between different Notes databases, for instance, between the fault management DB and test document management DB. However, since these databases share the basic technology and the company is very familiar with the Notes technology, the integration has been fairly easy to implement.

The agile methods have been under active research for a decade. There are a number of commercial and open source tools that support the methods. In our case, the company had the challenges of increasing globalisation and efficiency demands. Therefore, the company started to seek more integrated solutions and methods to coordinate distinct project phases and to provide visibility into development projects. In practice, this meant that the SW teams deployed a commercial ALM tool, Team Foundation Server (TFS), with the Scrum process. The successful use of TFS to support Scrum methodology has been reported in [4]. However, Moore et al. [4] stated that they needed to considerably tailor the TFS process template for their purposes. The same problem was also noticed in our case [11, 12]. A challenge with the commercial ALM solution was to find a suitable template for the projects. Since each organisation has its own characteristics and needs, the challenge is to find efficient implementations of lifecycle management for complicated, real-life situations. If the ALM suite's process template library does not include a suitable process template for an organisation, the modifications to a standard template or creation of a new template from scratch might need significant effort. Therefore, teams wanted to keep the changes in a standard template minor even though the basic template was not optimal. This was the opposite approach if compared to Moore et al. [4] since in their study the company made considerable modifications. One interesting study related to the adaptation of TFS process templates is presented in [24]. Medina-Domínguez et al. propose the project pattern concept and a model to support process improvement based on patterns in a TFS environment.

Recently SW Team 1 moved the management of Scrum items (i.e. PBI and SBI) from TFS into the proprietary Notes database. However, our study shows that it was beneficial to use a commercial ALM tool (TFS) in both teams a few years ago when starting to deploy the new working method, Scrum. TFS had a ready process template for handling Scrum work items and, therefore, it worked as a ready-to-use platform for experimenting with Scrum in a SW project even though the solution was not optimal. This facilitated the deployment of the Scrum method. After successful deployment it was feasible to start to optimise the solution for the organisation. Now SW Team 2 uses TFS with the Scrum template for managing Scrum work items, whereas, SW Team 1 has moved the management of Scrum items into the proprietary Notes database (feature management DB) that is also used by other platform projects. In both solutions Scrum items are managed as separate configuration items and can be associated with each other and, therefore, can be used for automated reporting, etc. This fine-grained management of configuration items has advantages compared to file-based management of product information (see e.g. [25, 26]).

5.2 Elaboration of ALM Framework

The documentation of the ALM solution and the collection of improvement ideas have been facilitated by using an ALM framework that supported the improvement activities in a company. When comparing the practical implementations of ALM solutions in a case company and ALM elements in the framework, it was possible to find relations between the elements (Figure 4). "Creation and management of lifecycle artefacts" is the foundation for ALM. The product information collected and managed by this element is needed, for instance, for traceability and reporting activities. "Traceability of lifecycle artefacts" provides a means to identify and maintain relationships between managed lifecycle artefacts and, therefore, facilitates reporting, change impact analysis and information visibility through the development lifecycle. "Reporting of lifecycle artefacts" utilises managed lifecycle artefacts and traceability information to generate needed reports from the lifecycle product information to support SW development and management. "Communication" provides communication tools (e.g. chat) as well as channels for distributing information about product lifecycle artefacts, links and reports and thus facilitates product information visibility for the whole SW project. "Process support" and "Tool integration" are the elements that are used to configure the ALM solution to support SW development procedures and to facilitate a productive development environment by enabling the user to easily launch tools and transfer information between different tools and databases. An example in the TFS environment that reflects these relations is the generation of a "Product backlog composition" -report for Project Portal. The TFS Scrum process template contains a "Product backlog composition" –report. The report collects managed Scrum items (PBIs, SBIs) as well as their relations to generate a report that presents PBIs and their related SBIs as well as their realization related information (hours). This report can then be made visible through a Project Portal that facilitates the real-time information visibility via a web browser for the whole SW project.

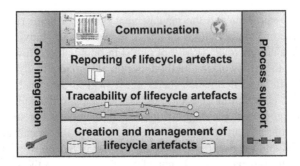

Fig. 4. Principal elements of Application Lifecycle Management

6 Conclusions

This paper presents the experiences of ALM improvement in an automation company. The improvement of Application Lifecycle Management in a case company has been iterative. The paper reports the history, current state and experiences from the improvement effort. The common feature that characterises product development in a company is the global development environment. Globalisation has been the main reason that has forced a company to seek more effective solutions to support product development. For two SW teams, the case company started to pilot the ALM solution to support global SW development with the agile development method, Scrum. The teams ended up with quite different ALM solutions based on their special needs for product development and management. One team ended up with a Notes-dominant ALM solution, whereas the other with a TFS-dominant solution.

The following list presents the summary of experiences about ALM improvement from a company producing complex multi-discipline products:

- Interfaces with system level product information management tools affect SW project's ALM solution (company/organisation constraints for SW project). In this case, lead to the use of several databases. Inter-project product information management practices and solutions need to be collectively agreed and compatible between development projects.
- A single central ALM tool was found feasible when there were not many relations to organization's other information management systems. Central database allowed the whole SW team to have a consistent view of project data.
- The integration of different technologies is still difficult. Therefore, it is more feasible to focus on certain technology and build the solution around it (e.g. TFS or Notes).
- Teams had specific needs for ALM that lead to different solutions. Iterative improvement of ALM practices and solutions produced feasible solutions for each team.
- In practice, ALM solution can be a central database or the collection of databases. In the case of several databases, the interoperability of databases is essential to maintain the consistency of product information (e.g. tight integration or loosely coupled integration with proper process).

- Commercial ALM solution with a process template that can be used to configure the whole system to support the selected development method facilitated the deployment of new development method (Scrum).
- ALM framework facilitated the documentation, understanding and analysis of ALM solution during the iterative improvement effort.
- During the research ALM was found to be an important topical concept to support global software development with the visibility and consistency of project information.

Future research will focus on further elaboration of the ALM framework and its usage in future ALM cases.

Acknowledgements. This work is funded by Tekes, Metso Automation and VTT. This work is being supported by the Academy of Finland under grant 130685. The authors would like to thank all the contributors for their assistance and cooperation.

References

1. Abrahamsson, P., Salo, O., Ronkainen, J., Warsta, J.: Agile software development methods: Review and Analysis. Espoo, Finland: Technical Research Centre of Finland, VTT Publications 478 (2002)
2. Ramesh, B., Cao, L., Mohan, K., Xu, P.: Can distributed software development be agile? Communications of the ACM 49(10) (2006)
3. Sutherland, J., Viktorov, A., Blount, J., Puntikov, J.: Distributed Scrum: Agile Project Management with Outsourced Development Teams. In: Proceedings of the 40th Annual Hawaii International Conference on System Sciences, HICSS (2007)
4. Moore, R., Reff, K., Graham, J., Hackerson, B.: Scrum at a Fortune 500 Manufacturing Company. In: AGILE 2007, pp. 175–180 (2007)
5. Sääksvuori, A., Immonen, A.: Product Lifecycle Management. Springer, Berlin (2004)
6. Stark, J.: Product Lifecycle Management – 21st Century Paradigm for Product Realisation. Springer, London (2005)
7. Abramovici, M.: Future Trends in Product Lifecycle Management (PLM). In: The Future of Product Development: Proceedings of the 17th CIRP Design Conference, Berlin, Germany, March 26-28 (2007)
8. Goth, G.: Agile Tool Market Growing with the Philosophy. IEEE Software 26(2), 88–91 (2009)
9. Schwaber, C.: The Expanding Purview Of Software Configuration Management. Forrester Research Inc., White paper, July 22 (2005)
10. Välimäki, A., Kääriäinen, J.: Product Managers' Requirement Management Practices As Patterns in Distributed Development. In: 8th International PROFES (Product Focused Software Development and Process Improvement) conference, Riga, Latvia, July 2-4 (2007)
11. Kääriäinen, J., Välimäki, A.: Impact of Application Lifecycle Management – a Case Study. In: International Conference on Interoperability of Enterprise, Software and Applications (I-ESA), Berlin, Germany, March 25-28, pp. 55–67 (2008)
12. Kääriäinen, J., Välimäki, A.: Get a Grip on your Distributed Software Development with Application Lifecycle Management. Accepted to be published in International Journal of Computer Applications in Technology, IJCAT (To be published, 2009)

13. Välimäki, A., Kääriäinen, J.: Patterns for Distributed Scrum – a Case Study. In: International Conference on Interoperability of Enterprise, Software and Applications (I-ESA), March 25-28, pp. 85–97 (2008)
14. Crnkovic, I., Asklund, U., Dahlqvist, A.: Implementing and Integrating Product Data Management and Software Configuration Management. Artech House, London (2003)
15. Kotonya, G., Sommerville, I.: Requirements Engineering: Process and Techniques. John Wiley & Sons, Chichester (1998)
16. Stevens, R., Brook, P., Jackson, K., Arnold, S.: Systems Engineering: Coping with Complexity. Pearson Education, London (1998)
17. Hooks, I., Farry, K.: Customer-centered products: creating successful products through smart requirements management. American Management Association, New York (2001)
18. Svensson, D.: Towards Product Structure Management in Heterogeneous Environments. In: Product and Production Development. Engineering and Industrial Design, Chalmers University of Technology, Göteborg, Sweden (2003)
19. Kääriäinen, J., Taramaa, J., Alenius, J.: Configuration management support for the development of an embedded system: experiences in the telecommunication industry. In: The Fifth International Symposium on Tools and Methods of Competitive Engineering (TMCE 2004), Lausanne, CH, April 13-17 (2004)
20. Lyon, D.: Practical CM – Best Configuration Management Practices for the 21st Century, 2nd edn. RAVEN Publishing Company (1999)
21. Leon, A.: A Guide to software configuration management. Artech House, Boston (2000)
22. Whitgift, D.: Methods and Tools for Software Configuration Management. John Wiley & Sons, England (1991)
23. Sommerville, I., Sawyer, P.: Requirements Engineering: A Good Practice Guide. John Wiley & Sons, Chichester (1997)
24. Medina-Domínguez, F., Sanchez-Segura, M., Amescua, A., García, J.: Extending Microsoft Team Foundation Server Architecture to Support Collaborative Product Patterns. In: Wang, Q., Pfahl, D., Raffo, D.M. (eds.) ICSP 2007. LNCS, vol. 4470, pp. 1–11. Springer, Heidelberg (2007)
25. Macfarlane, I.A., Reilly, I.: Requirements traceability in an integrated development environment. In: Proceedings of the Second IEEE International Symposium on Requirements Engineering, pp. 116–123 (1995)
26. Crnkovic, I., Funk, P., Larsson, M.: Processing requirements by software configuration management. In: Proceedings of the 25th EUROMICRO Conference, vol. 2, pp. 260–265 (1999)

Exploring the Role of Usability in the Software Process: A Study of Irish Software SMEs

Rory V. O'Connor

School of Computing, Dublin City University, Dublin, Ireland
and Lero, The Irish Software Engineering Research Centre
roconnor@computing.dcu.ie

Abstract. This paper explores the software processes and usability techniques used by Small and Medium Enterprises (SMEs) that develop web applications. The significance of this research is that it looks at development processes used by SMEs in order to assess to what degree usability is integrated into the process. This study seeks to gain an understanding into the level of awareness of usability within SMEs today and their commitment to usability in practice. The motivation for this research is to explore the current development processes used by SMEs in developing web applications and to understand how usability is represented in those processes. The background for this research is provided by the growth of the web application industry beyond informational web sites to more sophisticated applications delivering a broad range of functionality. This paper presents an analysis of the practices of several Irish SMEs that develop web applications through a series of case studies. With the focus on SMEs that develop web applications as Management Information Systems and not E-Commerce sites, informational sites, online communities or web portals. This study gathered data about the usability techniques practiced by these companies and their awareness of usability in the context of the software process in those SMEs. The contribution of this study is to further the understanding of the current role of usability within the software development processes of SMEs that develop web applications.

Keywords: Software process improvement, Software process, Usability, SME.

1 Introduction

Since the introduction of the Internet, web applications have moved beyond information sharing to a point where most traditional standalone applications have a web-enabled version [1]. Today the term web applications represent anything from information portals to online communities. This study focuses on web applications as Management Information Systems (MIS) accessed via a web browser with a central database backend. It focuses on the following definition of a web application proposed by [2]: *"These new web applications blend navigation and browsing capabilities, common to hypermedia, with 'classical' operations (or transactions), common to traditional information systems"*. This study does not consider in its scope E-Commerce sites, informational sites, online communities or web portals.

R.V. O'Connor et al. (Eds.): EuroSPI 2009, CCIS 42, pp. 161–172, 2009.
© Springer-Verlag Berlin Heidelberg 2009

With the growth of the software industry, many development process models have emerged, such as the waterfall, iterative and agile models. Companies are also placing an increasing emphasis on the importance of compliance with standards such as ISO 9001 or the use of best practice models such as the Capability Maturity Model Integration (CMMI). But despite the number and variety of models and frameworks, there is evidence that SMEs find it difficult to adhere fully to any one model or set of standards [3].

Recently there has been a call for new development process models that address the unique requirements of web application development [4]. Such requirements include a short development lifecycle and a shorter shelf life of new functionality. They must also keep pace with the rapidly changing technology on which they rely. There are general guidelines available on what a web application process should incorporate. Suggestions include combining the activities of traditional models with those of hypermedia design models [5]. Alternatively, an incremental process is recommended, incorporating activities that address the needs of web application development [6]. Despite these guidelines, there is evidence that most web development is still largely ad-hoc and researchers liken it to the early days of traditional software development [7, 8].

ISO 9241-11, a guidance on usability, defines usability in terms of measurable objectives, stating: *"the extent to which a product can be used by specified users to achieve specified goals with effectiveness, efficiency, and satisfaction in a specified context of use"*. Guidelines for web usability include: the degree of visual quality, degree of customization, tracking user activity, and degree of proactivity [5]. However, usability guidelines for the web focus almost exclusively on web sites and fail to identify usability issues unique to web applications. Even web application developers are confused about usability standards and whether they should conform to web site standards or Windows standards [19].

User-Centred Design (UCD) is an effort to involve the user in all stages of a software development process. There are many UCD models, such as ISO 13407 or industry models such as IBM's. Much research to date on the practice of UCD in companies assumes that a reasonably defined development process exists in the first place. For this reason, the significance of this study is that it investigates whether a well-defined development process indeed exists and if so, whether usability practices are incorporated into that process.

1.1 Research Aims

This study examines SMEs understanding of usability, what usability techniques they currently practice and how well they believe usability is represented in their development process. It analyses the software development process SMEs claim to use and looks at whether the process is actually followed in a typical project. By comparing results across several case study companies, this study investigates whether common issues and attitudes exist and how their practices compare to software development models and usability standards. By investigating the typical development process and what usability techniques are being used, the aim of this study is to set the groundwork for further investigation into whether SMEs find it difficult to follow software development process models and UCD models when developing web applications. Accordingly, the objectives of this study are to:

1. Explore the software development processes in practice by SMEs that develop web applications.
2. Investigate the SMEs understanding of usability and assess their level of commitment to it within the development process.
3. Investigate the gap between the development processes practiced by SMEs developing web applications and the proposed software development process models, standards and best practices.
4. Investigate the gap between usability awareness and practices among SMEs and usability standards and UCD guidelines.
5. Gain an understanding of why SMEs do, or do not, integrate usability into their web development process.

2   Usability and Web Development Processes

Although usability is gaining widespread recognition, confusion exists as to what is meant by the term usability [9]. For some it focuses on the User Interface, dealing with issues such as user of color, pleasing layout and consistent terminology. For others it deals with the software's overall structure, how productively it allows the user to complete their tasks and how easy it is to learn [10]. This study adopts the definitions put forward by the ISO (ISO 9241-11) which defines usability as: "the extent to which a product can be used by specified users to achieve specified goals with effectiveness, efficiency, and satisfaction in a specified context of use".

The process by which one achieves good usability in a product is known as User-Centred Design (UCD). This is also referred to as usability engineering or human-centred design. Many UCD design models put forward and all contain the key element of involving the user in all stages of the development process [11]. This is in contrast to a traditional software development process, which only involves the user in specific stages of the lifecycle, such as requirements analysis and acceptance testing.

Studies have shown that user-centred design techniques are still underused among development teams [12] and most usability issues are only detected during testing and after deployment [13, 14]. Of those practicing UCD, one investigation revealed that the majority of methods in practice were informal, low-cost user-centered design methods. The most commonly used methods were iterative design, usability evaluation, task analysis, informal expert review, and field studies [15]. Obstacles given for not implementing UCD techniques include a lack of awareness of usability across the company, lack of usability experience, poor management support and marketing pressures [16]. Another reason given is the fact that UCD techniques are developed in isolation from the software engineering community and real company environments and thus do not take into account how well they will work in terms of team buy-in, and resources [17].

2.1 Web Development Processes

Many current software development models have been criticized as not meeting the unique requirements of web application development [7, 4] and accordingly there is a need to develop new models that address the needs of web application development [4]. The absence of a well-defined model for web applications has been explained by two causes. Firstly, the scope of how a web application is defined varies greatly. Secondly, the web's legacy is as an information platform rather than an application platform [8].

There are some general guidelines available on creating a development process for web applications. [5] suggests combining the activities of traditional lifecycles with those suggested for hypermedia. [6] suggests an evolutionary, or incremental, process which addresses the needs of web application development through the following activities: formulation, planning, analysis, modelling, page generation, testing and customer evaluation. Finally, many agree that regardless of the type of application being developed, the basic principles of software engineering should always apply. Good design, solid testing and change control should all be used as they are historically proven to work [18, 6].

2.2   Role of Usability in Web Development Process

Web application usability goes beyond interface design and interaction issues specific to web pages. This study has found that research on usability standards for the web focuses almost exclusively on web sites and there is a lack of usability standards for web applications and developers admit to defining standards as they go. They also express confusion as to what standards they should conform to, those for web sites or traditional applications [19]. In the absence of clear recommendations, this study looks at how web applications share characteristics of both traditional applications and web sites.

Web application front ends are accessed via a browser, just as web sites are. As far as usability for the user interface is concerned, web applications can borrow from guidelines common to web sites. Web applications share other usability issues with web sites, such as: download times, browser preferences and access via different devices, such as PDAs [11]. On the other hand, web applications may differ from web sites when it comes to the importance of learnability. Learnability may be less critical in web applications compared to web sites as they are likely to be accessed on a more frequent basis. There is also a greater chance that some degree of training or documentation is available for web applications compared to informational web sites [20].

There is little evidence available on the level of usability being delivered in real web applications today and how today's end users feel about usability standards. This may be put down to the reluctance of companies to allow such information to become public. But usability concerns for web sites focus on the UI and interaction issues dealing with information, such as searching.

3   Case Studies

The case studies were restricted to companies that develop web applications. The definition of web applications presented in section 1 has formed the basis for selecting suitable companies. It was not limited to any genre of web application or to a geographical area. It was also considered immaterial if a company also developed traditional applications as long as a significant portion of development efforts focused on web application development. The primary source for identifying case studies was through the researchers contacts, with possible companies being assessed. Through this process, five companies were identified, who ranged in size from 15 to 2 softare development staff. The job titles of those interviewed included Web Development Manager, Product Manager and Software Development Manager among others.

An interview guide was prepared for use in the semi-structured interviews which comprised both factual questions and open-ended questions designed to explore the interviewee's attitudes and opinions. It was designed to be semi-structured based on the assumption that additional questions would be asked depending on the direction in which the answers went. The guide was deigned so that each interview would be completed within an hour, in order to ensure that interviewees would not lose focus. The five main topic area covered by the interview guide were:

1. General background information about the company and its business sector.
2. The organization's software development process and its practice.
3. The organization's understanding and awareness of usability.
4. Usability Practices: Usability activities within the development process.
5. The interviewee's opinion of usability in relation to the company's products.

Detailed notes were taken during each interview and any additional questions that were asked were also noted. Each interview was also recorded on tape. After each interview, the tape recordings were transcribed and the interview notes were reviewed and documented. This material was then used as the basis for within-case analysis. The researchers looked for interesting findings or contradictory answers and wrote a summary of observations for each case. All five interviews took place over a two month period. After all of the interviews had been completed, the researchers began within-case analysis. After the within-case analysis was complete, cross-case analysis was carried out.

4 Analysis

This section presents the cross-case analysis of the data collected during the case study interviews. It examines the findings of the interviews under the areas of Software Process, Usability Awareness, Usability Practices and Product Usability. Firstly, it looks at the software practices followed by the case study companies and compares them to recommended practices as discussed in the literature and whether they have adopted suggested practices for web application development. It then discusses the awareness of usability and investigate usability practices of the case study companies and examines the gap between their practices and suggested usability design techniques. Lastly, it discusses the opinions of the interviewees about the usability of their products and examines the lack of evidence available on the level of usability of today's web applications.

4.1 Software Process

Of the five case studies, two companies use RUP as their development method, one uses an Agile approach and the other two use an internally developed process based on a waterfall style model. Only the two companies using RUP had a fully documented process. The company using an Agile approach had a partially documented process and the two companies using an internally developed process had not documented it at all. Analysis of the development process revealed that all five companies were knowledgeable and clear in describing the steps that they follow, regardless of whether it was documented or not. All but one of the companies believed the process was being followed in all projects. However, four out of five companies also cited deviations from the process.

An interesting finding was that three of the companies had recently undergone significant improvements to their processes. One company had hired a project manager with the responsibility of establishing a more structured, repeatable development process. Another set up a new test team and formalized the build process. It was evident that these companies were moving in the right direction while still being aware that they had more improvements to make.

None of the companies were following any of the available development models without having customized it to their needs. When describing their development process, all five companies reported having a Requirements Analysis phase at the beginning of the lifecycle. Much of the literature cites poor requirements as the cause of many subsequent problems in the software. But [21] believe that in web projects, clients do not have a clear enough understanding of their requirements at the beginning of a project for existing software processes to be effective. They believe that web development companies should adopt an iterative approach that incorporates client developer interaction and that assesses partial designs in order to clarify the client's requirements. Although only one company cited poor Requirements Analysis as a problem in their process, there appears to be a lack of awareness that a key advantage of the iterative design process is its ability to involve the end user early in the product lifecycle. Of the three companies following an iterative process, only two delivered interim software builds to the client. But both of these companies described the client as a distinct entity to the end user of the system. Delivery of the builds appeared to be more to meet the contract deliverable rather than a design tool.

The literature suggested that web application development can be likened to the early days of traditional software development, when applications were mostly being developed in an ad-hoc manner. But this study has revealed that all five case studies have a defined development process. Although the process may not have been documented in two cases, all of the companies were able to clearly describe the steps involved in their process and believed it to be a clearly defined, repeatable process. They were also able to acknowledge deviations from the defined process. These findings suggest that although there appears to be a need for a process suitable to small companies developing web applications, practices are more formal than anecdotal evidence suggests.

4.2 Usability Awareness

All of the companies had very little awareness of usability standards, with only one company having a good knowledge of usability. Most of the companies believed usability was well represented in their development process and that usability awareness was good throughout the company. It emerged that two companies had a limited understanding of usability awareness, citing look and feel as the primary element. The other three companies had a deeper understanding, describing usability as the need to support the user tasks. An interesting finding was that those companies that showed a deeper understanding of usability were also the ones doing business on a tender basis. It is possible that in order to win tenders, companies must ensure that they respond to the client's needs. It is also possible that during the development process, the client has much deeper involvement compared to those companies who are selling their application on an off the shelf basis.

Analysis of users needs showed that the most commonly reported need was intuitive use. Two companies remarked that having to do as few clicks as possible was important for their users, while another phrased this as fast use. Other needs cited were easy navigation, quality of information and responsiveness. One company observed that their users simply like what they are used to. This is an interesting challenge when developing web applications because it is possible that users are used to desktop applications but have less experience with web applications. This is reflected in the fact that one company said that their biggest challenge was delivering more and more complex functionality via the web and still trying to maintain a high level of usability. The challenge is to develop a web application that delivers a high level of ease of use and learnability so that it becomes irrelevant to users that they achieve their goal in a slightly different way to before. The researchers also believes that novice users may benefit greatly from education from the development company on the advantages the web brings before assuming that the client wants a mirror image of the desktop application functionality.

Only one company reported that awareness of the user needs and their IT skills was poor. They acknowledged that this was reflected in the fact that they were still delivering new functionality with poor usability. Most of the companies felt that awareness among staff of the client needs grows with the experience of working on a project and through good requirement specifications.

Analysis of how the interviewees defined usability supports the evidence that confusion still exists as to what is meant by usability. For some usability refers to the UI and for others it means how productively the system allows users to complete their task. Two companies defined usability in terms of the UI and the other three defined it in terms of supporting the user's task. It is encouraging that three companies defined usability as the extent to which it supported the user tasks. But only one company mentioned efficiency as an element of usability. This is particularly interesting in terms of web applications because efficiency has been cited as one of the most important aspects of usability for the web. Also, none of the companies remarked on effectiveness or satisfaction as key elements of usability. Most of the companies have reached an understanding that a system should enable a user to reach his goal but they lack the awareness of the fact that it should enable them to do so in as productive and pleasing a manner possible.

Rather than dismissing those who defined usability primarily in terms of look and feel as having a poor understanding of usability, it is worth looking at the fact that most of the companies did not mention look and feel at all. Although industry definitions make it clear that usability is much more about the look of a product, [5] cites the 'degree of visual quality' as a key element of usability for web applications. This finding supports the observations by [19] who noted that developers are confused about whether they should conform to web site or traditional application standards. It is encouraging that three of the companies described usability in terms of reaching user goals but the importance of look and feel for web applications cannot be dismissed. This raises the need for a clearer definition of usability for web applications, one that embraces the need to support the user goals yet recognizes the visual elements web applications share with web sites.

Analysis of how the companies described the usability needs of their user shows a contradiction with their definitions of usability. For example, when describing their understanding of usability, no companies mentioned efficiency or productive use. But when discussing the needs of their user, two cited the most important element as efficient use of the product. Another example is that although two companies defined usability in terms of look and feel, none regarded it as a usability need for their users. Yet most companies recognized it as a key element in attracting new customers. The most common usability needs cited centered around ease of use, although it was described in different ways. One company described it as learnability, another as ease of use and two as intuitiveness. This is interesting when compared to claims by [20] who suggested that learnability is not as important in web applications compared to web sites because the user would be more likely to have undergone training or have documentation available.

4.3 Usability Practices

Only two of the five companies had internal staff dedicated to usability design practices and one of these was a part-time employee working from home. A third company used external consultants to conduct usability evaluations of their product during its initial development. Three of the five companies gathered usability requirements as part of requirements analysis. In two of these companies, they do not explicitly refer to them as usability requirements, rather they were gathered as part of the general task requirements for the user. These were the same companies that defined usability in terms of supporting the user's tasks. It is difficult to see how the user can explicitly provide all of their usability requirements without ever referring to them as such.

In terms of the overall product design, three of the companies had a formally established software design team in place and the other two had lead architects responsible for product design. They were responsible for the overall vision and direction of the product. It is of concern that there was no mention of usability being represented at this level of design. It appears that usability tasks are being practiced at grassroots level and are of less concern during the high level design of products. This suggests that usability is not a concern at the upper management level yet management support is critical for it to grow in importance. Although all five companies considered themselves to be offering a good level of usability, only one of the four companies had a management driven approach to practicing usability techniques.

Two of the five companies claimed to do usability testing, with one reporting that that this was done as part of Acceptance Testing. The researchers believes that there is a lack of understanding as to what usability testing is and it is confused with User Acceptance Testing. Two companies required that the client must sign off on the product based on acceptance testing. This is a positive step although not an efficient means in catching usability issues at the end of the project lifecycle.

When asked who was responsible for usability in the end product, two companies cited the client. This is interesting considering the fact that these companies never explicitly discuss usability with the client, so it is difficult to see to what degree they are responsible. Although all companies demonstrated a degree of collaboration with the client during Requirements Analysis, only one company sought approval from the client on the final set of requirements. The most interesting observation was that none of the companies openly discussed usability requirements with their clients but incorporated it into the task requirements. This suggests that companies expect their clients to be able to represent their usability needs without having explicitly referred to usability.

The lack of UCD practices was apparent across all of the case studies, regardless of whether they developed bespoke applications or software for sale to multiple customers. The findings revealed that the three companies developing bespoke software were the only ones who claimed to gather usability requirements. However, the evidence on overall usability practices in this sample size did not suggest that the nature of applications being developed had any bearing on the level of UCD techniques being practiced.

Analysis of the development process has shown that three of the companies are following an iterative process, which is encouraged by UCD experts as a critical factor in ensuring good usability in the end product. But during their iterative design phase, only two companies provide early prototypes to the clients for analysis. Evidence shows that finding usability issues at the end of a project life cycle is the most inefficient way to resolve them. For this reason, it is worrying that most of the companies are not involving their users from the early stages of the design process. It appears that between Requirements Analysis and Acceptance Testing, there is very little interaction between the client and the development team.

It should also be noted that there was almost no distinction in any company between client and end user. One company noted that the client might review the requirements despite the fact that they are not necessarily knowledgeable about the end user's needs. It was clear that these companies recognised the fact that they had to please the client first and foremost. But this assumes that the client will represent the end users needs and if the end user is not happy with the end product, it is unlikely that the client will take responsibility.

The evidence suggests that meeting usability needs is considered by companies to be a part of good functional and U.I design, rather than a set of independent tasks. These companies have not adopted specific usability techniques in their development process. This supports the evidence that UCD techniques as criticized as unsuitable due to the fact that they were developed outside the field of software development. Despite not using usability techniques, most of these companies demonstrated a belief that they are supporting the usability needs of the user through good task analysis. [21] believe that web-based applications place increased emphasis on user interactions. It suggests that the nature of web applications means that there is already more focus on the user experience compared to developing traditional applications.

4.4 Product Usability

All of the companies believed that usability was very important for attracting new customers. They unanimously claimed that the usability of their product was very good. However, it was outside the scope of this study to examine the usability of the products developed by the case study companies. For this reason, it was not possible to verify the claims made by the interviewees about the usability of their products. All five companies claimed that the usability of their product was better than the competition, another claim which could not be verified without assessing the usability of their products and their competitor's products.

This study found no evidence on the level of usability being delivered in web applications today. This has been justified by the fact that companies would naturally be reluctant to reveal negative feedback about their web applications. Accordingly, it was not possible to compare the opinions about the usability other companies products with those of the case study companies. As previously stated, this study also did not review the usability of the products developed by the case study companies as it was considered outside its scope. For this reason, it was not possible to compare the usability of the case studies products against those of other companies.

5 Discussion

The cross-case analysis has revealed differences between current practices among SMEs and industry standards for software development processes and usability practices. The key gaps between these standards and current practices are outlined below:

- SMEs are not using a development process designed to meet the specific needs of web application development.
- There is little use of UCD techniques in the development process: Usability requirements are not gathered independently; No formal usability testing; No involvement of end user in design process; and little practice of usability evaluations.
- The SMEs definition of usability is limited and inconsistent.
- There is a need for a definition of usability specifically for web applications.
- Uptake of, and interest in, best practice frameworks is poor.
- There is a need for open discussion with clients and end users on usability requirements.
- There is little awareness of usability standards and they are considered too vague to implement in real projects.
- Few staff members with UCD experience.

Other findings of less critical importance were:

- The definitions of usability made no provision for 'quality in use', such as satisfaction or efficiency.
- No usability representation during high level design of products.
- Descriptions of usability contradicted their awareness of the end user's usability needs.
- Regardless of the process model, interviewees demonstrated a good understanding of their process and acknowledged deviations.
- SMEs were positive in the direction they were taking through recent efforts to improve their process.

5.1 Conclusions

The findings show interesting similarities with our background literature review, which revealed that there were no proven process models available that met the specific needs of web development. This study showed that none of the companies were using a development process designed specifically for web application development. It also supported evidence that the use of best practice frameworks has been particularly slow among SMEs.

The literature also suggested that the practice of UCD techniques was slow, which was corroborated with the evidence from these case studies. The findings also uphold suggestions that web developers are confused about how to implement usability. Analysis of the interviews showed that the definitions of usability were inconsistent and that there is still is a need for a definition of usability specifically for web applications. There was also very little awareness of usability standards. Also of concern is the lack of involvement of end users in the development process.

There were positive findings in that the companies were demonstrating recent improvements in their process and an acknowledgement of process shortcomings. Interviewees demonstrated a good understanding of their process, regardless of whether it was documented or not. There was also a unanimously high level of pride in the end product.

5.2 Limitations

The primary limitation of this research is the small number of companies it analysed. It is difficult to draw firm conclusions from such a small set of case studies. However, it is still possible to draw tentative conclusions and a higher sample size of case study companies could be used to strengthen the validity of the findings. Further study would also benefit from a larger sample size of interviewees from each case study company. This would enable the researcher to investigate whether the practices and opinions differ according to different perspectives within the same company.

This study did not look at the products developed by any of the case study companies in order to assess their level of usability. When investigating usability awareness and practices in a company, it would be of merit to also measure the usability in the end product in order to see if the level of awareness has any bearing on the usability on the end product.

5.3 Future Research

As the number and complexity of web applications grow, and user interactions with these systems grow, the need for research in web application usability increases. The background research revealed a need for further research in software process models and UCD models that cater specifically to web application development. But before a suitable model can be established, there is a need to understand the current practices among web development companies and the difficulties they encounter. The scope of the research into usability practices among web application development companies could be widened to a larger number of case studies, based on an increased timeframe. This would increase the validity of the findings and set the groundwork for developing a suitable process model and UCD model for web application development by SMEs.

References

1. Ginige, A., Murugesan, S.: Web Engineering: An Introduction. IEEE Multimedia (January- March 2001)
2. Baresi, L., Garzotto, F., Paolini, P.: From Web Sites to Web Applications: New Issues for Conceptual Modeling. In: Mayr, H.C., Liddle, S.W., Thalheim, B. (eds.) ER Workshops 2000. LNCS, vol. 1921, p. 89. Springer, Heidelberg (2000)
3. Coleman, G., O'Connor, R.: Software Process in Practice: A Grounded Theory of the Irish Software Industry. In: Richardson, I., Runeson, P., Messnarz, R. (eds.) EuroSPI 2006. LNCS, vol. 4257, pp. 28–39. Springer, Heidelberg (2006)
4. Ginige, A., Murugesan, S.: The Essence of Web Engineering. IEEE Multimedia (April-June 2001)
5. Fraternali, P.: Tools and Approaches for Developing Data-Intensive Web Applications: A Survey. ACM Computer Surveys 31(3) (1999)
6. Pressman, R.: What a Tangled Web We Weave. IEEE Software (January-February 2000)
7. Avison, D., Fitzgerald, G.: Where now for Development Methodologies. Communications of the ACM 46(1) (2003)
8. Gellersen, H., Gaedke, M.: Object-Oriented Web Application Development. IEEE Internet Computing (Januaruy-February 1999)
9. Frokjar, E., Hertzum, M., Hornbak, K.: Measuring Usability: Are Effectiveness, Efficiency, and Satisfaction Really Correlated? In: Proceedings of the SIGCHI conference on Human factors in computing systems. ACM Press, New York (2000)
10. Juristo, N., Windl, H., Constantine, L.: Introducing Usability. IEEE Software (January-February 2001)
11. Mayhew, D.: The Usability Engineering Lifecycle. Morgan Kaufmann, San Francisco (1999)
12. Seffah, A., Metzker, E.: The Obstacles and Myths of Usability and Software Engineering. Communications of the ACM 47(12) (2004)
13. Folmer, E., van Gurp, J., Bosch, J.: A Framework for Capturing the Relationship between Usability and Software Architecture. Software Process Improvement and Practice 8(2) (2003)
14. Anderson, J., Fleek, F., Garrity, K., Drake, F.: Integrating Usability Techniques into Software Development. IEEE Software (January-February 2001)
15. Mao, J., Vredenburg, K., Smith, P., Carey, T.: The State of User-Centered Design Practice. Communications of the ACM 48(3) (2005)
16. Radle, K., Young, S.: Partnering Usability with Development: How Three Organizations Succeeded. IEEE Software (January-February 2001)
17. Wixon, D.: Evaluation Usability Methods: Why the Current Literature Fails the Practitioner. Interactions (July-August 2003)
18. Constantine, L., Lockwood, L.: Usage-Centered Engineering for Web Applications. IEEE Software (March-April 2002)
19. Cloyd, M.: Designing User-Centered Web Applications in Web Time. IEEE Software (January-February 2001)
20. Lazar, J.: User-Centred Web Development. Jones and Bartlett Computer Science (2000)
21. Lowe, D., Eklund, J.: Client Needs and the Design Process in Web Projects. Journal of Mobile Multimedia 1(1) (2005)

Quality Attribute Techniques Framework

Yin Kia Chiam[1,2,3], Liming Zhu[1,2], and Mark Staples[1,2]

[1] NICTA, Locked Bag 9013, Alexandria NSW 1435, Australia
{yinkia.chiam,liming.zhu,mark.staples}@nicta.com.au
[2] School of Computer Science and Engineering, K17, University of New South Wales,
Sydney, NSW 2052, Australia
[3] School of Computer Science, University of Malaya, 50603 Kuala Lumpur, Malaysia

Abstract. The quality of software is achieved during its development. Development teams use various techniques to investigate, evaluate and control potential quality problems in their systems. These "Quality Attribute Techniques" target specific product qualities such as safety or security. This paper proposes a framework to capture important characteristics of these techniques. The framework is intended to support process tailoring, by facilitating the selection of techniques for inclusion into process models that target specific product qualities. We use risk management as a theory to accommodate techniques for many product qualities and lifecycle phases. Safety techniques have motivated the framework, and safety and performance techniques have been used to evaluate the framework. The evaluation demonstrates the ability of quality risk management to cover the development lifecycle and to accommodate two different product qualities. We identify advantages and limitations of the framework, and discuss future research on the framework.

Keywords: Quality Attribute Techniques, Product Quality, Software Process Improvement, Process Tailoring.

1 Introduction

The process research framework presented by SEI's IPRC states that "In an ideal future state, the use of processes is part of accepted practice to ensure that acceptable levels of product qualities are in place during all stages of the software and system development life cycle" [1, p.24]. It is during software development that product qualities such as safety, performance, reliability and security are determined. It is costly and time consuming to fix quality problems at later development stages if a system fails to meet specified levels of product quality. Research questions identified by the IPRC [1, p.27] in this area highlight the importance of understanding how software processes can be created to target product quality goals: "How do we select processes to meet specific product quality requirements?" and "What process steps significantly influence the achievement of a specified level of product quality?".

Software engineers use a variety of specific techniques to investigate, evaluate, and control potential quality problems throughout the development of a system.

R.V. O'Connor et al. (Eds.): EuroSPI 2009, CCIS 42, pp. 173–184, 2009.

In this paper, we call these "Quality Attribute Techniques" (QAT). These QATs are usually technical engineering techniques [2] that are specific to individual product quality issues. Examples of QATs for safety include hazard analysis techniques such as Failure Mode and Effect Analysis (FMEA) and Fault Tree Analysis (FTA). QATs may be specific to a single phase of the development lifecycle, or span multiple phases. However, QATs are usually not explicitly detailed in software process models, and the relationship between QATs and other process elements are not usually clearly shown. In order to create software process models that target specific quality attributes, it is important to first understand the important characteristics of QATs and how they relate to the development process. If quality procedures are left implicit in software process models, then tasks related to quality problems can be forgotten when individuals leave development teams [3, p.2].

Most software process tailoring methodologies are designed to address variations in project context such as customer characteristics or the size of the product or development team [4,5,6]. The research literature has not normally regarded product quality as an important characteristic for software process tailoring. So, although QATs are used in practice by software engineers, they are not currently represented in detail or incorporated well in software development process models [2,7]. In practice, such information is usually informally described in process documentation. The existence of a repository of codified knowledge about QATs could help development teams to better understand the potential effect of using various QATs to target key product qualities across all phases of the software development process.

This paper proposes and evaluates a Quality Attribute Technique Framework (QATF) for capturing important information about QATs. The QATF is intended to provide a basis for creating a catalogue of QATs to support software process tailoring to target a specific product quality attribute. Elements of the QATF focus on information required for decision making during QAT selection and integration with development processes. We have used safety techniques to motivate the framework, and evaluate the framework using safety and performance techniques. We use risk management as a general theory to encompass a variety of product qualities. The following two research questions are the focus of this paper:

1. What characteristics of QATs are useful to select QATs for inclusion in a tailored software process that targets a specific product quality attribute?
2. What characteristics of QATs are useful to integrate QATs into software development process models?

The outline of this report is as follows. Section 2 discusses work related to this research. Section 3 describes the QATF. Section 4 presents an evaluation of the QATF using safety and performance techniques. Section 5 discusses limitations and advantages of the QATF arising from the evaluation. Section 6 presents conclusions and discusses future research.

2   Related Work

Most earlier research on helping development teams to achieve specific product qualities has focused on techniques and guidelines for specific quality attributes (e.g. [8,9,10,11,12]) or specific lifecycle phases (e.g. [13]). It is important to address quality throughout the entire development process. Process engineers select appropriate techniques and incorporate them into development processes created or tailored for new projects. The selection and integration of techniques into defined process models requires relevant information about those techniques to be available and presented to process engineers.

There are some efforts in the safety area to describe information about safety techniques. The EWICS TC7 Software Sub-group [14] and Leveson [15, p.313-358] provide general descriptions of safety techniques and highlight advantages and disadvantages of using each technique. Characteristics related to process information have been discussed by Alberico et al. [11]) and Stephans [16]. Zurich Risk Engineering [17] has compared hazard analysis techniques from the resource perspective (team approach, documentation, time required and team leader expertise) and the scope perspective (result, analysis approach, depth of analysis, emphasize single or multiple failures). These (especially the resource perspective) are closely related to project characteristics. Some approaches in software performance engineering (SPE) such as [18,19] discuss integration of performance activities into the software development process. Vegas [20] has proposed a characterisation schema to identify the relevant information for testing techniques.

Previous approaches do not attempt to systematically capture and document the important information about QATs and their relationship with other process elements. Most of the safety guidelines and approaches still lack information which is important for QAT integration and process tailoring. Some attributes identified in [20] and [14] are only suitable for testing techniques and are not relevant to other types of QATs. Development teams need appropriate information to understand the characteristics of QATs, how they are incorporated into process models, and how they function to identify, analyse or control potential quality problems.

QATs for safety-critical system have been selected to motivate this initial framework because the area of system safety is well-established. There are many existing procedures, handbooks, standards, books and other references. In safety-critical systems, techniques are available to perform hazard evaluation, hazard control and hazard analysis. This does not affect the validity of the whole framework as all extracted characteristics are non-safety specific.

3   QATF

The ultimate goal of this research is to improve product quality by better integrating appropriate QATs into software process models. Information about QATs can support decision making during QAT selection and integration with development processes. The QAT framework (QATF) captures and presents information about QATs in a format intended to be suitable for process engineers to understand QATs and to highlight the relationship between QATs and other process elements. This is to support development teams select appropriate QATs and incorporate them into process models and related process guides. The framework is intended to encompass QATs from many quality domains.

3.1   QAT Overview

QATs are used to identify, analyze, and control potential quality problems in the development of critical systems. For examples, safety critical systems are concerned with hazards to life, property or the environment, security-critical systems focus on resistance to external threats and malicious actions against integrity [15], and performance-critical systems emphasize response time or throughput [18]. However, despite their importance in practice, QATs are not usually represented in detail in software development process models. They are not well integrated with other process elements such as tasks, roles and work products across the different phases of process models.

3.2   Identifying Important Characteristics of QATs

The QATF was constructed using the following approach. An initial review of the software safety literature identified the QATs in the safety area. The review also provided information about characteristics of these QATs, such as aims, description, benefits, limitations and expertise required [15,21,16,22,17]. By referring to the software process modeling literature and simulation literature [23,24][23] and the safety literature [11,16], process characteristics such as input, output and performer have been identified and populated.

We analysed the differences and similarities between various types of safety techniques. Based on the purpose of selecting QATs and integrating them into process models, characteristics which are generic for all the QATs have been selected. These characteristics have been grouped into three perspectives: General Information, Process Tailoring and QAT selection. Metamodels such as SPEM [23] can be used to define software processes and their components. The Process Tailoring characteristics in our framework have been selected based on the basic process entities defined in SPEM: roles, activities, work products and guidance. According to SPEM, a software development process is a collaboration between multiple roles that execute operations called activities and have work products as inputs and outputs [23]. Guidance elements such as tools, guidelines and examples can be used to support or automate the execution of an activity. The QATF and the three perspectives are as follows.

General Information. The General Information perspective provides an overview of the functionality of a QAT.

- Technique Name: *Short and full name of the QAT.*
- Aims: *What the QAT helps or enables us to do.*
- Description: *A brief overview of the QAT.*

Process Tailoring Characteristics. The Process Tailoring perspective highlights the relationship of a QAT with elements in software process models.

- Main performer(s): *The roles of people who typically perform the QAT.*
- Optional Performer(s): *Other roles which can optionally perform or assist the QAT.*
- Phase(s): *The development process phase(s) in which the QAT is applied.*
- Input: *The work products (information or artefacts) needed to apply the QAT.*
- Output: *The temporary, intermediate or final products created or modified during the performance of the QAT.*
- Guidance Documents: *Additional documents (e.g. guidelines, templates or examples) that can be used to assist the performer to execute the QAT.*
- As Source Data for (optional): *Other techniques or process activities that rely on the outputs from the QAT.*

QAT Selection Characteristics. The QAT Selection perspective provides a more detailed and structured view of a QAT, including costs, benefits, and quality impact in terms of our risk-based theory of quality management.

- Category: *The quality risk to which the QAT belongs (refer to Section 3.3).*
- Benefits: *Principal benefits claimed for the QAT.*
- Limitations: *Specific difficulties or limitations associated with the QAT.*
- Cost of Application: *The level of effort and resources needed to perform the QAT.*
- Expertise: *The level of expertise or training required to perform this QAT.*
- Team/Individual approach: *Whether the QAT is a team approach or is performed by an individual.*
- Single/Multiple Failures Analysis: *Whether the QAT emphasizes single failures in isolation or is geared toward multiple failures in combination.*
- Tool(s): *Tool(s) that can be used to support this QAT.*

3.3   QAT Categorisation Based on Risk Management Process

Most prior research has focused on techniques for individual quality attributes or specific lifecycle phases. We are attempting to provide a more general framework for QATs, using risk management as a general theory for managing quality during development. We have found risk management to be useful in understanding how QATs function to affect quality by identifying, analyzing, and controlling potential quality problems. In the QATF, categories classify QATs according to the method by which they address quality risks. We believe this will help process engineers to incorporate appropriate QATs to better manage quality throughout the development process. For example, FMEA is useful for hazard analysis (safety risk analysis). Process engineers may include FMEA into process activities which require hazard analysis during the design phase.

According to [25, p.7], the risk management process is "a continuous process for systematically addressing risk throughout the life cycle of a product or service". The risk-driven quality management process is inter-related with the normal software development processes. After defining quality objectives, potential quality risks can be identified. The impact of each potential risk can be analysed and ranked according to its probability of occurrence and severity of damage. The amount of effort to monitor, eliminate or prevent specific risks can be determined by the level of risks.

Based on the studies that discusses software risk management processes [26,25,15], QATs have been grouped into two main categories: Quality Assessment and Quality Control (see Fig. 1). Below, safety techniques are used as case examples in the description of these categories.

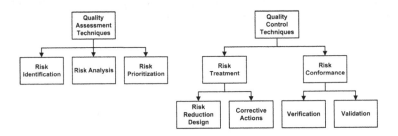

Fig. 1. Categorisation of QATs: Quality Assessment and Quality Control

Quality Assessment Techniques

1. Risk Identification - Involve QATs which produce lists of the project-specific quality risk items may compromise a project's satisfactory outcome. Typical QATs for safety include hazard identification techniques such as Hazard and Operability Study (HAZOP), "What if" Checklist.
2. Risk Analysis - Involve QATs which produce assessments of the probability and magnitude of losses associated with each of the identified quality risk items, and assessments of compound risks involved in risk-item interactions. Typical QATs for safety include hazard analysis techniques such as Failure Mode and Effect Analysis (FMEA), Fault Tree Analysis (FTA).
3. Risk Prioritisation - Involve QATs which produce a prioritised ordering of the quality risk items identified and analysed. Typical QATs for safety include techniques used to rank the impact of identified hazards such as Consequence Analysis, Criticality Analysis.

Quality Control Techniques

1. Risk Treatment - Involve QATs which resolve, reduce or eliminate risk items and take corrective action when appropriate. Typical QATs for safety include hazard reduction design such as simplification and decoupling or corrective actions such as improve error recovery (e.g. feedback, checking procedures, treating system failures and supervision).

2. Risk Conformance - Involve process of determining (verification) and confirming (validation) the quality specification of either a phase or that the complete system is fulfilled and is consistent with the quality requirements. Typical QATs for safety include verification and validation techniques such as Sneak Circuit Analysis, Control Flow Analysis and Boundary Value Analysis to ensure that the software product meet precise safety objectives.

4   Evaluation of QATF

This section provides an initial evaluation of the QATF in assessing its support for the integration of QATs into software development process models. Various types of QATs are available to identify, analyze, and control potential quality problems during software development. In this evaluation, the QATF has been used to capture information for some safety and performance techniques.

Table 1. Organising Safety QATs into Different Software Development Phases

Development Phase	Safety Activities	Safety Techniques
Requirements	Preliminary Hazard Identification (PHI)	ETBA, HAZOP, Checklist
	Preliminary Hazard Analysis (PHA)	ETBA, HAZOP
Architecture	Hazard Analysis (SSHA, SHA)	FMEA, FMECA, FTA, ETA
	Design Pattern	Homogeneous Redundancy Pattern, Diverse Redundancy Pattern, Monitor-Actuator Pattern
Design	Hazard Analysis (SSHA, SHA)	FMEA, FMECA, FTA, ETA
	Hazard Analysis (O&SHA)	PET, Procedural audits
	Safety Design	Design for controllability, Barriers (Lockouts, Lockins, Interlocks), fail-safe design
	Safety Design Review	Walkthroughs, Checklists, Fagan inspection, State transition diagrams, Time Petri nets
Coding	Safety Code Design	Error prevention (e.g. interlock); Error deduction (e.g. stepladder); Error recovery (e.g. warning)
	Safety Code Review	Emulation Analysis, Symbolic execution
	Design Patterns	Homogeneous Redundancy, Diverse Redundancy, Monitor-Actuator
Testing	Safety Testing	Sneak circuit analysis, Software common work analysis
	Hazard Analysis	FMEA, FMECA, FTA, ETA
	Independent Safety Audit	Safety Management Organisation Review Technique (SMORT)

4.1 Methodology

The first part of the evaluation organises these QATs into different development phases. The process tailoring information (e.g. phase, artifacts) captured by QATF is used to incorporate QATs into relevant development process phases. Safety and performance activities are used to describe the common purpose of using these QATs. The second part of evaluation organises QATs into different risk categories in Section 3.3 according to their aims in risk management. Safety and performance techniques are again used as examples for this evaluation.

4.2 Results of Evaluation

Table 1 shows some examples of the safety QATs and their fit into development process phases. For example, FMEA is suitable for subsystem hazard analysis (SSHA) and system hazard analysis (SHA) during the architecture and design phases. This QAT is not appropriate for hazard identification or preliminary hazard analysis (PHA) in earlier phases because it is intended to help to analyse potential failure causes and their effects. Corrective actions will be recommended to the potential hazards based on an assessment of their criticality. Detailed system information and descriptions are needed in order to perform this QAT.

Table 2. Organising Performance QATs into Different Software Development Phases

Development Phase	Performance Activities	Performance Techniques
Requirements	Define and Analyse Performance Requirements	Execution graphs (EG), Use Case Maps (UCM), Layered Queueing Network (LQN)
Architecture	Performance Prediction	Performance Assessment for Software Architecture (PASA), LQN, Performance Evaluation Process Algebra (PEPA), Stochastic Petri Nets (SPN)
	Performance-oriented design Principles and Patterns	Principles (e.g. Centering Principles, Shared Resource Principle), Patterns (e.g. Fast Path, Batching)
	Identify Performance Antipatterns	Antipatterns (e.g. Excessive Dynamic Allocation)
Design	Performance Prediction	LQN, Markov Chain
	Performance Principles	Principles (e.g. Locality Principle, Parallel Processing Principles)
	Identify Performance Antipatterns	Antipatterns (e.g. Circuitous Treasure Hunt)
Coding	Performance Solutions	Performance Patterns (e.g. Fast Path, Batching)
Testing	Performance Testing and Measurement	Load Test, Instrumentation (e.g. ARM, Paradyn), Benchmark
	Performance Enhancement	Performance Tuning

Table 3. Organising QATs into Different Risk Management Categories

Risk Category	Safety Techniques	Performance Techniques
Risk Identification	HAZOP, Checklist, ETBA	EG, UCM, Interactive Tree Algorithm, Performance Antipatterns
Risk Analysis	FMEA, FMECA, FTA, ETA	Software Architecture Analysis Method (SAAM), PASA; Layered queuing network (LQN), Stochastic Petri Nets, Markov Chains
Risk Prioritisation	FMEA, FMECA, Criticality Analysis, Consequence Analysis	Layered queueing network (LQN), Markov Chains
Risk Treatment - Risk Reduction Design	Hazard Reduction Design (e.g. Simplification and decoupling)	Principles (e.g. Locality, Parallel Processing)
Risk Treatment - Corrective Actions	Error Recovery (e.g. feedback, checking procedures)	Performance Tuning, Performance Patterns (e.g. Fast Path Speed-Up)
Risk Conformance - Verification	Sneak Circuit Analysis, Control Flow Analysis and Boundary Value Analysis	Load Testing, Stress Testing, Instrumentation
Risk Conformance - Validation	SMORT, Safety Review, Fagan Inspection	Benchmark, Profilers

Development teams can use the QATF to help them compare FMEA with other safety QATs such as FTA and ETA, to determine a sequence of using QATs by referring to the process information captured by the QATF. The most appropriate QATs can be selected to execute specific safety tasks. For example, FTA and ETA can be used when the design is completed. FTA begins with all hazards identified from other QATs such as FMEA and HAZOP and works backwards to determine their possible causes until reaching a base event. ETA uses inputs from QATs such as FTA to analyse all possible consequences and determine the percentage of consequences which lead to the desired result.

As with safety, there are various performance techniques available to identify and address performance problems throught development processes. These QATs include performance estimation techniques, performance modelling techniques, performance evaluation techniques to ensure that the implementation meets performance objectives and also some principles and patterns for performance design. Table 2 organises some performance QATs into different development phases. For example, there are a set of performance-oriented principles to identify design alternatives that help to meet specific performance objectives. Design engineers can use the QATF to help choose the most suitable principle by referring to the definition and examples of applying these principles.

Table 3 organises some of the safety and performance QATs into different quality risk management types (refer to Section 3.3). QATs are categorised based on their aims and description captured by QATF. Development teams can choose QATs based on their action in quality risk management process, and then integrate them into their software processes.

5   Discussion

The section discusses some of the benefits and limitations of using QATF that we have observed to date. The QATF provides a systematic way to capture important information about QATs. The template provides some information about how QATs impact quality during development, and how QATs can be related to software development processes. The first part of our evaluation suggests that QATs can be integrated into process models by referring to the process tailoring characteristics in the QATF. Although the QATF was initially motivated and developed using safety techniques, our evaluation has shown that the framework is also relevant for other quality attributes (performance).

The risk management categories provide a way for development team to choose QATs based on the means by which they impact quality risks. Table 3 shows some examples of QATs which are been organised into different risk management categories. We expect that process improvements to identify, analyse, and control quality risks could be undertaken by integrating corresponding QATs into the appropriate development phases or activities. These tables also indicate that quality management processes are iterative and ongoing. For example, FMEA and FTA not only can be used for hazard analysis in the early development phases but also can been applied later during testing. New hazards will have been identified during the testing phase. These hazards can be analysed to decide on suitable risk treatments to control the identified hazards according to their severity and frequency of occurrence. However, the selection of QATs can be determined in practice by other considerations. For example, available expertise may be a limiting condition in adopting a new QAT. The framework contains elements to describe the resources and expertise required to use each QAT.

In the development of the QATF, we have catalogued some QATs for safety and performance, but the catalogue is incomplete. Joint efforts will be required between between researchers, process engineers, and quality experts in development teams to obtain a more complete catalogue of QATs across a wider range of product qualities. We intend that QAT selection strategies and process tailoring methods will be supported by this framework, but they are outside of the scope of the framework itself. Some selection strategies (e.g. [20,13]) and tailoring methods may be able to be extended to select and integrate QATs more effectively into development processes. Process modelling tools such as EPF or WAGNER may be able to be used to represent QAT information and tailor development process models using selected QATs.

6   Conclusions and Future Work

Quality Attribute Techniques (QATs) are used by development teams to create software with specific qualities. Potential quality problems can be identified, analyzed and controlled by using appropriate QATs throughout the development process. Development teams need appropriate information about QATs to better understand their impact on quality and to better integrate QATs into process models. Previous process tailoring approaches do not attempt to systematically capture and document how QATs can be incorporated into process models. This study has investigated important characteristics of QATs and has proposed a framework to capture and present significant QAT information to support QAT selection and process tailoring.

On the basis of this characterisation, development teams can use the QATF to help identify important information about QATs and to place QATs into development phases. We have used risk management theory as a basis to characterise QATs according to the means by which they impact potential quality risks. This has let us develop a framework that addresses a variety product qualities. Although the QATF was motivated and developed using safety techniques, our initial evaluation has showed that the framework can be used for performance, and we expect that other product qualities will also be able to be treated within the framework. This framework has been generated according to our own view, further theoretical and empirical evaluation is required for this initial framework.

Our future work will develop process tailoring methods to select appropriate QATs according to the product quality goals in a development project, and to incorporate those QATs into software development process models. The SPEM metamodel and EPF Composer will be investigated in terms of their ability to support the representation of QAT information captured by QATF and also integration of QATs.

Acknowledgements. NICTA is funded by the Australian Government as represented by the Department of Broadband, Communications and the Digital Economy and the Australian Research Council through the ICT Centre of Excellence program.

References

1. Forrester, E.: A Process Research Framework. The International Process Research Consortium (IPRC) (2006)
2. Zhu, L., Jeffery, D.R., Staples, M., Huo, M., Tran, T.T.: Effects of Architecture and Technical Development Process on Micro-process. In: Wang, Q., Pfahl, D., Raffo, D.M. (eds.) ICSP 2007. LNCS, vol. 4470, pp. 49–60. Springer, Heidelberg (2007)
3. Smith, C.U., Williams, L.G.: Best Practices for Software Performance Engineering. Technical report, Performance Engineering Services and Software Engineering Research (2003)
4. Basili, V.R., Rombach, H.D.: Tailoring the Software Process to Project Goals and Environments. In: International Conference on Software Engineering (ICSP), pp. 345–357 (1987)
5. Bowers, J., May, J., Melander, E., Baarman, M., Ayoob, A.: Tailoring XP for Large System Mission Critical Software Development. In: Wells, D., Williams, L. (eds.) XP 2002. LNCS, vol. 2418, pp. 100–111. Springer, Heidelberg (2002)

6. Pedreira, O., Piattini, M., Luaces, M.R., Brisaboa, N.R.: A Systematic Review of Software Process Tailoring. SIGSOFT Software Engineering Notes 32(3), 1–6 (2007)
7. Zhu, L., Tran, T.T., Staples, M., Jeffery, D.R.: Technical Development Process in the XML Domain. In: International Conference of Software Process, ICSP (2009)
8. Juristo, N., Ferre, X.: How to Integrate Usability into The Software Development Process. In: International Conference on Software engineering (ICSE 2006), pp. 1079–1080. ACM, New York (2006)
9. Lutz, R.R.: Targeting Safety-related Errors During Software Requirements Analysis. SIGSOFT Softw. Eng. Notes 18(5), 99–106 (1993)
10. Lawrence, J. D.: Software Safety Hazard Analysis Version 2.0. Technical report, Lawrence Livermore National Laboratory (1995)
11. Alberico, D., Bozarth, J., Brown, M., Gill, J., Mattern, S., McKinlay VI, A.: Software System Safety Handbook. A Technical and Managerial Team Approach (1999)
12. Borcsok, J., Schaefer, S.: Software Development for Safety-related Systems. In: International Conference on Systems (ICONS 2007), pp. 38–42 (2007)
13. Wojcicki, M.A., Strooper, P.: An Iterative Empirical Strategy for the Systematic Selection of a Combination of Verification and Validation Technologies. In: International Workshop on Software Quality (WoSQ 2007), p. 9 (2007)
14. EWICS TC7 Software Sub-group: Techniques for Verification and Validation of Safety-related Software. Computers and Standards 4(2), 101–112 (1985)
15. Leveson, N.: Safeware: System Safety and Computers. Addison-Wesley, Reading (1995)
16. Stephans, R.A.: System Safety for the 21st Century. Wiley, Chichester (2004)
17. Zurich Risk Engineering: Which Hazard Analysis? - A Selection Guide (1998)
18. Smith, C., Williams, L.: Performance Solutions: A Practical Guide to Creating Responsive, Scalable Software. Addison-Wesley, Reading (2002)
19. Fox, G.: Performance Engineering as A Part of The Development Life Cycle for Large-Scale Software Systems. In: International Conference on Software Engineering (ICSP), pp. 85–94. ACM Press, New York (1989)
20. Vegas, S.: Identifying The Relevant Information for Software Testing Technique Selection. In: International Symposium on Empirical Software Engineering (2004)
21. Storey, N.: Safety Critical Computer Systems. Addison Wesley, Reading (1996)
22. Vincoli, J.W.: Basic Guide to System Safety. Wiley, Chichester (2006)
23. OMG: Software Process Engineering Metamodel (SPEM) Version 2.0 (2008)
24. Pfahl, D., Ruhe, G., Lebsanft, K., Stupperich, M.: Software Process Simulation with System Dynamics - A Tool for Learning and Decision Support. New Trends in Software Process Modelling. World Scientific 18, 57–90 (2006)
25. AS/NZS ISO/IEC 16085:2007: Risk Management (2007)
26. Boehm, B.W.: Software Risk Management. IEEE Computer Society, Los Alamitos (1989)

Building an Observatory of Course-of-Action in Software Engineering: Towards a Link between ISO/IEC Software Engineering Standards and a Reflective Practice

François-Xavier Bru[1], Gaëlle Frappin[2], Ludovic Legrand[1], Estéban Merrer[1], Sylvain Piteau[3], Guillaume Salou[4], Philippe Saliou[5], and Vincent Ribaud[5]

[1] Thales Airborne System, 29283 Brest Cedex 2
{François-Xavier.Bru,Ludovic.Legrand,
Esteban.Merrer}@thalesgroup.com
[2] Teamlog, Rue Fulgence Bienvenüe, 22300 Lannion
Gaëlle.Frappin@teamlog.com
[3] Direction des Constructions Navales - DCNS, route de la corniche, 29200 Brest
Sylvain.Piteau@dcnsgroup.com
[4] Groupe Arkéa, 32 rue Mirabeau 29480 Le Relecq Kerhuon
Guillaume.Salou@arkea.com
[5] University of Brest, CS 93837, 29238 Brest Cedex, France
Vincent.Ribaud@univ-brest.fr, Philippe.Saliou@univ-brest.fr

Abstract. As a help to compete in an evolving market, small software companies may use an observatory of their course-of-action. The course of action considers the observable aspect of the actor's activity. Its analysis provides a description of actors' activity and it can express recommendations concerning both the individual situations and the collective situation. The observatory is an articulated set of data collecting methods supported with semantic wikis and a dedicated application. A case study, based on the activity of a team of 6 young software engineers, depicts some aspects of the building and the filling of the course-of-action observatory. As primary results of this work, we may think that observing and analyzing software engineer's activity help to reveal his/her theory-in-use – what governs engineers' behavior and tends to be tacit structures – That may help engineers to establish links between "Project Processes-in-use" and a simplified Process Reference Model and contribute to reduce the fit between a project-in-action and espoused SE standards.

Keywords: Course-of-action, theory-in-use, espoused theory, reflective practitioner, software engineering processes.

1 Introduction

For many small software companies, software process improvement (SPI) is often out of reach due to prohibitive costs and lack of SPI knowledge. However, to survive in this competitive market, software developers must improve their productivity, time to

R.V. O'Connor et al. (Eds.): EuroSPI 2009, CCIS 42, pp. 185–200, 2009.

market and customer satisfaction. A help could be provided through a reflective attitude (D. Schön [1]). A question occurs: "How to bring this reflective (and learning) attitude into organizations and everyday work?"

Theories of action study what an actor do, in a given situation, in order to achieve consequence or objectives. A distinction can be made between two kinds of theories of action. Espoused theories are those that an individual claims to follow. Theories-in-use are those that can be inferred from action [2]. Espoused theory and theory-in-use may be inconsistent, and the agent may or may not be aware of any inconsistency. By definition, the agent is aware of espoused theory. Theories-in-use can be made explicit by reflecting on action [2]. In the software engineering field - and especially in Very Small Enterprises – the horizon of standards or the corporate baseline of processes and practices constitute the espoused theory, since it is what engineers claim to follow. Although an emerging standard "Software Engineering - Lifecycle Profiles for Very Small Enterprises (VSE)" [2] may facilitate the use of SE standards in a VSE, what engineers do (and this action is designed and do not "just happen") may reveal a different theory-in-use. We believe that making explicit theories-in-use may help software engineers to learn more suitable theories-in-use, thus contributes to improve productivity and performance.

In this perspective, after several years of informal methods to analyze and improve software engineers' activities, we are now using the course-of-action analysis in order to understand the structural coupling of a software engineer with his/her environment and especially lifecycle software processes. Let us cite a short definition of course-of-action: "the activity of one (or several) specific actor(s), engaged in a specific situation, belonging to a specific culture, which is significant for the latter, in other words, that can be related or commented by him (or them) at any moment [4]." The course-of-action analysis is based on an observatory that we consider in this introduction as a system of data collecting methods. The data necessary to study the course of action includes continuous observations of the behavior of action and communication in a work situation as well as different traces of other elements such as interpretations, feelings, and judgments [4]. The analysis of this data produces a decomposition of the global dynamic in terms of smaller units and the relations of sequencing and embedding between these units. The results of this analysis may (i) help to design better interactions or corrective situations; (ii) facilitate the reconstruction by the actor of his/her own activity, i.e. going from "pre-reflective consciousness" towards a reflective attitude [1].

This paper is organized as follow. Section 2 presents the course-of-action framework and its application to software engineering. Section 3 drafts some related work. Section 4 discuss about the observatory of course-of-action of software engineers. Section 5 present excerpts of a case study. We finish with perspectives.

2 Course-of-Action Applied to Software Engineers' Activity

2.1 The Course-of-Action in a Nutshell

Pinsky and Theureau, ergonomists, initiated the theoretical and methodological framework of "course-of-action", summarized in one directing idea, that of the necessity of an analysis of the actual operators' activities in real work situations for the design of new work situations [5]. An important theoretical hypothesis that the course-of-action framework states about human activity, is that human activity is dynamically situated, i.e. always appeals to resources, individual as well as collectively shared to varied degrees, which stem from constantly changing material, social, and cultural circumstances. The course-of-action analysis add to various theories of "situated activity" the consideration of the domain of experience, i.e. that of the agent's course-of-experience, of the constructing process of this experience at any moment, and takes an interest in the articulation between the cognitive domain and the course-of-experience. Theureau in [6] defines the theoretical object called "course of action" as follows: *"what, in the observable activity of an agent in a defined state, actively engaged in a physically and socially defined environment and belonging to a defined culture, is pre-reflexive or again significant to this agent, i.e. presentable, accountable and commentable by him/her at any time during its happening to an observer-interlocutor in favourable conditions"*.

2.2 The Observatory of Course-of-Action

This paragraph is reproduced from [7].

The course-of-action analysis is based on an observatory that allows to specify the material conditions of situated recall (time, place, material elements of the situation), the follow up and the guiding of presentations, accounts and commentaries by the agents as well as the cultural, ethical, political and contractual conditions that are favorable to observation, interlocution, and creation of a consensus between the agent and the observer-interlocutor [6].

A methodology has been developed to collect data on the courses-of-action. It connects continuous observations and recordings of the agents' behavior, the provoked verbalizations of these agents in activity (from the "thinking aloud" for the observer-interlocutor to the interruptive verbalizations at privileged moments) and the agents' comments in self confrontation with recordings of their behavior [6].

Continuous observations and recordings together with verbalizations and self-confrontation let us access to a representation of dynamics of the structural coupling between the actor and his/her situation (including other actors) [9]. A "semiological framework" [6] provide us with a theory of activity allowing to describe the activity in abstract terms expressing hypothetical invariants. Explaining and using this theory is out of the scope of this paper focused on the observatory of course-of-action. It is sufficient to tell that this semiologic stems from the hypothesis that any period of course-of-action may be described in smaller units. This description of the intrinsic organisation of the course of action articulates two complementary descriptions: a description of its global dynamics, characterising the units of the course of action and the relations of sequencing and embedding between these units; a description of its local dynamics, characterising the underlying structure of the elementary units [5].

2.3 An Observatory of Software Engineers' Activity

The intervention of an ergonomist in an organization intended to produce software concern the analysis of human-system interaction – of the software engineer with his/her organization's processes – and the design of the system in order to optimize human well-being and overall system performance. In our case, we use the theoretical and methodological framework of course-of-action in order to analyze the activity of software engineers within Very Small Enterprises (VSEs, up to 15-25 employees).

Recall the definition of the course-of-action in §2.1: what, in the observable activity of an agent [...] is pre-reflexive or again significant to this agent, i.e. (i) presentable, (ii) accountable and (iii) commentable by him/her at any time during its happening [...]. Software workers do not achieve complex technical gestures or do not have to progress along a detailed procedure. So (i) presentations to an observer are quite difficult to reproduce and presentable artifacts that are most notable and representative of the job are the outputs of software activities and tasks. (ii) Accounts are easier to collect and observe because a minimum of traceability and reporting is performed in any organization and if it is not sufficient, accounting can be provoked without significantly modify the course of the activities. (iii) Comments are not natural objects and have to be provoked: reports, self competency assessment (§ 4.3).

The course-of-action framework proposes self confrontation as an indirect means to document actor's experience or pre-reflective consciousness or immediate understanding of his/her activity at every instant t; the fact is highlighted that the experience at instant t differs from what is called the reflective consciousness, which concerns particular and situated periods of the actor's activity, when he/she considers his/her past activity with a given purpose [8].

However, considering these two levels of consciousness, we may think that there are two different levels of description of software processes. The first level – on which this paper is focused – is concerned with the day-to-day course of a software project and its associated activities while the second level – on which most Software Engineering standards are focused – is concerned with a description of these activities. We believe that the first level is related with theories-in-use, those that can be inferred from action [2]. And we think that the second level is related with espoused theories, those that an individual claims to follow. The purpose of our work is to provide an observatory of existing processes and practices that could help to situate project processes and practices in-use regarding to espoused standards.

2.4 Application for Software Engineers in VSEs

The semiological framework of course-of-action makes it possible to describe the courses of action in general structural terms, expressing underlying regularities. It allows on the one hand, such a description of the global dynamics of the courses of action, and on the other hand, such a description of their local dynamics. It also links these two descriptions. As we discuss in §5.3, the smaller units, based on individual courses-of-action, describe the carrying out of all or part of software engineering base practices. Hence, the global dynamic, which is related to the composition of these performed practices, is a description of what we may call process-in-action.

The course-of-action analysis operates on what, in the observable activity of an agent, is presentable, accountable and commentable by him/her. A sound analysis may work only with sound collected data and, because most accurate data are collected by the team itself, it requires the team commitment to this self-observation. This team commitment can only be effective if the team is the main beneficiary of this overwork, collectively - with a valuable result on team processes-in-action - and individually - with an added-value on competency development -.

Thus, as presented in figure 1, this analysis shall lead to (i) help to specify the modalities of engineers' interaction with project processes leading to the design of better interactions or of corrective situations; (ii) contradict or support the reconstruction by the engineer of his/her own activity, i.e. going from "pre-reflective consciousness" of the actor towards a reflective practitioner attitude [1]. Both results have a valued impact on the project processes.

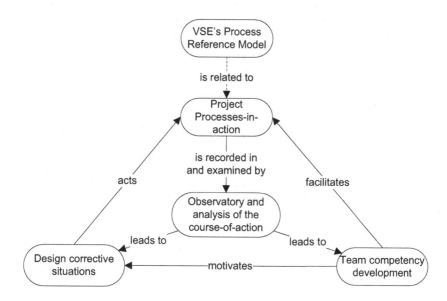

Fig. 1. The project's observable activities are self-recorded by team members. The analysis of the project-in-action provides a decomposition of the global dynamic in terms of smaller units and the relations of sequencing and embedding between these units. Two benefits are expected: (i) a reflective consciousness of competency maturity level; (ii) a support to design corrective actions. Both consequences may improve and facilitate the project processes.

3   Related Work

The "course-of-action" research framework [6] consists in several empirical and technological research programs in various domains (work analysis [4], traffic control [5], sport [8], and music composition [21]). The work described in this paper uses plentifully results of these research programs.

It would be impossible to reference all the research work that has been inseminated by Argyris and Schön's theories [10]. In the software engineering field, Halloran [11] investigates the relationship between a software process assessment and improvement model and organizational learning. This work points out the difference between "engineer's espoused theory" and his/her "theory in use" but it does not develop this matter as we did and rather focuses on the use of organizational learning to promote a proactive approach culturally to continuous improvement and learning procedures.

Many propositions have been made for Process Improvement or Process Assessment in small software companies ([12], [13], [14]). Many small organizations are unaware of existing SPI& SPA standards and assumes that assessments conformant to these standards can be expensive and time consuming, difficult to perform in small companies. We think that while building the observatory of course-of-action, foundations are set-up that will facilitate further SPI & SPA programs. There are similitude with the SPA process proposed in [13] based on an initial self-evaluation and following structured interviews and the observatory as we use it.

4 Observing Software Activities

4.1 Software Engineering Standards

A very concise definition of the objects of software engineering is "a project uses resources in performing processes to produce products for a customer [15]." It gives a model in figure 2, centered on the software engineering project as the focal point for applying software engineering standards. This suggests a categorization of standards in four major areas: customer, process, product, and resource.

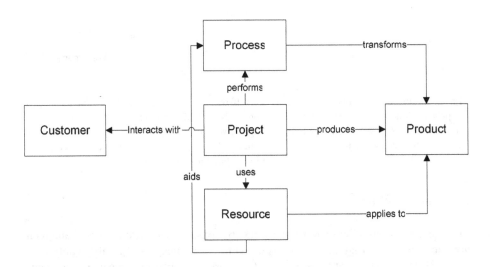

Fig. 2. The objects of software engineering, suggesting a categorization of standards in the subject areas of customer, process, product, and resource [15]

For VSEs, each category contains a number of standards that put them out of reach. There is a need for an umbrella standard within each category. The IEEE/IEC 12207, Software Life Cycle Processes [16], provides this umbrella for all of the customer and process standards. An on-going initiative of ISO should provide lifecycle profiles for Very Small Enterprises (VSEs) [7].

4.2 VSEs Faced to the 12207

Confronted to the 12207, a software engineer in a VSE is at a loss ([1]"like a goose finding a knife" as French people say). First, this standard has received major changes since 1995: Amendment 1 in 2002, Amendment 2 in 2004, and a complete revision in 2008. Secondly, there are currently 43 processes in the 12207:2008 [16], organized in 7 process groups. As an example of the gap with the VSEs needs, the emerging standard "Software Engineering - Lifecycle Profiles for Very Small Enterprises (VSE)" [7] contains 2 processes: Project Management (PM.1) and Software Implementation (SD.1). PM.1 is subdivided in 4 sub-processes (Project Planning, Project Plan Execution, Project Assessment and Control, Project Closure) and SD.1 is subdivided in 6 sub-processes (Software Implementation Initiation, Software Requirements Analysis, Software Architecture and Detailed Design, Software Construction, Software Integration and Tests Product Delivery).

It is not sure that a software engineer in a VSE share the same meaning of these 10 names of sub-processes (from Project Planning to Software Integration and Tests Product Delivery) with a client or a colleague of a major company engaged in any SPI program such as ISO/IEC 15504 or CMMI. However, they will try to communicate and may sign a contract, but they don't speak about the same things. This lack of understanding illustrates the existence of two theories of action – for a software engineer as for any practitioner -, as defined by Argyris and Schön. They have established a distinction between those theories that are implicit in what we do as practitioners and managers (theories-in-use), and those on which we call to speak of our actions to others (espoused theory). "When someone is asked how he would behave under certain circumstances, the answer he usually gives is his espoused theory of action for that situation. This is the theory of action to which he gives allegiance, and which, upon request, he communicates to others. However, the theory that actually governs his actions is this theory-in-use [10]." We may ask question about the extent to which theory-in-use fits espoused theory. Reflection may be a help to discover the theory-in-use and to reveal the nature of the 'fit'. We believe that the observatory of course-of-action – adapted to the software engineering field – may support this process.

4.3 What Can Be Observed?

This significant activity for the actors includes action and communication, but also other elements: interpretations, feelings, judgments, …The data necessary to study the course of action must include continuous observations of the behavior of action and communication in a work situation as well as different kinds of instigated verbalizations from the actors which would provide access to other elements [4].

Software development never uses a repeated scheme and it may be difficult to interrupt a software engineer at work and to provoke a verbalization of what he/she is doing and why. In §2.3 we gave an overview of what, in the observable activity is (i) presentable, (ii) accountable and (iii) commentable by the actor.

Products and documentary resources are main objects of (i) presentation as they describe the inputs and outputs of the activity. The "historical" context of resources' use and products' production has to be recorded too. This can be described in terms of events and processes, involving occurrences of agents (people) and artifacts (products and resources) meeting in space (in case of distributed cooperation) and time. As a first stage, we may consider individual courses of action of the various participants. At a second level, a collective action involves parts of several individual courses of action which take place synchronically or sequentially. We need to divide individual course-of-action in smaller units, that we call course-of-action unit. Each event of interest has to be (ii) accounted in an instance of Course-of-action Unit in relation with people and artifacts involved. It provides a kind of project journal. A journal may be seen as a kind of reflective practice that is a device for working with events and experiences in order to write (iii) comments and extract meaning from them.

5 A Case Study

5.1 Introduction

In spring 2007, local employers in Brest decided to implement a recent French law on professional training. This law requires that 3% of employees be under 'sandwich' (or work placement) conditions. A lot of companies choose to use a system called "Contrat de professionnalisation" (professionalization contract) over a period of 12 months. During these 12 months, the full-paid employee is attending university for certain periods. For contracts involving our computing department, we dedicated an innovative program called "Software Engineering by Immersion" ('Ingénierie du Logiciel par Immersion'). The main feature of this last year of the Masters programme is to learn software engineering by doing, without any computing course but with a long-term project as the foundation of all apprenticeships. Alternating employees are attending university in 9 periods of 2 consecutive weeks and work in team of 6 in order to build a complete information system.

The program's rhythm is based on the lifecycle of a project organized into stages. Each stage was arbitrary sized to 2 weeks due to the constraints of alternation. The cycle is: Stage 0: Warm-up; Stage 1: Project set-up; Stage 2: Requirement capture; Stage 3: Requirement analysis; Stage 4: Design; Stage 5: Software construction; Stage 6: Software construction; Stage 7: Integration and Verification; Stage 8: Qualification and Deployment.

This case study is based on the activity of a team of 6 young software engineers (the six former authors) accompanied with the two latter authors acting as participants-to-observe: one having a direct contact of the team members, sharing their environment and taking part in the activities of the team, the other one conducting reviews and formal assessments as they happen. This case study depicts some aspects of the building and the filling of the course-of-action observatory.

The whole observatory is supported with several electronic tools such as semantic wikis, content management system and dedicated applications. Semantic wikis offers a lightweight authoring plate-form and will be used to record most events of the day-to-day life in the project journal.

5.2   The Horizon of Software Engineering Standard

As told in section 4.1, the 12207:2008 standard acts as a standard umbrella and was used during the introductory stage to define the framework of a software engineer's activity. The 12207:2008 was preferred to CMMI because the former (used jointly with the 15504 standard [17]) separates processes and capability levels in two dimensions while CMMI handles them in one dimension. This separation was preferred because it defines processes "(set of interrelated or interacting activities which transforms inputs into outputs" [16]) independently from base practices ("an activity that, when consistently performed, contributes to achieving a specific process purpose [17]").

The 43 processes are too many and complex to be used as the reference model and we concentrate on 16, those related to the software development cycle, that is: 6.2.2 Infrastructure Management, 6.3.1 Project Planning, 6.3.2 Project Assessment and Control, 6.4.1 Stakeholder Requirements Definition, 6.4.4 Implementation Process replaced by 7.1.1 Software (SW) Implementation Process and its 6 sub-processes, 7.2.1 SW Documentation Management, 7.2.2 SW Configuration Management, 7.2.3 SW Quality Assurance, 7.2.4 and 7.2.5 SW Verification & Validation, 6.4.7 SW Installation. Processes are grouped into process groups (five 12207 group processes are concerned that we regrouped in three).

The 6 young engineers chosen for this case study have a Bachelor in Information Technology (4-year studies in the field) and they work in large companies with a structured corporate baseline. However, there is a need for a common reference of the terms used, either because they have different significations in the different companies, or because their signification is unknown or fuzzy. We choose to use the ISO/IEC FCD 24765, "Systems and software engineering – Vocabulary [18]".

We dispose of a PDF version of the 12207:2008, licensed by ISO and of a electronic version of the 24765, copyrighted by ISO but free of use as long as the copyright is cited. As the project goes along and its events are recorded in the project journal, and in order to facilitate links between the project journal and Software Engineering standards used at the horizon, the whole team filled two semantic wikis with a subset of the two standards used:

- the 12207 wiki (http://oysterz.univ-brest.fr/12207) is an hypertext reference of the ISO/IEC 12207:2008 for the process level : title, purpose, list of outcomes and process decomposition in activities and tasks;
- the 24765 wiki (http://oysterz.univ-brest.fr/24765) is a subset of the ISO/IEC 24765 vocabulary, it is actually under reengineering but on-line SEVOCAB is provided by ISO (http://pascal.computer.org/sev_display).

The structure of these two semantic wikis is given in figure 3.

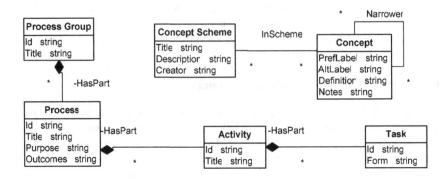

Fig. 3. A model of 12207 and 24765 semantic wikis

5.3   The Project in Action

The two latter authors both worked for nearly ten years at Thales Information System (formerly Syseca Inc), a software services company. They led projects and developed several management information systems under the control of Thales Information System corporate baseline.

The authors have defined an apprenticeship/production framework called ILI (*Ingénierie du Logiciel par Immersion*, Software Engineering by Immersion), based on a reference model, a development cycle and a typical WBS (Working Breakdown Structure: a deliverable-oriented hierarchical decomposition of the work to be executed by the project team to accomplish the project objectives and create the required deliverables. It organizes and defines the total scope of the project [18]).

The Process Reference Model (PRM) is adapted and simplified from ISO/IEC 12207; we are using 3 *process groups* organizing 13 processes: *Software Development Engineering* (Requirements capture, Software Requirements Analysis, Software Architectural Design, Software Detailed Design, Software Construction, Software integration; Software qualification testing); *Software Project Management* (Project Management, Quality Assurance, Configuration Management); and *Software Development Support* (Infrastructure Management, Life Cycle Model Management, Documentation Management, Installation-Operation).

We use a Y-shaped life cycle that separates resolution of technical issues from resolution of feature issues [19]. First, the cycle is divided into two branches (tracks): a functional track and a technical track. Then these two tracks amalgamate for the realization of the system.

The WBS has a structural and a temporal decomposition. Each process is structurally decomposed in Software Engineering activities (to distinguish it from the activities in the 12207 sense) that may have slightly variation from a project to another. Each Software Engineering activity is further decomposed in sub-activities that can be fully specified or just named, depending of the scope and goals of the project. The WBS is temporally organized in stages (in our case, 9 of 2 week each). The planning of each stage is divided in several work scenes that carry on SE activities. Scenes will be performed by team members and ought to produce artifacts.

The course-of-action forms a whole that is concerned with all aspects described in previous paragraphs but we need to divide the continuous development of the course of action into significant units (cf. §2.3). We decide to divide the whole course-of-action by replying to the question: "What is this about, from the point of view of the engineer?" This division is recorded through the central event Course-of-action Unit. Complex or collective interactions require an intermediate level, called Step-of-action sequencing and embedding Course-of-action units. Links with PRM are provided.

A picture of all these interlinked concerns is given in figure 4.

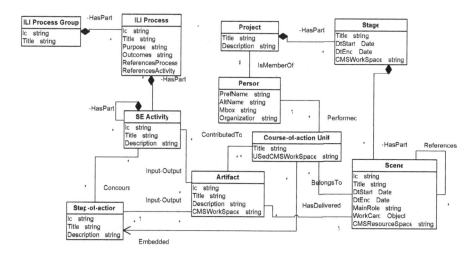

Fig. 4. A model of Process Reference Model -PRM- (on the left) and WBS (on the right). Artifacts are shared between PRM and WBS. The Course-of-action Unit is used as central link. Steps-in-action characterize the relations of sequencing and embedding between these units.

The project journal uses a semantic wiki in order to record the progress of the project. The project manager initially fills and updates the WBS of his/her project. Team members can record events as they happen but have to systematically fill the wiki at the end of each phase. Semantic wiki is the most flexible tool in order to record and shape a structured content. Properties (modifying the underlying data model) can be added, updated or deleted as the project goes along. Information (data) can be recorded in a bulk mode and the typesetting performed later. Things to do or to report are created in one Wiki word to indicate that they have to be filled. Information can be temporary missing or incomplete.

5.4 Recording Assessments

Several kinds of assessment occur in the life of a project. Assessment may be focused on products or services, on processes or on persons. Assessment itself provides information on action performed but many other elements significant for the actors and the course-of-action analysis: interpretations, feelings, judgments, actors' commitment to the situation and their use of past experience in the course-of- action.

Recording project assessment. The project has to record artifacts produced by project progress: lecture notes, progress meeting report, peer review reports which constitute valuable inputs for further analysis.

Recording competency assessment. We argue that personal capability determination (rather than process capability determination) is more suitable to VSEs because employees may perceive it as a valuable benefit. Using the 2-level structure of our Process Reference Model (on the left part of figure 4), we analyze carefully SE activities in order to define abilities mobilized (or competencies: "the ability of a person to act in a pertinent way in a given situation in order to achieve specific purposes [20]"). For each process, we defined a family of competencies constituted with a list of knowledge topics and a set of abilities or skills required to perform the process (see an example in table 1).

Table 1. An example of a competency family: "Software detailed design'

Knowledge topics	Abilities or skills
Software Design Fundamentals : concepts and principles, design role in a development cycle, top-level and detailed design	To use design methods and tools (in relation with requirements) to produce design documents: system and software architecture and detailed design
Software decomposition configuration item, software component, software unit	To implement methods and modeling tools of various aspects of a system (architecture and decomposition software, data structure)
Software architecture through different views: conceptual, dynamic, physical, data.	To implement J2EE development and technology of associated framework
UML diagrams to describe static and dynamic views	To implement DBMS concepts, techniques and tools
Object-oriented design	

We believe that a first step in competency development should be made by the engineer him/herself through a self-assessment of abilities at a maturity level. The assessment scale grows from 1 to 5: - 1: Smog - 2: Notion - 3: User - 4: Autonomous - 5: Expert. Each young engineer is required to periodically fill the 13 competency families while auto-analyzing the tasks performed and him/her achievement level with the abilities defined in the family. This periodic inventory is supported by eCompas, a tool intended to manage development, assessment and value-added of competencies over the course of a curriculum or a professional career.

The eCompas tool is intended to store artifacts that may be interesting to illustrate the ability determination. Each time a software engineer self-assesses a process's ability level, he/she has to write an entry associated with the process and may link this entry with artifacts stored. It constitutes a rudimentary portfolio, but sufficient for our purposes. This tool needs to be reengineered to work with the wikis' architecture.

5.5   Focus on a Process: The Design Process

Recording the project in action. According to ISO/IEC 12207, outcomes of the 7.1.3 Architectural Design and 7.1.4 Software Detailed Design Processes are: a) a software architectural design is developed and baselined that describes the software items that will implement the software requirements; b) internal and external interfaces of each software item are defined; c) consistency and traceability are established between software requirements and software design and d) a detailed design of each software component, describing the software units to be built, is developed.

For the Design Process, 12207 recommended tasks and 15504 base practices are roughly the same:

1) transformation of the requirements for the software item into an architecture that describes its top-level structure and identifies the software components.
2) development and documentation of a top-level design for the interfaces external to the software item and between the software components of the software item.
3) development and documentation of a top-level design for the database.
4) development and documentation of preliminary versions of user documentation.
5) definition and documentation of preliminary test requirements and the schedule for Software Integration.

Our ILI framework, considered as representative of VSEs processes, decompose the Design Process in 3 SE Activities: Adjusting the Design, Exemplary Software Design, and Software Design (including Database Design as a sub-activity).

If we have a look at the information recorded in the observatory by team members, they performed two kinds of self-confrontations. The structure of self-confrontations of the former kind, performed at the end of the task, reflects the structure of recommended tasks as they may be found in the SE Activity description. For instance, for the Exemplary Software Design Activity, the description stresses the identification of Computer Software Components, the requirements allocation to the components and the components specification. So, each participant to this activity recorded its own participation in a Course-of-action unit kept to the Activity description. The latter kind of self-confrontation was performed as team members prepared the Software Design Process Review, a formal review. They have to create a synthetic description of the Design Process and to record it in its associated Work Scenes (see figure 4). Participants created Steps-in-action embedding individual Course-of-action units and established inter-wikis links with the corresponding 12207 Processes. It is not sure that the 12207 outcomes and tasks were confronted to the performed actions, but it indicates an attempt to link the course-of-action at the horizon of SE standards.

Recording team competency development. Periodic inventories of team members are recorded within the eCompas tool. A copy (in a Word format) is stored into the observatory. Focusing on the Design Process, we may note that a team member has participated to the 3 SE Activities defined for the Design Process (see above). As the year started, he assesses himself at the maturity level - 1 - (or - none) for the process as a whole and for each associated abilities. Inside his company, he acts as a software developer and has very little opportunity to improve design skills. After the Software

Design Process Review (6th stage), he assesses himself to a maturity level of 4 - Autonomous - (level 2 - Notions - was reached at the end of the 3rd stage, and level 3 - User – after the Exemplary Design Activity). The availability of accurate competency level provides valuable information for the project manager in order to assign tasks to team members.

Recording other assessments. The most valuable information is provided with the meeting report. They are recorded using a semantic wiki through a semantic form. Links to other resources (person, artifact, process ...) are very easy to establish and to update. It provides an ordering scheme and new navigation features.

6 Conclusion and Perspectives

We proposed to adapt the course-of-action framework to software engineers' activity in Very Small Enterprises (VSEs). An observatory collects the data necessary to study the course of action therefore including continuous observations of the behavior of action and communication in a work situation as well as different kinds of instigated verbalizations (transcript in a written form) from the actors which would provide access to other elements such as interpretations, feelings, judgments. As a case study, the activity of a team of 6 young software engineers accompanied with two participants-to-observe is currently recorded in the observatory. As units of courses of action are significant units for the actor, we choose to breakdown the whole course-of-action in units based on individual performed activities.

A further study will use these data to proceed with the analysis of course-of-action, using a theoretical framework, described as semio-logical. This framework will make possible to explain the global dynamics - or composition - of the courses of action units, their local dynamics - or generation - and the linkage between these two dynamics.

The current state of this work – the building and the filling of an observatory of the part of the agent's observable activity that is pre-reflexive (i.e. presentable, accountable and commentable) – let suggest that analysis will lead (1) to specify the modalities of engineers' interaction with life cycle processes leading to the design of better interaction or of corrective situations and (2) to contradict or support the reconstruction by the engineer of his/her own activity, i.e. going from "pre-reflective consciousness" of the actor towards a reflective attitude.

Thus, we may think that observing and analyzing software engineer's activity help to reveal his/her theory-in-use [10] - what governs engineers' behavior and tends to be tacit structures - that we may call Project Processes-in-use in a VSE. The unit breakdown of course-of-action is based on performed activities related to a simple Process Reference Model issued from the ISO/IEC 12207:2008 standard. We made the hypothesis that this standard constitutes the "espoused theory" of software engineers. So, the course-of-action framework may help engineers to establish a link between his/her "Project Processes-in-use" and "espoused Process Reference Model" and contribute to reduce the fit between a project-in-action and SE standards. When the upcoming standard "Software Engineering - Lifecycle Profiles for Very Small Enterprises (VSE)" [7] will be available, we will consider how this standard fits in this proposition.

Argyris and Schön explored the nature of organizational learning and defined two kind of learning: simple-loop learning and double-loop learning [22]. Then they set up two models (Model I and Model II) that describe features of theories-in-use that either inhibit or enhance double-loop learning. Further work is required to consider how course-of-action analysis is related with these organizational learning models and hence, on the VSE's ability to cope with innovations and changes.

References

1. Schön, D.: The Reflective Practitioner. Basic Books, New York (1983)
2. Argyris, C., Putnam, R., McLain Smith, D.: Action Science, Concepts, methods, and skills for research and intervention. Jossey-Bass, San Francisco (1985)
3. Software Engineering - Lifecycle Profiles for Very Small Enterprises (VSE) – Part 1, `http://www.iso.org/iso/iso_catalogue/catalogue_tc/ catalogue_detail.htm?csnumber=51150`
4. Theureau, J., Filippi, G., Gaillard, I.: From semio-logical analysis to design: the case of traffic control, communication. In: Colloquium Work activity in the perspective of organization and design, M.S.H., Paris (1992)
5. Theureau, J., Filippi, G.: Analysing cooperative work in an urban traffic control room for the design of a coordination support system. In: Luff, P., Hindmarsh, J., Heath, C. (eds.) Workplace studies, ch. 4, pp. 68–91. Cambridge Univ. Press, Cambridge (2000)
6. Theureau, J.: Course-of-action analysis & course-of-action centered design. In: Hollnagel, E. (ed.) Handbook of Cognitive Task Design. Lawrence Erlbaum Ass., New Haven (2003)
7. Ribaud, V., Saliou, P.: Revealing Software Engineering Theory-in-Use through the Observation of Software Engineering Apprentices' Course-of-action. In: 4th International Multi-Conference on Computing in the Global Information Technology. IEEE Press, New York (2009)
8. Theureau, J.: Selfconfrontation interview as a component of an empirical and technological research programme. In: II° Journées internationales des sciences du sport, Paris (2002)
9. Varela, F.: Principles of biological autonomy. Elsevier, New York (1980)
10. Argyris, C., Schön, D.: Theory in practice: Increasing professional effectiveness. Jossey-Bass, San Fransisco (1974)
11. Halloran, P.: Organisational Learning from the Perspective of a Software Process Assessment & Improvement Program. In: 32nd Hawaii International Conference on System Sciences. IEEE Press, New York (1999)
12. Cater-Steel, A.P.: Process improvement in four small software companies. In: Software Engineering Conference, pp. 262–272. IEEE Press, New York (1999)
13. Grunbacher, P.: A software assessment process for small software enterprises. In: Euromicro 1997. New Frontiers of Information Technology, pp. 123–128. IEEE Press, New York (1997)
14. von Wangenheim, C.G., Anacleto, A., Salviano, C.F.: Helping small companies assess software processes. IEEE Software 23, 91–98 (2006)
15. Moore, J.W.: An integrated collection of software engineering standards. IEEE Software 16(6), 51–57 (1999)
16. ISO/IEC 12207:2008, Information technology – Software life cycle processes. International Organization for Standardization (ISO), Geneva (2008)
17. ISO/IEC 15504:2004, Information technology – Process assessment. International Organization for Standardization (ISO), Geneva (2004)

18. ISO/IEC FCD 24765, Systems and software engineering – Vocabulary. International Organization for Standardization (ISO), Geneva (2009)
19. Roques, P., Vallée, F.: UML en action. Eyrolles, Paris (2002)
20. Meirieu, P.: Si la compétence n'existait pas, il faudrait l'inventer In IUFM de Paris Collège des CPE (2005),
    http://cpe.paris.iufm.fr/spip.php?article1150 (2007)
21. Donin, N., Theureau, J.: Music composition in the wild: from the horizon of creative cognition to the time & situation of inquiry. In: EACE 2005, Crète, pp. 57–64 (2005)
22. Argyris, C., Schön, D.: Organizational learning: A theory of action perspective. Addison Wesley, Reading (1978)

Tailoring ISO/IEC 27001 for SMEs:
A Guide to Implement an Information Security
Management System in Small Settings

Thierry Valdevit, Nicolas Mayer, and Béatrix Barafort

CRP Henri Tudor, 29 avenue John F. Kennedy, L-1855 Luxembourg, Luxembourg
{thierry.valdevit,nicolas.mayer,beatrix.barafort}@tudor.lu

Abstract. While Information Security Management Systems (ISMS) are being adopted by the biggest IT companies, it remains quite difficult for smaller entities to implement and maintain all the requirements of ISO/IEC 27001. In order to increase information security in Luxembourg, the Public Research Centre Henri Tudor has been charged by the Luxembourg Ministry of Economy and Foreign Trade to find solutions to facilitate ISMS deployment for SMEs. After an initial experiment aiming at assisting a SME in getting the first national ISO/IEC 27001 certification for a private company, an implementation guide for deploying an ISMS, validated by local experts and experimented in SMEs, has been released and is presented in this paper.

Keywords: Information security, ISO/IEC 27001, SME, implementation guide.

1 Introduction

In 2008, financial frauds were displayed at the top of security incidents charts [1]. Nowadays viruses are becoming less alarming than notebook thefts. However, organisations tend to buy additional security products when security incidents occur. There is currently a strong need for a reliable and managed information security that does not focus only on technical solutions. Since 1995, the interest in risk management standards never ceased to grow. The British standards BS 7799 [2][3], which gave birth to both ISO/IEC 27001 [4] and ISO/IEC 27002 [5] ten years later, became more and more successful among organisations concerned by information security management.

Since their international development through ISO/IEC 27001, Information Security Management Systems (ISMS) [4] are known to be the systematic organisational answer to information security problems. They set the requirements for a global and self-improving environment to manage information security. In 2009, over 5000 organisations worldwide have already certified their ISMS [6].

To enhance the promotion of innovation and improve the overall maturity of organisations [7], Luxembourg's Ministry of Economy and Foreign Trade has charged the Public Research Centre Henri Tudor to establish a strong link between standardisation and end-users by spreading ISMS to SMEs (companies with less than 250 employees) in Luxembourg. As they represent 90% of the country's organisations, it

R.V. O'Connor et al. (Eds.): EuroSPI 2009, CCIS 42, pp. 201–212, 2009.

is legitimate to evaluate how easily could ISO/IEC 27001 be deployed across SMEs. This research work lies on the expertise that has been developed for several years in CRP Henri Tudor in Information Security [8], assessment and improvement of processes using the ISO/IEC 15504 standard (Process assessment) in several sectors and disciplines [9][10][11], downsizing standards for SMEs and transferring competences to the market via the development of labels and/or certifications [12].

The particular underlying research project developing the ISMS implementation guide for SMEs aims at helping them to go towards the implementation of a simpler ISMS. The focus of this paper is thus based on the following research questions:

1. What are the specific needs of SMEs regarding ISMS?
2. How can we adapt ISO/IEC 27001 to best suit SMEs?

The paper is structured as follows: Section 2 presents the ISO/IEC 27001 standard. Then, Section 3 presents our research method. Section 4 discusses the initial experiment that triggered the definition of our particular objectives for an ISMS implementation guide adapted to SMEs. Section 5 reports the various steps of the elaboration of the guide. Section 6 presents the future work required by the project. Finally, Section 7 concludes this paper and opens discussions regarding the research method and the strengths and weaknesses of the results.

2   The ISO/IEC 27001 Standard

The outcome of an ISO/IEC 27001 certification is the effective establishment and management of an ISMS. Relying upon quality management and ISO 9001 [13] principles, it is built around a PDCA (Plan-Do-Check-Act) cycle, which objective is a continual improvement of information security.

For an organisation to be certified, it is necessary to be compliant with the set of normative requirements defined in the ISO/IEC 27001 standard. Those requirements are expressed from Section 4 to Section 8 of the standard [4]. The other sections are considered to be informative, and thus are not mandatory for the certification. The set of normative requirements can be summarised as represented in Figure 1. This figure presents the different parts of the standard, structured by sections.

First of all, it is necessary to establish and manage the ISMS by following the PDCA cycle, composed of four iterative steps (described from Section 4.2.1 to Section 4.2.4). These steps are supported by a specific documentation, whose requirements are explained in Section 4.3. Along with the documentation, they represent the core requirements that one should satisfy to be certified. Additionally, some requirements are especially developed in a dedicated section, because of their importance or complexity. The first one in this case is the management responsibility, describing where it is necessary for the management to be specifically involved (Section 5). A part is dedicated to the way to perform the internal ISMS audits, which are mandatory (Section 6). Regular management reviews are also necessary in the cycle (Section 7). Finally, the normative requirements sections end with requirements on how to perform the ISMS improvement (Section 8).

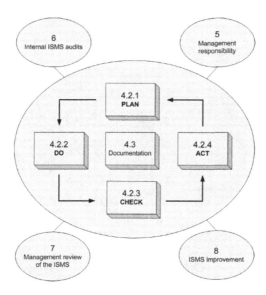

Fig. 1. The ISO/IEC 27001 group of requirements

3 Research Method

In order to answer our research questions in a structured way, we propose a research method following an action research approach [14]. It can be defined as "an iterative process involving researchers and practitioners acting together on a particular cycle of activities, including problem diagnosis, action intervention and reflective learning" [15]. The research method, presented in Figure 2, consists of three steps.

Step 1 – *Initial experiment*: An initial experiment is performed in a Luxembourger SME. In order to identify the issues related to the implementation of an ISMS in such an entity, many feedbacks are gathered from this experiment. Then, they are summarised to put emphasis on the major issues encountered. Hence, our research objectives are defined so as to address those issues. This step answers our first research question.

Step 2 – *Building the guide*: The guide is written in order to achieve the objectives identified during the first step of the research method. To ensure the relevance and the viability of the document, it is validated through experts' reviews. To do so, Luxembourger experts in information security are mandated to theoretically evaluate the guide. This process, closely tied with field experiments (Step 3), gives feedbacks in order to improve the guide.

Step 3 – *Experimenting the guide*: As theoretical validation cannot bring an insurance of effectiveness and adaptability of the guide, experiments are required within the research method. They take place in several SMEs with different security backgrounds and from different activity sectors. These experiments are not only conducted by our team, but also by external individuals, in order to assess the usability of the guide by people not involved in its development process. Each experiment leads to several feedbacks and initiates upgrades to the guide.

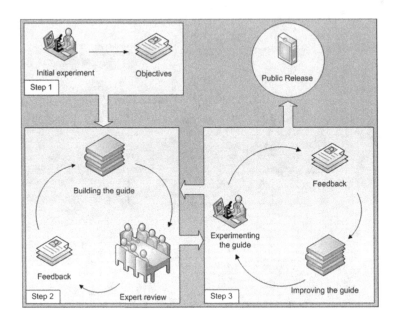

Fig. 2. Research method

Step 2 and 3 are performed iteratively, with consecutive updates of the guide. After each reviewing process, a concrete experiment is planned bringing feedbacks and updates to the guide. These modifications are then validated or modified through another expert review and a new experiment can be started. After several iterations, the guide should be freely available to SMEs.

4   Initial Experiment

The initial experiment was conducted in a SME in Luxembourg called Codasystem [16]. This company offers innovative security services based on new information technologies. The value proposition associated to their services is based on the management of the authenticity of digital documents. The Codasystem product addresses the need for a reliable, secure and easy to use system capable of circumventing falsification risks both on electronic documents and exchanges. Currently, solutions available on the market are focused on securing exchanges (authentication, email signatures, cryptography). No solution exists that could provide indisputable proof in court for both the electronic document and its exchange. Codasystem offers the first integrated solution for the creation of digital proofs and their secure distribution (see Figure 3). The solution of Codasystem has been examined by a law firm expert in digitalisation and legal property, and has received approval regarding its legal value. The technology of Codasystem is patented in France and extended worldwide.

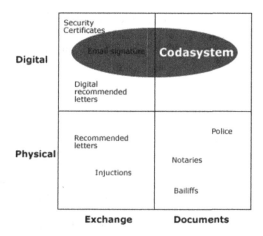

Fig. 3. Proposed product of Codasystem

Although the product proposed by Codasystem has been approved by experts, the security of their processes is also at the heart of their concern. That is why the improvements in terms of security and the trust granted by the ISO/IEC 27001 certification were raising strong interests.

4.1 Implementation of Codasystem's ISMS

The initial experiment (Figure 2) at Codasystem started in June 2006 and ended in May 2008. The collaboration between our team and Codasystem is evaluated at about 100 CRP Henri Tudor man-days. The total documentation produced was over 300 pages.

The complete process was very long and time-consuming. This is actually due to several issues. First, the set of ISO/IEC 27001 requirements to satisfy is very important, especially for a SME like Codasystem with few human resources to allocate on this project. Moreover, the gap between the current state of an SME and the state to reach for the certification is generally more important in SMEs. For example, a resource management process is typically in place in large organisations, as opposed to SMEs where it is usual to develop it "from scratch". Very few formalised policies or procedures were already available in Codasystem.

The average knowledge of people involved in the setting up of the ISMS is also generally lower in a SME than in a large company. Where large companies are able to hire experienced and skilled human resources with regards to management systems, SMEs generally choose internal employees who include their effort on the ISMS in their day-to-day work. That was the case within Codasystem, where people had not much knowledge in quality and process management. Many training sessions were performed during the early meetings of the experiment, in order to familiarise the team with the standard.

The time needed to develop the documentation and to satisfy all the requirements was also very important. Hopefully, our knowledge was an added value to the Codasystem's team, because they had very few experiences on what to implement in order to satisfy the requirements.

After nearly two years of experimentation, Codasystem became the first private company ISO/IEC 27001 certified in Luxembourg, thus successfully concluding the first step of our project. Moreover, all the lessons learnt during this experiment have provided significant inputs for Step 2 of the project. They are summarised in the next section.

4.2 Identification of the Objectives of the Guide

As seen in the previous section of the paper, this first experiment with Codasystem brought us interesting feedback regarding the implementation of an ISMS in a SME. Those inputs have been analysed in order to highlight some key issues and thus have shown the challenges of such a research project. As a result, a methodological guidance is indeed necessary, in order to achieve the following objectives:

- Objective 1: *Downsize the requirements in order to reduce the cost and the complexity of an ISMS*. The set of ISO/IEC 27001 requirements has to be scaled down, in order to fit with the limited resources of most SMEs.
- Objective 2: *Smooth the approach to the users*. Implementing an ISMS should not be perceived as a constraint imposed by business strategy. Therefore, a smooth approach has to be developed introducing processes, PDCA paradigm and management systems benefits to users.
- Objective 3: *Give the major recommendations and generic tasks to ensure the proper operation of the ISMS*. Part of the work is transversal, like documentation management and management responsibility: it takes place all along the successive PDCA tasks. Therefore, the guide should start by presenting these specific actions, detailing how they affect the whole system.
- Objective 4: *Provide implementation guidance for each process of the PDCA cycle*. ISO/IEC 27001 presents all those requirements in a rough listing while the presentation of these items should require a simple, standard and clear pattern. All the inputs needed to ease fulfilment should also be provided.
- Objective 5: *Ensure coherence and reliability of this tailored handbook*. The goal is to allow the possibility of having a smooth transition towards ISO/IEC 27001 certification. Therefore, the guide has to remain strictly aligned with the original requirements, in order to necessitate only simple improvements if a SME wants to achieve a certification.
- Objective 6: *Provide tool support*. A framework of documentation tools and templates should be proposed as a support for the implementation. The aim is to accelerate the process of implementation and decrease the cost involved (particularly for documentation). It should also serve as a basis for packaged market-oriented solutions and services (next transfer part of the research project).

5 Building the Guide

In order to achieve the objectives set in Section 4.2 of this paper, the guide has been built with these specific aspects in mind. The following paragraphs explain how we tackle the issues highlighted in the preceding ones.

5.1 Selective Coverage

As an answer to the first objective, we propose in the guide a tailored version of the ISO/IEC 27001 requirements. The complete set of standard requirements was first modelled as a list of 32 major activities. Each of them was annotated, if applicable, with its key outputs in term of document production. This list was then split over a 5-column matrix representing various progressive configurations, giving five coherent set of activities. Those five choices have been established through multiple experts' opinions in order to find a consensus that would maintain coherence for each column and keep the smoothest progression from implementing level 1 to 5.

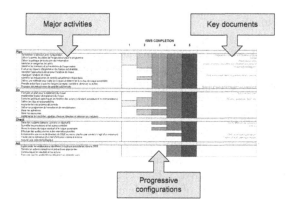

Fig. 4. ISMS completion matrix

The criteria used to define these configurations were essentially in connection with resources consumption, importance of the activity within the ISMS and therefore return on security investment. However, the impact of each choice was taken into account for its relevance with regards to the whole ISMS's efficiency. Indeed, numerous activities are strongly tied together and cannot be removed nor added without others. For instance, the risk assessment requires half a dozen of activities, which have no meaning by themselves.

Finally, a given level was chosen: implementation level 4. It basically consists of a complete ISMS, without audits requirements, nor technical surveys. On one hand, level 3 was rejected as it lacked most "check/act" activities. On the other hand, level 5 was too close to the original standard to bring any added value to the guide. Furthermore, as audits were probably one of the most expensive and time-consuming part in Codasystem's experiment, it made sense to remove them.

Decisions made with this matrix conducted to the definition of the ISO/IEC 27001 coverage of the guide. This modelling of the standard also served as guidelines regarding how the guide should be organised, as explained in Section 5.4.

5.2 Raising Awareness and Maturity to Lower Apprehension

As stated in Objective 2, initial apprehension can be critical regarding ISMS implementation. That is to say, if the management perceives an ISMS as a long, costly or useless approach, it will not fund its implementation. Therefore, the guide starts with some introduction chapters, which aim at answering most common doubts and misconceptions, and motivate the use of the guide.

First, 10 key concepts are explained such as "asset" or "residual risk". This introduction page covers the most important concepts used all along the document into a convenient condensed form. It gives the prerequisites to understand the guide and keep it self-sufficient. Then, the reader is introduced to ISMS, by providing more information on their goals and reducing common misconceptions regarding information security. In order to highlight the scope of the guide, the gap with the actual ISO/IEC 27001 is detailed and explained. Subsequently, quality management and process approaches are presented by giving the necessary knowledge to understand the PDCA paradigm.

In the end, raising awareness is tackled with some advices about the state of mind and maturity required before implementing an ISMS. A whole chapter dedicated to the estimated implementation period supports this last part. A generic distribution of each stage is given as an example of how PDCA iterations should be conducted.

5.3   Transversal Guidelines

ISMS deployment does not only rely on the successive tasks recurring within the PDCA cycle. Indeed, the standard contains requirements supporting the whole PDCA chapters, as mentioned in Objective 3. Four chapters focus on those specific concerns and serve as the very first steps of the implementation, prior to the beginning of the "Plan" stage.

First, the guide insists on the importance of obtaining a written management commitment regarding the requirements and consequences of ISMS. Indeed, the management often takes lightly all the implications of such a project in the company. By asking for this document, the guide ensures that management has considered those aspects.

Second, it gives all the required information on how to manage documentation within the system. Focus is made on the importance of having a proper documentation policy and generic guidelines are given to classify each document regarding its origin, access restriction, storage and disposal.

Third, users are invited to build a document referencing and assigning human resources. The guide proposes four generic categories of actors involved in the various tasks of an ISMS. Assigning people on those roles eases the implementation because each step is linked to those categories.

As a conclusion to transversal guidelines, the guide insists on deontological ethics all along the life cycle of the management system.

5.4   Key Steps Presentation

The standard is not user-friendly enough to be handled by most SMEs (Objective 4). Consequently, in order to facilitate the readability and comprehension of the guide, each process is presented using a simple pattern inspired by Process Reference Models (PRM) [17].

B. Implement anomaly management process

Details	The efficiency of the ISMS is insured by detection mechanisms, monitoring, records and anomaly correction.
Tasks	Define and apply anomaly management process including the following items: 1. Identify the anomaly (incident, non conformity, etc.) 2. Diagnostic method 3. Creation of anomaly ticket (synthetic record containing useful information regarding the anomaly) 4. Possible escalation 5. Anomaly resolution procedure 6. Anomaly enclosing
Inputs	Enterprise's organisation
Outputs	Anomaly management process Anomaly tickets
Actors	Every level of management ISMS accountable Employees

Fig. 5. Process description example

For each process selected in the guide (see Section 5.1), the guide presents:

- Its name

Most processes are named like their ISO/IEC 27001 equivalent, but little adjustments were made to obtain more generic and global terms, which represents more clearly their content.

- Its description

In order to facilitate comprehension and enhance efficiency, the guide includes awareness-raising elements all along its content. It explains for each process its motivations, utility and consequences.

- The detailed tasks

Processes are split across a simple set of tasks containing the sub-actions that should be completed. They are first aggregated according to Codasystem's feedbacks for readability and understanding, and will be improved after the next experiments.

- Input/output documents and records

Linking the various steps to each other is complex. Thus, to facilitate organisation of documents and "out of the box" deployment, each process directly refers to its inputs and lists its own outputs. In this way, it is easier to mesh all the processes together and facilitate templates production and use.

- The people involved

As stated previously (Section 5.3), four categories of actors are defined. Those key roles are assigned to each process when needed, giving immediate information regarding who should be involved and what are the hierarchical implications.

5.5 Experts Validation

ANSIL is the Luxembourg Information Society Standardisation Association. This national association contributes to IT standardisation activities in Luxembourg, from the creation of experts committees to the promotion of standardisation. Within this association lies the CNLSI (Information Security Standardisation Committee: mirror group of ISO/IEC JTC1 SC27 in Luxembourg) which is composed of a dozen of experts in information security. They were mandated to review and comment the guide (theoretical review) twice, thus ensuring the achievement of Objective 5.

On the first validation cycle, in November 2008, they conducted 3 iterative reviews in the same way as ISO standards are reviewed. Overall, they issued 156 comments requiring various modifications of the guide. Prior to the first experimentation stages, this initial validation ensured the document's reliability, coherence and alignment with ISO/IEC 27001.

The second reviewing process is planned to take place after the first SME experiment (see Figure 2). It will expectantly give new feedbacks, thus ensuring the quality of the final version of the guide.

5.6 Tool Support

In agreement with Objective 6, a methodological guidance does not help enough the users in order to implement an ISMS. To cope with this issue, we have developed numerous templates and documentation tools mostly based on Codasystem's experiment. They ease and speed up the implementation of the ISMS, enabling users to focus on more complex tasks, thus reducing the amount of human resources required.

Regarding documentation, we created numerous generic procedures to be completed and tailored by end-users. Our templates (i.e. management commitment, ISMS policy, anomaly management procedure, etc.) only require to fill a few blanks, and sometimes to be slightly adapted to the context of the organisation, before being used.

For the most complex part of the 'Plan' phase, that is to say risk assessment, a specific tool has been developed following an innovative model for risk management [18]. It assists the user all along the risk assessment steps and is compliant with ISO/IEC 27005 [19].

6 Further Experiments and Upgrades

Experimental results in Codasystem showed numerous opportunities to improve and scale down an ISMS to fit to SMEs' needs. That is why the project's method integrates two experimentation stages.

After 6 months of development and reviews, the guide is currently assessed in a public (SME-sized) administration. Later on, a complete experimentation panel will take place by supervising the deployment of the guide among three candidate SMEs from various sizes and businesses. This second experimentation stage will be conducted in a mutualised and interactive manner. Indeed, the ISMS implementation of the three SME's will be synchronised. Collective training sessions will be performed and completed with individual on-site coaching. During combined courses, the three SMEs will discuss their progress together, bringing new ideas and more feedbacks to improve the guide even further.

7 Discussion and Conclusion

In this paper, we have first analysed what are the specific needs of SMEs regarding ISMS. Then, we have proposed a research method in order to tailor the ISO/IEC 27001 standard to an adapted way for SMEs. The two first steps of this research method have been already performed and the third step is currently in progress. Furthermore, the theoretical validation, that is part of the second step, will be performed again, in order to improve the guide iteratively after experiments. The outcome of this research work is a guide providing a more affordable, easier and faster way to implement an ISMS that is still covering a vast majority of ISO/IEC 27001 requirements. This way, this research project brings combined benefits for the Luxembourger market: it promotes information security to SMEs through the guide, and it provides local IT consultants with a wider range of methodological support.

Regarding strengths of our approach, the systematic research method proposed in Section 3 blends theoretical reviews and experiments. Furthermore, the experiments are not only conducted by our teams, but also by individuals apprehending the guide for the first time. We thus ensure objective feedbacks about our research work.

Moreover, this guide looks convenient on many aspects. Indeed, by approaching management systems from the very beginning and dispensing the required knowledge to understand why and how ISMS should be deployed, the guide gets a strong head start when compared to the raw ISO/IEC 27001 document. The presentation pattern listing both human and documentary resources eases the understanding and speeds up the deployment of an ISMS. Combined with the limited coverage of the standard, the guide grants the possibility to easily focus on the core elements of an ISMS implementation and therefore increases overall efficiency.

However, each action to make the guide simpler is one step away from the initial standard. Certainly, the reduced scope causes potential troubles. Audits are definitely a good mean of detecting problems within one's organisation and helps setting milestones regarding ISMS status.

Finally, individuals could wonder why they should implement such a guide instead of targeting a direct ISO/IEC 27001 certificate. Given this statement, the guide should be part of a complete labelling framework for SMEs, supported by the Ministry of Economy and Foreign Trade, and potentially a national certification dedicated to SMEs. The development of this framework is part of our future work.

References

1. CSI, 2008 CSI Computer Crime and Security Survey (2009)
2. BSI, BS7799-1: Information Security Management Systems – Code of Practice for Information Security Management Systems (1995)
3. BSI, BS7799-2: Information Security Management Systems – Specification with guidance for use (1999)
4. ISO, ISO/IEC 27001: Information technology – Security techniques – Information security management systems – Requirements (2005)
5. ISO, ISO/IEC 27002: Information technology – Security techniques – Code of practice for information security management (2005)

6. ISO, Information security management systems for small and medium-sized enterprises. ISO Management Systems 9(1) (2009)
7. Information Security Portal in Luxembourg (2009), http://www.cases.public.lu
8. Barafort, B., Humbert, J-P., Poggi, S.: Information Security Management and ISO/IEC 15504: the link opportunity between Security and Quality. In: SPICE 2006, Luxembourg (2006)
9. Hilbert, R., Renault, A.: Assessing IT Service Management Processes with AIDA – Experience Feedback. In: EuroSPI 2007, Potsdam, Germany (2007)
10. Di Renzo, B., Valoggia, P.: Assessment and Improvement of Firm's Knowledge Management Capabilities by using a KM Process Assessment compliant to ISO/IEC 15504. A Case Study. In: SPICE 2007, Seoul, South Korea (2007)
11. Di Renzo, B., Hillairet, M., Picard, M., Rifaut, A., Bernard, C., Hagen, D., Maar, P., Reinard, D.: Operational Risk Management in Financial Institutions: Process Assessment in Concordance with Basel II. In: SPICE 2005, Klagenfurt, Austria (2005)
12. Renault, S., Dubois, E., Barafort, B., Krystkowiak, M.: Improving SME trust into IT consultancy: a network of certified consultants case study. In: EuroSPI 2007, Postdam, Germany (2007)
13. ISO, ISO 9001: Quality Management Systems – Requirements (2000)
14. Susman, G., Evered, R.: An Assessment of the Scientific Merits of Action Research. Administrative Science Quarterly 23(4) (1978)
15. Avison, D., Lau, F., Myers, M., Nielsen, P.A.: Action Research. Communications of the ACM 42(1) (1999)
16. Codasystem (2009), http://www.codasystem.com
17. ISO, ISO/IEC 15504-2: Information technology – Process assessment – Part 2: Performing an assessment (2003)
18. Mayer, N.: Model-based Management of Information System Security Risk. PhD thesis, University of Namur, Belgium (2009)
19. ISO, ISO/IEC 27005: Information technology – Security techniques – Information security risk management (2008)

An Integrated Framework to Guide Software Process Improvement in Small Organizations

Francisco J. Pino[1,2], Félix García[2], and Mario Piattini[2]

[1] IDIS Research Group – Electronic and Telecommunications Engineering Faculty
University of Cauca, Street 5 # 4 – 70 Popayán, Colombia
fjpino@unicauca.edu.co
[2] Alarcos Research Group – Institute of Information Technologies & Systems
University of Castilla-La Mancha, Paseo de la Universidad, 4, 13071, Ciudad Real, Spain
{Felix.Garcia,Mario.Piattini}@uclm.es

Abstract. When a small organization (VSE) tackles a software process improvement (SPI) initiative, the model that is used least is the one that would guide the process improvement. We believe that this is a great failing, because it is precisely a model of this type that is the guide which is needed to articulate all the activities related to that improvement. In this vein, to support VSEs, as well as to guide them in detail when they wish to carry out SPI initiatives, we have developed an integrated improvement framework. We have done this by taking into account widely recognized frameworks and the special characteristics of VSEs. This paper introduces that improvement framework, its components and its relationship with the COMPETISOFT project. Furthermore, through case studies, it describes our experience of the application of the proposed framework in eight firms. The initial results show that it is useful, practical and suitable for addressing SPI initiatives in VSEs.

Keywords: Improvement framework, Software process improvement, Small companies, SPI, SMEs, COMPETISOFT.

1 Introduction

Although process reference models (e.g. ISO/IEC 12207, CMMI and ISO/IEC 15504-5), process assessment methods (such as ISO/IEC 15504-2 and SCAMPI) and improvement models (like ISO/IEC 15504-4 and IDEAL) used for Software Process Improvement -SPI- are available to all enterprises, studies such as [1-4] show that these proposals from SEI or ISO are difficult for the vast majority of the very small software enterprises -VSEs (i.e. firms with fewer than 25 employees, according to [5]), to apply. This difficulty comes about because of the complexity of the recommendations of the models and the consequent large investment in terms of time and resources. In addition, many organizations remain unaware of these proposals [6].

Regarding the model that guides process improvement (improvement model), we have found in [7] that this type of model is the one used least by small companies. This type of model was used by 23 (of 122) companies involved in some SPI initiative, that is in only 19% of the companies. This is a low percentage and we believe

R.V. O'Connor et al. (Eds.): EuroSPI 2009, CCIS 42, pp. 213–224, 2009.
© Springer-Verlag Berlin Heidelberg 2009

that this is something to be regretted and dealt with. An improvement model is precisely the guide which is needed to articulate all the activities related to the improvement, as well as all the other models involved, of course.

In this sense, and aiming to support the SPI initiatives within a VSE, we have developed the COMPETISOFT project [8]. In this project great importance was given to the model for guiding SPI activities, the goal being to carry out SPI initiatives following a systematic and coherent approach. COMPETISOFT maintains that if we are to help small companies set up and pursue process improvement, then a guideline which will address the improvement activities is needed. We should also point out that one success factor for SPI initiatives in VSEs is for the improvement effort to be guided by means of specific procedures and the combination of different approaches [7]. Given all this, one of the components of the Methodological Framework developed by COMPETISOFT is a specific *framework for guiding SPI activities* (*improvement framework*). The other two components are a Process Reference Model (based on MoProSoft [12]) and a Process Evaluation Model (this conforms with the ISO/IEC 15504 standard [9]). The aim of this paper is simply to show the different components of *the improvement framework* (proposed by COMPETISOFT's Methodological Framework) and its application in eight VSEs.

The paper is structured as follows. The next section presents related works. The Methodological Framework of COMPETISOFT is then described. Section 4 explains the *improvement framework* and its different components, and section 5 gives a description of its application in eight case studies. Lastly, an analysis is given and our conclusions are set out.

2 Related Work

There are several proposals that present a set of processes which small companies could use to reach significant benefit from process improvement. Among others, these include: MoProSoft [9], MPS.BR [10], Adept [11] and Rapid [12]. All of these proposals are related to assessment methods or process reference models and all of them define a group of processes that should be taken into account by small companies in their improvement efforts. Nevertheless, only in some of these proposals is a process related to the activities to guide process improvement described. We could mention, for instance, MoProSoft, which describes Process Management and MPS.BR, which describes Process Assessment and Improvement.

With regard to research on models that direct improvement implementation for small companies, several proposals have emerged in recent years. These include, amongst others: IMPACT [13], MESOPyME [14], PROCESSUS [15], and the application of the IDEAL model to small and medium enterprises [16, 17].

However, these proposals do not describe in detail a framework that integrates different components (such as strategies, methodologies, processes and tools) in guiding the execution of SPI initiatives on small companies. The main contribution to the subject of SPI in VSEs that this work intends to make is to guide the implementation of process improvement in detail, by means of an integrated *improvement framework* which VSEs would be able to take on.

The *improvement framework* describes five components which have been defined by taking into account: (i) widely recognized frameworks, such as ISO/IEC 15504-4 [18], IDEAL and SCRUM; and (ii) special characteristics of the VSEs, such as that: they are generally extremely reactive and flexible; they typically have a flat structure and a free-flowing management style that encourages entrepreneurship and innovation; they have limited economic movement and lightweight processes; and they do not usually have enough staff to be able to develop specialized functions that would enable them to perform complex tasks and to develop secondary products [6].

These components describe tailored and integrated improvement practices, strategies and tools aiming to offer the VSEs a framework which is useful and practical for addressing SPI initiatives. Furthermore, according to [7], the proposals that have been used to SPI on VSEs are diverse and include: adaptation and use of SPI models, establishment of software processes to guide the SPI efforts, prioritization of the SPI efforts and evaluation of a SPI programme. Only the *improvement framework* addresses (by means of its components) these improvement proposals in an integrated and explicit manner.

3 Methodological Framework of COMPETISOFT

COMPETISOFT seeks to provide a strategy for increasing the level of competitiveness of Latin-American small software organizations by means of the creation and dissemination of a common Methodological Framework for the improvement and certification of the software processes of the small enterprises. An overview of the components of this Methodological Framework is shown in Fig. 1.

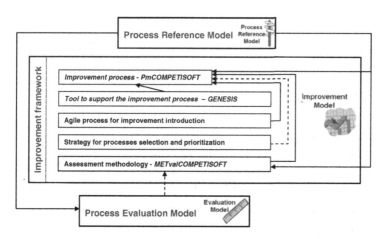

Fig. 1. Methodological Framework of COMPETISOFT

The process reference model is based on MoProSoft. In fact, we can view this process reference model as an evolution of MoProSoft, coming from the experience of researchers and practitioners in software process development and improvement. It is important to highlight that this evolution of MoProSoft has been used as a basis for the subsequent publication of what has been called ISO/IEC 29110 Software Engineering - Lifecycle Profiles for VSE [5], by the WG 24 / SC7 of ISO.

To allow mutual recognition of formal evaluations of COMPETISOFT across Latin American countries, we suggest that each country should define its own Assessment Model, which must be in accordance with ISO/IEC 15504. In this sense, and bearing in mind the new ISO/IEC 15504-7 standard [19], AENOR (Spanish Association for Standardisation and Certification) from Spain and IRAM (Argentine Institute for Standardisation and Certification) from Argentina are currently establishing an organizational maturity model and a process assessment model to give the small software companies a new strategy for certification by maturity levels.

For the definition, refinement and application of these components of the Methodological Framework of COMPETISOFT the A-R (Action-Research) and case study research methods have been used. For the application of the A-R research method we divided the project participants into two groups: a first one, made up of *researchers* from different universities, and a second one, called the *critical reference group*, which included the information technology professionals from VSEs. Through the application of A-R we obtained continual feedback between the *researchers* and the VSEs involved, aiming to develop and refine the Methodological Framework.

4   Improvement Framework

The aim of the *improvement framework* is to provide improvement practices, strategies and tools to support improvement initiatives in small companies. This framework is influenced by the ISO/IEC 15504 (Part 2, Part 4 and Part 5), IDEAL and SCRUM models. From these proposals we have analyzed, integrated and tailored several improvement practices, in order to offer a specialized and suitable framework which meets the needs of the VSEs when leading SPI initiatives. This *improvement framework* defines five components: (i) a process called PmCOMPETISOFT, (ii) a methodology for software process assessment called METvalCOMPETISOFT, (iii) an agile process for improvement introduction, (iv) a strategy for process selection and prioritization and (v) tools to support the improvement process (see Fig. 1). All the process of this framework are described in terms of purpose, objectives, roles, activity diagram, activities, work products, and tools support, according to the process pattern established by COMPETISOFT. In the following section we give a summarised description of these elements, its brevity due to restrictions on space.

4.1   Improvement Process – PmCOMPETISOFT

This process has been defined to provide the VSEs with a guide with which to manage and lead the SPI initiatives step-by-step. The purpose of this process is to improve an organization's processes according to its business objectives, along with assisting it to carry out its SPI initiatives. This process is the backbone as well as the component integrator of the *improvement framework*. Fig. 2 shows the PmCOMPETISOFT activity diagram, which includes roles, activities and work products. A complete description of this process is presented in [20].

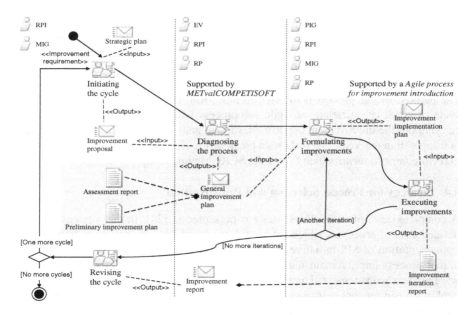

Fig. 2. PmCOMPETISOFT Activity Diagram

4.2 Assessment Methodological – METvalCOMPETISOFT

METvalCOMPETISOFT has been defined to give support to the activity of *diagnosing processes* from PmCOMPETISOFT, so as to help VSEs in the execution of an internal, non-formal process assessment. This methodology allows us to obtain reliable information about the strengths and weaknesses of software processes, along with information on opportunities for improvement. The purpose is for that information to serve as a basis for decision making about process improvement within the organization. This methodology defines:

- A process for software process assessment, called PvalCOMPETISOFT, which offers a step-by-step guide to the execution of the activity of processes diagnosis. This process breaks down into detail the activity of *diagnosing processes*. In Fig. 3, the activities, roles and work products are shown.
- A light assessment method to determine the capability of software processes and the maturity of a small organization [21]. The assessment method defines a measurement framework (conformance with ISO 15504 Part 2), which in the capability dimension has got only three levels of capability, making the model lighter, so that it can be easily applied to small organizations.
- A tool to support the execution of the assessment process and method [22].

4.3 Agile Process for Improvement Introduction

This process has been defined in such a way as to give a detailed guideline for supporting the management and performance of the activities of the cycle made up by the *formulating and executing improvement* activities of PmCOMPETISOFT. We developed this process because in the early applications we observed that it is the iteration, composed of the *formulation and execution of improvements*, which requires the greatest amount of effort in the SPI initiative. What is more, this load falls mainly upon the organization. For the definition of this process we have used the SCRUM agile method because it provides support for project management and it focused on small teams [23]. The purpose of this process is to offer all those who are involved in the improvement cycle of small organizations an agile sub-process which allows them to take part in carrying out the improvement opportunities found and with which they have some relationship within the VSE. Fig. 4 shows a break-down of the activities for *formulating* and *executing improvements* which follow the SCRUM philosophy.

4.4 Strategy for Process Selection and Prioritization

A complete description of this strategy is presented in [24]. In this strategy we have defined a set of processes which we consider to be of high-priority when initiating the implementation of SPI initiative in VSEs. The fundamental principle of the proposal is that process improvement must be connected to the other responsibilities of software process management. The prioritization of these processes is established so as to deploy a basic process management infrastructure (as the process improvement is not an isolated activity, but is closely related to other activities of the software process management). The processes selected and their priorities are:

- First of all, the process improvement process group (PIM.1 Process establishment, PIM.2 Process assessment, and PIM.3 Process improvement)
- Secondly, the management process group (MAN.1 Organizational alignment, MAN.3 Project management and MAN.6 Measurement)
- Thirdly, the support process group (SUP.10 Change request management, SUP.8 Configuration management, SUP.7 Documentation, and SUP.1 Quality assurance).
- Finally, the engineering process group (ENG.1 Requirements elicitation, ENG.2 System requirements analysis, ENG.3 System architectural design, ENG.4 Software requirements analysis, ENG.5 Software design, ENG.6 Software construction, ENG.7 Software integration, ENG.8 Software testing, ENG.11 Software maintenance)

Base practices of the process groups of engineering and support are described in the process reference model of COMPETISOFT. The main practices of the process groups of improvement and management are likewise described in the three components of the *improvement framework* described above.

4.5 Tools to Support the Improvement Process

We have also developed a tool called GENESIS [25], which is used to support the person Responsible for process improvement (RPI) in the management and implementation of an SPI initiative and in the administration of generated knowledge.

We might add that this framework has been described with the standard SPEM 2.0 and edited with the EPF Composer, thereby generating documentation in a standard format which is updated and available to organizations through the Web.

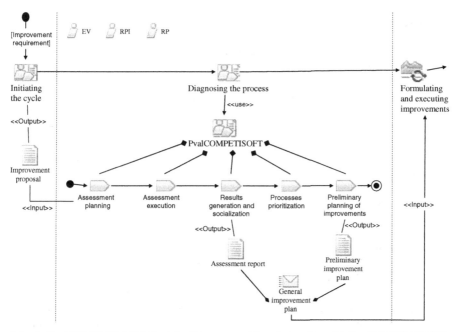

Fig. 3. PvalCOMPETISOFT Activity Diagram and its relationship with PmCOMPETISOFT

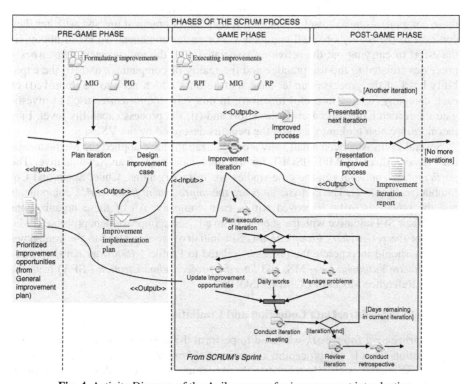

Fig. 4. Activity Diagram of the Agile process for improvement introduction

5 Case Studies

In COMPETISOFT the *researchers* carried out the intervention with the new proposals in the *critical reference group*, using the empirical variant for the execution of the action activity of A-R. That is, the *improvement framework* developed was applied by the *researchers* in the small companies (*critical reference group*) by means of the use of the case study research method. To apply the proposed framework, we have conducted eight case studies by following the protocol template for case studies presented in [26]. Lack of space means that we will then give just an overview of the case studies in terms of design, subjects, analysis unit, field procedures, data collection and limitations.

5.1 Design, Subjects and Analysis Unit

Taking into account the focus presented by [27], the *design type* of the case study in this work is multiple cases – holistic, since the strategy has been applied in the context of eight small companies. The *object of study* is a new integrated *improvement framework* through which to guide SPI in VSEs.

The *main research question* addressed by this study is: Is the *improvement framework* suitable (useful and practical) for leading Software Process Improvement efforts in small software enterprises? We identified an *additional research question* and various *sub-questions* (derived from each research question) for each component of the *improvement framework*. By means of these questions we seek to know whether these components have a useful function, if they are of practical use and whether they conform to the reality of small companies. For each component we asked about: (i) the effort of carrying out the activities associated with the *improvement framework*'s processes (related to the use practice and the reality of companies), and (ii) the capability level of the processes under analysis (the ones which need to be improved) of each company (related to useful function). In this vein, the *measures* used to investigate the research question are: (i) the effort and (ii) the process capability level. Furthermore, we also took into account the benefits described by the VSEs.

Several Latin American small software organizations have applied the Methodological Framework of COMPETISOFT for the implementation of an SPI initiative. The *participating companies* in the case studies are from Argentina, Chile, Spain and Colombia (see Table 1). The *analysis units* are the *improvement framework*'s components and the processes to be improved within each company. All of these organizations started their SPI initiative with the support of an adviser in improvement processes (who is part of the *researchers group*). In this SPI initiative we suggested to the companies that they should incorporate the processes related to Profile 1 (*Software development - SD, Software maintenance – MS, and Specific project administration - SPA*) from the Process Reference Model of COMPETISOFT.

5.2 Field Procedure, Data Collection and Limitations

The *improvement framework* was used to perform the improvement activities in each organization. That is, the procedure governing *field procedure* and the *data collection* of the case studies is closely related to the strategies, activities, roles and work products described in each of the processes defined by the *improvement framework* of

COMPETISOFT (see Fig. 2, 3 and 4 from Section 4). At the beginning and at the end of the SPI initiative in each company, an internal assessment was performed and the amount of effort used to carry out the improvement cycle (see Table 2) was also established. The information related to the process capability was obtained after analyzing and synthesizing the data of the processes chosen (those to be improved by the companies) with respect to the three process attributes and the process capability level ratings defined by the light assessment method of METvalCOMPETISOFT. The COMPETISOFT adviser played the role of evaluator (EV) and he evaluated the processes by applying interview and survey techniques.

Table 1. VSEs from the critical reference group involved in the case studies

Com.	Country	Emplo.	Path	Main areas of professional activity
E1	Argentina	8 (7)	16 years / N&I	Development of new tailored information systems with ongoing integration of new technology
E2	Chile	18 (12)	10 years / N&I	Computer Engineering projects for the agricultural (wine and food) industry.
E3	Spain	7 (6)	5 years / N	Software development on WEB.
E4	Spain	21 (15)	13 years / N	Software development through contracts and agreements with public organizations.
E5	Colombia	4 (4)	3 years. N	Software to manage and control the ISO 9001-2000 quality management system.
E6	Colombia	6 (6)	3 years. N	Web application development-oriented agricultural services.
E7	Colombia	4 (4)	3 years. N	Software to mobile telephony and devices.
E8	Argentina	12 (5)	4 years. N&I	Custom software development.

Emplo.: Number of employees in the enterprise (People in software development and maintenance)
Path: Number of years of existence of the company / scope of the market for its products (National–N / International–I)

Table 2. Initial and final capability of the organization's process and cycle effort

Comp.	Assessment	SD	SPA	SM	BM	PM	PjM	HRM	KM	IM	Cycle length (weeks)	Adviser (A)	Comp. (C)	Total
E1	Initial	-	2	-	-	-	-	-	-	-	24	40	264	304
	Final	1	2	*	1	1	1	1	1	1				
E2	Initial	0	1	0	-	-	-	-	-	-	20	89	255	344
	Final	1	2	*	*	-	-	-	-	-				
E3	Initial	0	0	-	-	-	-	-	-	-	12	15	39	54
	Final	1	*	-	-	-	-	-	-	-				
E4	Initial	0	0	-	-	-	-	-	-	-	12	41	47	88
	Final	1	*	-	-	-	-	-	-	-				
E5	Initial	1	0	-	-	-	-	-	-	-	10	42	27	69
	Final	1*	1	-	-	-	-	-	-	-				
E6	Initial	1	1	-	-	-	-	-	-	-	10	38	11	49
	Final	1	1*	-	-	-	-	-	-	-				
E7	Initial	0	0	-	-	-	-	-	-	-	10	65	23	88
	Final	1	1	-	-	-	-	-	-	-				
E8	Initial	0	0	-	-	-	-	-	-	-	16	71	16	87
	Final	0*	1	-	-	-	-	-	-	-				

Processes: SD (Software Development), SPA (Specific Project Administration), SM (Software Maintenance), BM (Business Management), PM (Process Management), PjM (Project Management), HRM (Human Resources Management), IM (Goods, Services and Infrastructure Management) and KM (Knowledge Management).
* Base practices of this process have been put into operation;   - Process not assessed.

The case studies carried out to use the *improvement framework* of COMPETISOFT in VSEs presented in this paper have some limits:

- The observations and conclusions presented are based on eight case studies, which can limit the power of generalization. Although these companies are representative of the software industry in Latin America, the number of companies taking part in the case studies is a low percentage of the overall population.
- The bias of the case studies, because the development of daily activities by employees may proceed differently precisely because they are being observed or due to some particular kind of handling of events and data by the advisers.

6 Analysis and Conclusions

Table 2 shows that the eight VSEs have increased the capability level of their SD and SPA processes, among others. It is important to highlight that enterprises E1 and E2 have also increased the capability of processes SM and BM. It can also be observed that E1 was the company which increased its level of capability in the greatest number of processes. This increase can be observed in the established base practices, which have been reported in the Improvement Reports of each company. Through the application of the *improvement framework,* the small companies have introduced new base practices to their processes, thus allowing them to increase their capability. Based on the collected data, there is evidence that the *improvement framework* has enabled these small companies to increase the capability of their processes.

From Table 2 we can also draw the conclusion that the effort spent on improving processes per week for each organization is: E1 12.7 h, E2 17.2 h, E3 4.5 h, E4 7.3 h, E5 6.9 h, E6 4.9 h, E7 8.8 h and E8 5.4 h (including the adviser's time). We consider that the effort of applying the proposed *improvement framework* has been suitable for the characteristics of each one of the organizations involved in the improvement initiative, since employees involved in the processes improvement of each enterprise were able to take on this effort without any negative effect on their daily activities.

Some benefits which the firms have reported are:

- The companies had moved from a chaotic and unpredictable software process to a tangible one, which is currently being used on development projects.
- The companies begin to generate a knowledge base which means historic data are available when decisions are being taken.
- The companies have a more specific vision of the organization itself which has helped and motivated them to set out on the road to quality certification. For instance, E1 is currently conducting an ISO 9001:2000 certification, and E3 has started to work towards a formal assessment at CMMI level 2.

Based on the case studies carried out, the increase of the capability of the processes to be improved, the effort of applying the proposed process and the benefits described by VSEs, we consider that the *improvement framework* is suitable for leading SPI initiatives in VSEs. The results, in terms of effort, increase of capability and benefits, are an indicator that the proposed framework can be a practical and useful strategy when facing the difficulty of carrying out SPI in VSEs. Furthermore, from the case studies we have been able to confirm that the proposed *improvement framework* was executed properly by the VSEs involved in the improvement initiatives.

On the basis of the application of the *improvement framework* in the VSEs, we have obtained some lessons which are described below:

- When performing the activity of *Initiating the cycle* we had difficulty in aligning the *Improvement Proposal* with the strategic planning of the firm (see Fig. 2), because there was no Strategic Plan. However, this fact should not be viewed as a problem but rather as an improvement opportunity, since it highlights the company's 'raison d'être', goals and its strategies for attaining them, i.e., Business Management.
- Obtaining the expected results in relatively short periods was an important aspect for the motivation and involvement of the participants in a project like this. Seeing such rapid results and taking part directly of these, allowed the employees to realize the possibilities of process improvement in general, and COMPETISOFT in particular, despite the initial reticence that these projects may have caused.
- Applying the improvements in pilot projects significantly reduced the resources needed, as well as the risk associated with the implementation of improvements in the companies' key processes.
- A-R is strengthened by the Case Study because it allows more control in the execution of the proposals developed. This means an increase in the reliability of the results. By means of the integration of these two methods, a well defined structure has been obtained for the development and application of the framework in VSEs.

Given that the results of the case studies are encouraging, new SPI initiatives are planned for the eight organizations. We shall conduct a follow-up in the companies, to attempt to determine whether this strategy has made an impact on the companies' success in terms of market attributes.

Acknowledgements. This work has been funded by the projects: INGENIO (PAC08-0154-9262 of JCCM of Spain) and ARMONIAS (PII2109-0223-7948 of JCCM of Spain). By the first author to the research fellowships granted by JCCM and funded by European Regional Development Fund (ERDF).

References

[1] Saiedian, H., Carr, N.: Characterizing a software process maturity model for small organizations. ACM SIGICE Bulletin 23(1), 2–11 (1997)

[2] Johnson, D.L., Brodman, J.G.: Tailoring the CMM for Small Businesses, Small Organizations, and Small Projects. In: El Emam, K., Madhavji, N.H. (eds.) Elements of Software Process Assessment and Improvement, pp. 239–259. IEEE CS Press, Los Alamitos (1999)

[3] Hareton, L., Terence, Y.: A process framework for small projects. Software Process: Improvement and Practice 6(2), 67–83 (2001)

[4] Staples, M., Niazi, M., Jeffery, R., Abrahams, A., Byatt, P., Murphy, R.: An exploratory study of why organizations do not adopt CMMI. Journal of Systems and Software 80(6), 883–895 (2007)

[5] Laporte, C., Alexandre, S., Renault, A.: Developing International Standards for Very Small Enterprises. IEEE Computer 41(3), 98–101 (2008)

[6] Richardson, I., Wangenheim, C.G.v.: Why are Small Software Organizations Different? IEEE Software 24(1), 18–22 (2007)

[7] Pino, F., Garcia, F., Piattini, M.: Software Process Improvement in Small and Medium Software Enterprises: A Systematic Review. Soft. Quality Journal 16(2), 237–261 (2008)

[8] Oktaba, H., Garcia, F., Piattini, M., Pino, F., Alquicira, C., Ruiz, F.: Software Process Improvement: The COMPETISOFT Project. IEEE Computer 40(10), 21–28 (2007)

[9] Oktaba, H.: MoProSoft®: A Software Process Model for Small Enterprises. In: Proceedings of the First International Research Workshop for Process Improvement in Small Settings, pp. 93–101. Carnegie Mellon University, Pittsburgh (2006)

[10] Weber, K., Araújo, E., Rocha, A., Machado, C., Scalet, D., Salviano, C.: Brazilian Software Process Reference Model and Assessment Method. In: Yolum, p., Güngör, T., Gürgen, F., Özturan, C. (eds.) ISCIS 2005. LNCS, vol. 3733, pp. 402–411. Springer, Heidelberg (2005)

[11] McCaffery, F., Taylor, P., Coleman, G.: Adept: A Unified Assessment Method for Small Software Companies. IEEE Software 24(1), 24–31 (2007)

[12] Cater-Steel, A.P., Toleman, M., Rout, T.: Process improvement for small firms: An evaluation of the RAPID assessment-based method. Information and Software Technology, 1–12 (2005) (in press)

[13] Scott, L., Jeffery, R., Carvalho, L., D'Ambra, J., Rutherford, P.: Practical Software Process Improvement -The IMPACT Project. In: Proceedings of the Australian Software Engineering Conference, pp. 182–189 (2001)

[14] Calvo-Manzano, J.A., Cuevas, G., San Feliu, T., De Amescua, A., Pérez, M.: Experiences in the Application of Software Process Improvement in SMES. Software Quality Journal 10(3), 261–273 (2002)

[15] Horvat, R.V., Rozman, I., Györkös, J.: Managing the complexity of SPI in small companies. Software Process: Improvement and Practice 5(1), 45–54 (2000)

[16] Casey, V., Richardson, I.: A practical application of the IDEAL model. Software Process: Improvement and Practice 9(3), 123–132 (2004)

[17] Kautz, K., Hansen, H.W., Thaysen, K.: Applying and adjusting a software process improvement model in practice: the use of the IDEAL model in a small software enterprise. In: Proceedings ICSE 2000, Limerick, Ireland, pp. 626–633 (2000)

[18] ISO, ISO/IEC 15504-4 - Information technology - Process assessment - Part 4: Guidance on use for process improvement and process capability determination, Geneva (2004)

[19] ISO, ISO/IEC TR 15504-7 - Information Technology - Process Assessment - Part 7: Assessment of Organizational Maturity, Montreal (2008)

[20] Pino, F., Hurtado, J., Vidal, J., García, F., Piattini, M.: A process for driving process improvement in VSEs. In: ICSP 2009. LNCS, vol. 5543, pp. 342–353. Springer, Heidelberg (2009)

[21] Pino, F., Garcia, F., Ruiz, F., Piattini, M.: A Lightweight Model for the Assessment of Software Processes. In: EuroSPI 2006, Joensuu, Finland. pp. 7.1–7.12 (2006)

[22] Martinez, T., Pino, F., León, E., Garcia, F., Piattini, M.: EVALTOOL: A flexible environment for the capability assessment of software processes. In: 3rd International Conference on Soft. and Data Tech (ICSOFT 2008), Oporto, Portugal, pp. 73–80 (2008)

[23] Abrahamsson, P., Salo, O., Rankainen, J., Warsta, J.: Agil software development methods: review and analysis. VTT Publications 478, Finland (2002)

[24] Pino, F., Garcia, F., Piattini, M.: Key processes to start software process improvement in small companies. In: SAC 2009, Honolulu, Hawaii, U.S.A, pp. 509–516 (2009)

[25] Hernández, M., Florez, A., Pino, F., Garcia, F., Piattini, M., Ibargüengoitia, G., Oktaba, H.: Supporting the Improvement Process for Small Software Enterprises through a software tool. In: IEEE Proceed., SES during ENC 2008, Mexicali, México (2008) (in press)

[26] Brereton, P., Kitchenham, B., Budgen, D., Li, Z.: Using a protocol template for case study planning. In: Evaluation and assessment in Soft. Engineering, Bari, Italia, pp. 1–8 (2008)

[27] Yin, R.K.: Case Study Research: Design and Methods. Sage Publications, Thousand Oaks (2003)

Author Index